I0453911

Contents

The Ungrateful Beggar

(The Author's Journal, 1892-1895)

The most beautiful names borne by men were the names given to them by their enemies. – Jules Barbey d'Aurevilly

Léon Bloy

Translated by Richard Robinson

Sunny Lou Publishing Company
Portland, Oregon, USA
http://www.sunnyloupublishing.com

Last Corrected Date: 2025 February 4
Original Publication Date: 2025 January 6

ISBN: 978-1-955392-74-7

This translation from French is based on *Le Mendiant Ingrat (Journal de l'Auteur, 1892-1895)*, by Léon Bloy, published by Edmond Deman, Brussels, 1898.

Translator's Preface

I first began reading *Le Mendiant Ingrat* [The Ungrateful Beggar] at the Portland State University library in February, 2019, an eon ago.

I would go there during my lunch hour. My lunch I would eat at work, in the office, before noon; and at the stroke of twelve, I would walk several blocks away, past the "park blocks," across the quad, and in through the doors of the library, where, on the 3rd floor, like a faithful lover, *Le Mendiant Ingrat* was always waiting for me, untouched, on the shelves where I had left her the day before. Thirty minutes of reading, a ten-minute nap, and back I walked to work, several blocks away.

Those were the halcyon days before COVID-19, before the face masks, lockdowns, and social distancing, before the Portland riots: the city has yet to fully recover. I haven't stepped foot in the office since March 2020, and I don't expect to do so any time soon. I almost never go downtown anymore, but, when I do, invariably I see a boarded window or two, homeless, beggars, graffiti, etc. The downtown was never so depressing and dismal, or less safe, than it is today.

Reading Bloy, of 130 years ago, today, sometimes feels as though I am reading a contemporary, as if he were alive to see our catastrophe. Such was the deterioration of his society then, and such is the deterioration of ours now. Will it ever end?

To borrow from the epilog of this work, with small

adjustments for time and place:

*The wheel of several **years**, as heavy as the Prophets' chariots, has crushed my heart.*

Ah! you there! you wanted to say something. You have taken the Words and the Promises seriously, and you have scorned men, forgetting that they themselves have become Gods! You sought Mightiness, Justice, Splendor! You sought Love!

*Well now! here is the abyss, here is your abyss, **Portland**. It's name is SILENCE...*

It is not an ordinary pit, this one. No need to ask it for that mercy of a bed of hard rock where the wretch, hurled down into it, might be broken. Its walls are ever expanding, on the contrary, its gob grows vaster and vaster, and the fall becomes infinite. There is no adieu comparable to that swallowing.

He has fallen, the blasphemer of the Riffraff, forever, undoubtedly. One dares to believe it.

Who knows, however? In the places of the deep there are, sometimes, strange surprises.

*Who knows, really, among the Riffraff, the satisfied and reveling Riffraff, whether that **Portlander** will not reappear, one day, on the surface of the darkness, holding a mysterious flower in his hand, – the flower of Silence, the flower of the Abyss?*

– Richard Robinson, New Year's Day, 2025.

To My Two Daughters

VÉRONIQUE and
MADELEINE

Foreword

Mendicus sum et Pauper[1] – Psalm, XXXIX.

Woe to him who has not begged! There is nothing so great as begging. God begs. Angels beg. Kings, Prophets, and Saints beg. The Dead beg. Everything that is in the Glory and in the Light begs. Why would anyone not want me to honor myself by having been a beggar, and, above all, an "ungrateful beggar"?...

The first and most terrible part of my life has been recounted in *The Desperate Man*. Here are the next four years which could appear equally as dark. I thought it would be good to publish some of the reflections that my torment daily suggests to me. From the viewpoint of French Letters alone, it is not without utility for people to know just how the generation of those conquered in 1870 could treat a proud Writer who did not wish to prostitute himself.

– Léon Bloy, Grand Montrouge, Saint Lazarus' feast day, 1895.

---

[1]*Mendicus sum...*: Latin for "I am a beggar and poor." Psalm 39:18 (Douay-Rheims).

1892

Seigneur Jésus ayez pitié des lampes misérables
qui se consument devant votre douloureuse
FACE. – Le Désespéré.[2]

February

14. – Visit by Georges L... who lies like a Musulman. Lively discussion on the subject of Barbey d'Aurevilly's tomb. Axiom. *I must always be wrong and I always see wrong,* no matter what I do or say. Of course, Georges L., a friend of thirty years now, will not hesitate to sacrifice me gelatinously to Mlle. R., perhaps even to Huysmans, whose most recent opinion is this: "*Bloy is an arid brain.*"

17. – Resolution to write for *The Figaro* an article on Henry de Groux's *Christ aux outrages.* Will Magnard accept it?

18. – Montparnasse Cemetery. Still no cross on d'Aurevilly's tomb!

19. – Have begun with great effort and fatigue the article on *Christ aux outrages. "In propria venit et sui eum non receperunt."*[3] These words by St. John oppress me.

22. – De Groux departs in search of a millionaire art lover indicated to him by an imbecile among our friends. The millionaire is a horrible boor who does

---

[3]*In propria venit*...: Latin for "He came unto his own, and his own received him not." John 1:11 (Douay-Rheims).

not even receive him.

24. – The sending to Magnard of an article undertaken the week before and happily completed while dying of hunger.

25. – Two abandoners in one single day!

26. – Response by Magnard's secretary, sending my copy back to me. The old pasha consents to inserting a short note about de Groux's tableau, but not a long article. Construction of that note. The article is handed over to the young Signoret to be published in the "Saint-Graal" and put before the eyes of its *fifteen* readers. Here it is:

THE CHRIST AUX OUTRAGES[4]

[4]Original footnote: *Le Christ aux outrages*: Two months earlier, I had announced a new work by Henry de Groux, in the several lines that follow (*La Plume,* January 1, 1892).

"*Les Vendanges!* [The Grape Harvests!] What a title for the new work by Henry de Groux, the terrifying painter of the *Christ aux outrages*, – immense outburst of madmen against a poor God who trembles!

"Henry de Groux appears, today, to be the only painter tormented enough by the insomnia of his own heart to express profound realities in his art.

"Ah! The bourgeois, the phoenixes among the bourgeois, those who can still shudder on seeing a desperate man's bosom heave, will feel, this time, the ineffable danger of having always been swine in a society that sobs to see its end draw near.

His Majesty Leopold II, likely tired of the renown of Boeotians *whom several of his more faithful subjects have grown exasperated with, just sent, out of the goodness of his heart, "free and clear," to Henry de Groux, in the outskirts of Paris, in the distant Vaugirard, where this extraordinary artist has provisionally set himself up, the immense tableau of desolation and anger that so profoundly derailed Brabantian imaginations when it was exhibited for the first time, last year, in the Triennial Salon of Brussels.*

The enormous size of the canvas and

"The visionary Artist, simplifying everything in a genial way, digs a unique bed for himself in the torrent of catastrophes. He chose, for the willing and satisfied cretins, for the sowers of bitterness and gardeners of ignominy, the very plausible extermination by torments.

"Thence, more pity for the spectator struck by fright. This panic and assaulting tableau never stops exhaling the terrible anguish of a multitude who, for the first time, humbly confabulate with the mountains in the ignoble hope of being crushed by them.

"It is the great Paschal carillon of the bellowing of grief, the frightening Pentecost of tongues torn out and the calcinating effusions of Justice, the lugubrious All Saints of capstans and scorpions. That, in a conflagration of colors crushed on the brightest and most-finely carven oaken palette ever seen since Delacroix. Such is, in as few words as possible, the breathless impression of a man permitted to contemplate the terrible sketch of the tableau that Henry de Groux proposes to expose this coming spring, under the redoubtable foliage of the manchineel of criticism."

the immense weight of such a package, which discouraged the movers, had compelled the errant painter to abandon it to the protection of the Belgian State for an indeterminate period of time, like an unmovable elephant.

You can, in fact, imagine for yourself the strange predicament of an artist deprived of any princely vestibule and condemned constantly to drag behind him, without respite, a neglected piece of art so colossal that it would require a basilica to house it comfortably.

But finally, thanks to the munificence of the Belgian king, the Christ aux outrages, having *escaped its catacomb in Brussels, is now visible – while waiting for a public and a resounding exposition – in the provincial rue Alain Chartier, at the back of a vast hangar known mostly by a few pigeons, where the sun makes it dazzle each morning like a blaze for the inexpressible astonishment of visitors.*

The Christ aux outrages, *an "immense outburst of madmen on a poor, trembling God," as someone once described it, is almost untranslatable into writing, so full of sorrow is it!...*

It is difficult to know exactly just what contemporary souls are capable of

*bearing. Doubtless, one can believe
them prepared for the sensation of the
most terrible images after so many
moral experiments or aesthetic operations inflicted on the human intelligence these last thirty or forty years.*

*But in this case, however, I am no
longer certain.*

*This painting is so frighteningly anor-
mal, so prodigiously outside known
traditions or processes, so resolutely
sequestered in its concepts and the*
anachronic *religious inspiration from
which it exited, it showcases its lamps
of cruelty so savagely that one fails to
conjecture in any precise manner the
effect of a like vision on beings little
disposed to sharing in the agony of a
truly tortured Redeemer.*

*The celebrated tableau by Munkacsy
upset nobody. His* Jesus before Pilate
*was the anodyne Savior preconized by
such apostles as Renan and the Rev-
erend Father Didon, a reassuring and
cosmetic Christ, raised in the salons
and who knew what he owed to the
people of high society.*

*The elegance of his manners and the
irreproachable rectitude of his presen-
tation happily did away with the goth-
ic and popular idea of a Lord God*

streaming with blood.

Lastly, he was a wily Christ, very mid- dle *of the century, respectful towards the rich, completely up to the task of his mission and possessing a surprising sense of poise, whom the most exquisite ladies could contemplate without terror and who had taken great pains to avoid the inconvenience of a rigorous suffering.*

Renown, therefore, was bound to blare all its trumpets and burst all its tambours for him.

From the point of view of perfumery and savoir-vivre, *Henry de Groux's tableau evidently holds a place of deep and deplorable inferiority. I believe, nevertheless, in the resounding success of this work, and here is why:*

First of all, people are really bored today. Entertainments grow sparse, and emotions become rarer and rarer.

People's faces are not slapped in Parliament every day of the week, and ministerial jostlings lack carnage, the theaters visibly crack, and sar Péladan himself, vexed by Russia, interrupts his farces.

On the other hand, a strange new current manifests and clarifies itself.

Intellectuals ask for a God. Many are not afraid even to ask openly and publicly for Our Lord Jesus Christ, "the most incontestable of Gods," as Baudelaire said.

It is an infinitely worthy thing to be observed, this mysterious impulse of young minds in the sense of a renewal of Christianity. Entirely literary evolution until now, which the Fleurs du Mal *appears to have initiated and which Paul Verlaine has recently miraculously accelerated.*

This latter poet, the only *great poet who after half a dozen centuries openly gave his heart to the Church, – rejuvenating by a* tour de force *of genius all the old images that atheism or habit had etiolated to the point of ridicule, – glorified the Holy Sacrament and Prayer in verses so beautiful that the incredulous youth of contemporary poetry was forced to admire them with enthusiasm and become the students thereof.*

It has gotten to such a point these days that Catholicism has become a kind of aristocracy for thought.

Let us add that modern artists, and especially painters, offer few consolations to the petitioners of the Sublime.

A recent, too-famous exposition served only to demonstrate, once again, the decrepit childishness of these so-called innovators, pointillists, *or* luminarists, *whom Rembrandt would not have allowed to crush his chocolate and who appeared, in the last analysis, merely to be uncultivated laborers of materialism.*

For all these reasons, I deem the triumph of the Christ aux outrages *to be twenty-times assured, the most formidable attempt at Christian spiritualism that has ever been achieved, in painting, since the predecessors of that watered-down paganism that is called the Renaissance.*

Note well that this has nothing at all to do with a subject that the imagination of critics could easily conjecture and whose more or less divine execution would save it from banality. It lies, on the contrary, at telescopic distances from all supposable commonplaces of religious iconography.

It is the Passion of Christ, just as visionary saints have recounted for us in diamantine books that will survive the last judgment of literatures; just as the Ancient Witnesses certified, who had their "throats cut" in order to obey the command to be "configured to his death"; just, finally, as the Church, not that of the Middle Ages, but of every century, has taught in its terrifying Liturgy.

It is the storm of unimaginable tortures without the counterweight of any efficacious pity for the voluntary Moribund whose Last Sigh extinguishes the sun and beclouds the constellations.

We have all heard speak of stain glass and the Primitives, of nightmare and the somber genius of Flanders; we have heard speak of Rubens and Delacroix. Of what, then, have we not heard speak, O Lord! since the entire Belgian press has bellowed about this monster of magnificence whose appearance has discountenanced the wisdom of a painter-race immobilized for two hundred years?

Ah! but it is quite simple and does not require so much erudition, since it is precisely what is needed for an old fishmonger from the Basque country or West Flanders to prostrate himself on the ground, exhaling moans of pity, as if some triptych by Jean de Bruges or some bleeding Ecce Homo *by Alonzo Cane! had been put before his eyes.*

For it is quite incontestable, I suppose,

that such [a response] must be the supreme objective of every exclusively religious work of art. A pious image before which no poor person could pray, – could anything be more identical to a sacrilegious prevarication than this?

Behold, then, the tableau by Henry de Groux in its extremely powerful simplicity:

The Man of Sorrows *stands on the famous Mount that tradition designates as the tumulus of the first Disobedient One.*

To his right is an impassible and mocking Praetorian brute wearing a bright panache, who could be the shepherd of that military flock, of so complete a brutification, which is seen in the background.

To his left, an indescribable individual, a cross between a eunuch and a butcher, whom one might believe to be the living monstrance or reliquary of several thousand years of human debauchery.

That man there... he is the mahout of the lamentable Lord whom they are about to crucify, the ineffably abject cicerone of ignominies, maledictions, and terrors.

He vociferates, while pointing out the Victim to the crowd. And such is the signal of the most demoniacal attack of riffraff that a painter, burning internally like a fumarole, has ever had the audacity to represent.

The rage of that populace with clenched fists seems to possess, in the mind of the four Evangelists, something prophetic and superhuman.

Even the small children, – panic detail! – howl at death and brandish their feeble arms against the ravaged bosom of the divine Lamb.

Clovis and his Franks are devilishly far, yes, to be sure! And the more one looks, the more one perceives that they are indiscernibly far away, at the other end of the centuries, in the seethe of barbarous chaos!

Jesus is alone, absolutely alone and face to face with that world condemned by him, horrible world which is nothing but the sweepings of the ancient, lost Paradise, made clean by Cherubim.

That God-made man has been so completely divested himself that he did not wish to keep even a single atom of Divinity which would have been necessary for him to ward off fear. He suf-

fers and trembles in his Skin like the most feeble among feeble.

May he hold on as best he can. The Angels themselves have decamped, the brilliant Angels come down from heaven for his recomfort.

It is time for all that to end, otherwise he would have, for the possessed, no more Blood left in him to spill on the poor salutary Cross.

Indeed, he bleeds terribly, through each of the pricks from his Crown and especially through the innumerable wounds from that miraculous Flagellation that the Franciscan Maria d'Agreda estimated at more than five hundred thousand blows with an iron-barbed strap. He is so crimson beneath the purple of his rags that one might think, in truth, that it is he who is the torturer of others...

But his Hands, which will soon be pierced, his exsanguious hands of a torture victim, so ardent with pain that it is easy to imagine them capable of consuming the firmament, – I recommend them particularly to the explorers of abysses who are not afraid to lean out over infinite Misery.

The very imminent public exposition of that extraordinary work whose intensity surpasses the most vaunted paroxysms will likely oblige the critic to modify his expressions slightly.

Some will understand, doubtless, not only that it has to do with a canvas that resembles nothing at all in all of contemporary painting, but, even more so, that we are in the presence of an absolute force represented by a stranger to whom the future belongs.

But is he really a stranger, this Henry de Groux, born in Brussels, twenty-five years ago, to a French father, a Breton even originally, who was himself a painter of very high merit, whom the national museums there are proud to possess several tableaux of? – for Belgium is perhaps the first country in the world to glorify its artists... when they die in obscurity and their carcasses have no more need of anyone.

With the exception of some young writers whom Belgium is surprised by, it would seem that King Leopold was just about the only one of his people to divine the greatness of this adolescent of genius, copiously insulted by the multitude, hideously renounced by some and forced to take refuge in Paris, which is the eternal pavilion of those sublime victims of a stoning.

It is in Paris, then, exclusively, in this intellectual Paris where just glory is not always economized, where it is fitting, going forward, to boast of a like castaway from heaven.[5]

– LÉON BLOY.

27. – Our idea of operating a pensione for young Scandinavian girls has decidedly gone belly up. Here is the second to the last of these goslings leaving us in the lurch... It is true that there is very little amusement

---

[5]Original footnote: What has become of the *Christ aux outrages*? Today, December 2, 1897, even Henry de Groux does not know!!!

About five years ago, this extraordinary canvas was entrusted to a sire X, merchant of tableaux, in Paris, for an exposition in London, at the "Hanover Gallery," where it obtained a considerable success, and fructuous for the unscrupulous dealer only, the unfortunate painter never having obtained what was indicated on the receipts, *nor even did anyone bother to tell him what had become of his work!!!!*

No amount of effort could vanquish the stubborn silence of the equitable industrialist who abuses the indigence of an artist in order to fleece him, to skin him alive, but who will, clearly, be forced to explain himself, one of these days, before the tribunal of correctional police.

The prejudice is all the more monstrous given that at the time of the exposition in London, toward the end of '92, de Groux had received a formal promise for the acquisition of his tableau by the College of the Cathedral of Senlis, where everyone would be able to admire it today, if the subtile second-hand goods dealer had not run away with it.

in our home.

28. – Letter from an affectionate and wealthy old man
for whom I had the occasion to perform some difficult tasks that have gone unpaid. He consoles himself
for being "unable" to help me by reminding me that
previously, – when I was, without question, a shoe-
less beggar, – he had prophesied my *ruin.*

March

6. – High mass at Saint-Sulpice for the first Sunday of Lent. *Sub pennis ejus sperabis.*[6]

      Our housekeeper is a drunk. Insufferable bother to look for another. I give this warrior her one-week notice.

8. – "*Montparnasse Cemetery.* – Why is there no cross on the tomb of one of the greatest Catholic writers of all time: Jules Barbey d'Aurevilly?" – in the *Saint-Graal*. (Liminary note in the March 8 issue.)

11. – De Groux, solicited, would perhaps exhibit at the Rosicrucians. But the frightful boredom of being a "Templar!"

19. – Rough day.

22. – This morning, De Groux goes after Léon Deschamps (*Plume*) who owes me seven or eight hundred francs, spends an hour explaining to him that I need money. This evening, a letter of five lines from the said Deschamps asking me "*how* he can help."

---

[6]*Sub pennis ejus sperabis*: Latin for "Under his wings thou shalt trust." Psalm 90:4 (Douay-Rheims).

23. – I have had quite enough of this street hawker. I write him:

My God! dear friend, it's very simple. At this moment I am given to religious meditations on the nothingness of life and I would have need of your person-al opinion about friends *on the road to prosperity, who leave behind very poor wretches amply and* gratuitously *employed on nefast days.*

The uniformity of that snub, which I was the victim of, by Rodolphe Salis, for example, who owes his scandalous success in part to me, and by several others as well, surprises me a little. That is due undoubtedly to my having a "chimerical" wit, as your good sense has informed me.

In return for your reflections on this matter, he whom you have seen fit to style "the first prosateur of France" and who willingly went out of his way for you, promises to drop into your fi-ancée's basket a formal quittance for the 800 francs that you owe him for services rendered in the form of liter-ary merchandise, according to the terms of a verbal contract entered into between us on the date of April 15, 1890 or thereabouts, if memory serves.

Cordially,

– LÉON BLOY.

P.S. To be published in the next issue of the Plume*: "Our eminent collaborator Léon Bloy renounces providing us with a follow-up to the* Secret *of M. Pérégrin Germinal. He informs us that his conscience reproaches him for sharing with the public a secret of such importance."*

24. – I handed our silverware over to the Mont-de-Piété. Took lunch, rue Copernic, at a well-to-do Englishwoman's house, who introduces her two girls to me. Naturally, they speak to me about Bourget and Daudet. I declare, with absolute simplicity, that those are readings for domestics. I am no longer welcome in that house.

Read, this morning, in the *Echo de Paris*, a long article by Scholl on the "dinner" at the *Plume*. The old ruffian protects his youngins.

26. – Letter from Prince Ourousof who believes me incapable of writing a novel because life is flat and pale, and my style appears dazzling and mamelonate. Flaubertian opinion.

27. – Huysmans would have apparently proposed to

the *Plume* to finish *Pérégrin Germinal* in my place!!!

29. – Despite my horrible sadness, meditated on the prodigious words of Ecclesiastes, needing to serve as an epigraph to my book on Napoleon: *Quid est quod fuit? ipsum quod futurum est. Quid est quod factum est, ipsum quod faciendum est.*[7] And these: *Vidi cuncta quae fiunt sub sole, et ecce universa vanitas et afflictio spiritus.*[8]

And to think that this word *Vanitas* is the exact translation of the name of *Abel!*...

30. – Montparnasse Cemetery. Still no cross on d'Aurevilly's tomb!

---

[7]*Quid est quod fuit?*...: Latin for "What is it that hath been? the same thing that shall be. What is it that hath been done? the same that shall be done." Ecclesiastes 1:9 (Douay-Rheims).

[8]*Vidi cuncta quae*...: Latin for "I have seen all things that are done under the sun, and behold all is vanity, and vexation of spirit." Ecclesiastes 1:14 (Douay-Rheims).

April

1st. – Montparnasse Cemetery. Still no cross. But surprising encounter. Two workers arrive, map in hand, looking for the tomb. Unquestionably, a cross and a grille will be installed, after *thirty-five* months! Effect of my liminary question in "Saint-Graal."

3. – Refusal of *Christ aux outrages* by the Champs de Mars jury. A word by President Stevens, long ago quite taken with de Groux's father, whom he was the pupil of: "A woman smelling a flower is far more difficult to paint than all your *Ecce Homo*."

Another word by a judge speaking directly to the man refused: "You would be the Ravachol[9] of the Champs de Mars."

4. – Received a copy of the March 20 issue of the "Saint-Graal," containing a letter by Charles Buet which affirms, in a pretty style, that I was mistaken to say there was never a cross on d'Aurevilly's tomb, and who jumps at the opportunity to reveal his own notoriety as a writer.

What a bother to have to respond to that idiot!

[9]Ravachol: François Claudius Koenigstein (AD 1859-1892), a French militant anarchist executed by guillotine for his crimes which included bombings and assassination.

5. – For the first time, I see de Groux weeping. Is it a sign that he will obtain something finally? I love those tears. Yesterday he ran aground everywhere.

6. – Not a sou and nothing to pawn at the Mont-de-Piété. I am saturated with sadness while re-reading old letters from my dead parents and from several old friends who have abandoned me. Thus do I work myself up, towards evening, into a sort of agony.

7. – De Groux has succeeded in having his two large tableaux, the *Christ aux outrages* and the *Procession des archers*, installed at the Pavilion of Liberal Arts (Champs de Mars). As for myself, I am received in a small cavern of hell. Horrible day.

8. – Letter to the "Saint-Graal" in response to Buet. Certain and irremediable falling out with a half-dozen people. General liquidation of questionable friends.

> *My dear Monsieur Signoret,*
>
> *I find in the March 20 issue of the "Saint-Graal" a letter by M. Charles Buet, accusing me of having "led you into error."*
>
> *That universal brochure writer, never failing to find an occasion to self-advertise a little, knows only too well that it is I who informed you, last*

*month, about the infinite absence of a
cross on Barbey d'Aurevilly's tomb.
Consequently, it is really at me that
that rectificative message is aimed.*

*You could perhaps have replied that
the contentious note by the "Saint-
Graal" was not handed over to the
printer except after an ocular verification of the surprising omission de-
nounced by your review.*

*You could even have observed that the
"Saint-Graal" did not say that there
had* never *been a cross, but that, not
seeing any vestige of the Sign of Redemption on the tomb of a great
Christian artist, an explanation was
naturally in order for that incredible*
refusal.

*M. Buet misrepresents the interroga-
tion and writes a sophistical letter to
you, of which he is not even the author, to try to whitewash the* only *person who might have, on this occasion,
the need to be disculpated.*

*I very sincerely acknowledge, with bit-
ter regrets, that until last January, I
had been completely unaware of this
monstruous* infidelity. *Having been
honored by twenty-three years of
friendship with Barbey d'Aurevilly
and knowing, better than anyone else,*

his thoughts and feelings, I estimated, in my quality as a Catholic, that it was more profitable and profound to pray for the dead in churches, in the presence of the Holy Sacrament, than to make hygienic pilgrimages to the cemetery, and I had not visited the sepulture of the dear great man who would have died desolate if he could have foreseen the horrible affront of being buried like an impious person.

How could I myself have foreseen a sacrilegious negligence that the most suspicious imagination would not have conceived of?

I add that my having stayed, for nearly one year, in a foreign country could, if needed, serve as my excuse.

So, on or around January 15, an anonymous correspondent, supposing me responsible, addressed indignant remonstrances to me, which I forwarded to the responsible party, with the expression of my most grievous astonishment.

I then received so ambiguous a response that I made an immediate inquiry into the matter, the result of which was, for me, the absolute certainty that no cross had ever been placed or requisitioned, and that someone was lying *by asserting the opposite; – certainty that the exiguous testimonies invoked by M. Buet under the said responsible party's dictation hardly shake.*

Finally, January 27, after earnest solicitations and having run out of patience, exasperated by these sinister jokes, I wrote the following letter:

Paris, January 27, 1892.

Mademoiselle, I received a letter from L., the person you hired to take care of the sepulture, who informs me that someone has just ordered a wrought-iron cross for d'Aurevilly's tomb; I suppose that this order was made by you, which you decided on finally, after *thirty-three months* of an inconceivable forgetfulness.

I had taken it upon myself several days earlier – even though I have no right over the sepulture – to order the construction of a more modest cross, with a view to repairing the odious negligence that would end, one day or another, in public scandal, and to avoid it being said anymore that the great Catholic writer had been interred like a dog or an atheist.

I stand back then, and cede place to you, happy, after all, that you have decided to listen to my advice. The cross, even if planted by idolaters, is always a Sign of Redemption.

If you did not love our great decedent enough to espouse his religious faith, I congratulate myself for having made you understand, at least, that you could not refuse to his poor tomb that supreme honor that the Church does not always refuse to parricides and apostates even.

Your,

– Léon Bloy.

Ah! I had little confidence in the order that someone had made me aware of, and I do not hesitate to confess that I was only pretending to take it seriously so as to obtain an effect of intimidation.

How naïve I was! Six weeks later, still

nothing had been done, and the intervention of "Saint-Graal" was needed to determine something. If the Christian admirers of Barbey d'Aurevilly notice a cross on his tomb, their recomfort will be owing to you, my dear Monsieur Signoret.

My last visit to Montparnasse cemetery was on April 1. I had the chance there of meeting two workers who showed me the plan of a pretentious grille surmounted by a cross; skillfully interrogated, they also informed me that the order dated from merely twelve days earlier.

We now hope that this work will be completed before six months. We also hope that I will be able to hold my patience, for I am fiendishly tempted by what the Gospel calls necessary scandals.

Do you not feel, dear sir, as I do, that the absence of the Cross on the tomb of such a Christian, – were it merely for twenty-four hours, *– is equivalent to a veritable profanation?*

– Cordially,

LÉON BLOY.

P.S. It goes without saying that I refuse any sort of verbal exchange

> *with M. Charles Buet who will proba-*
> *bly send you fifty pages in response, of*
> *which forty-nine at minimum are con-*
> *secrated to the enumeration of his*
> *works. One assures me that he is in*
> *the process now of putting the last*
> *touches on his 117th doorstop. – L.B.*[10]

10. – Palm Sunday. *Alios salvos fecit, seipsum non potest salvum* facere.[11] Only those who are of the Holy Spirit can appreciate the profundity of that Jewish expression.

11. – An appearance by Montchal, to whom *The Desperate Man* was dedicated. Poor Louis! Aged by ten years, ravaged by sorrow, half-destroyed by miseries... Germany consumes him.

13. – Montchal's departure for Dresden. But will I ever see him again, this "brother of election" whom I see disappear with great affliction.

---

[10]Original footnote: Published the following month by the "Saint-Graal" with this consoling addition: "May 4. The cross has finally been erected. Ugly, alas! but erected all the same and embedded in hard stone, extracted from what refractory depths! by the obstinate lapicides that we are, my very dear Monsieur Signoret. Therefore, *Laus Deo! –* L.B."

[11]*Alios salvos fecit*...: Latin for "He saved others; himself he could not save." Matthew 27:42 (Douay-Rheims).

15. – Silverware crisis. Installment unpaid. Crushing debts. I revisit the ancient tortures of *The Desperate Man*. I feel as if captive in some grimy prison with horn windows, through which I can barely detect the luminous forms of the Divine World which is really my fatherland.

16. – Office of Holy Saturday. Benediction of the paschal candle. *Flammas ejus Lucifer matutinus inveniat. Ille, inquam, LUCIFER, qui nescit occasum. Ille qui regressus ab inferis, humano generi serenus illuxit.[12]* Evidently, the Church *does not know what* it says, and it is for this reason that it is *infallible*.

17. – Easter. The joy of the Church penetrates me in an opposite sense to that of the common faithful. On this day of great joy, I feel my captivity more keenly. The idea of a prison obsesses me to the point where the great candles on the Altar seem to look like *bars*.

In the end, however, good tears, consoling tears come to me, with the memory of so many sad Easters when the most bitter Lent perdured for me, when I was alone and without assistance...

A pale hope is reborn. It is really not possible that God should abandon me, for in the end, whatever my faults may have been, I have practiced mercy of-

---

[12]*Flammas ejus Lucifer...*: Latin for "May the Morning Star [Lucifer] discover its flames. That Morning Star, I say, which knows no setting. Having returned from the lower world [Hell], it casts a serene light on humanity." From the *Exultet,* or *Praeconium Paschale (Easter Proclamation).*

ten and sometimes even to the point of heroism.
Nothing can erase that. Then also, *I know* things that
no one knows. They were not shown to me only to
make me suffer.

18. – Geometric exegesis. The Triangle is equivalent
to the Cross, that is to say, to two right angles.

19. – Lunched with Demay who is surprised to hear
me speak about Providence and foolishly counters it
with *chance*.

"Dear friend," I say to this poor fellow, "a
man will soon come for me and this man, perhaps,
will save me. I do not know his name, I do not know
whence he comes, but I feel that he will come. Will
you call this chance?"

Exclamations by Demay who declares himself
ready to see in me a prophet if things should turn out
as I say. A quarter of an hour later, the announced
person appears in the guise of an old friend from
more than a year ago, who asks about me and makes
me hope for stunning and imminent subsidies.

20. – De Groux received six hundred francs this
morning. He gives five hundred of them to me spontaneously, just as he would give me five hundred
thousand, that is to say, with the certitude and intention of remaining eternally in my debt.

Pavilion of Liberal Arts. The *Christ* [*aux outrages*] is admirably placed, the *Procession* too. Here I am standing under this latter which I am still not familiar with. Immense tableau that disconcerts me, and distresses me. I cannot discern any design, or color, or whatsoever it might be, when, after standing back from it, all of a sudden the astonishing beauty of this work hits me. What a visionary loved by God, my great and poor Henry De Groux!

It is a pleasure to see him enjoying his success, which is evident and considerable. But primarily it is the *Christ aux outrages* that draws the crowd. Despite the protestations of some women whom the absence of pomade and lavabo disconcert; despite the haughty reprobation by a visiting soutane whom I study, for several instants, the animal physiognomy of, the general impression is that there is only de Groux at this exposition.

21. – Visit to my landlady whose face is that of a big cheese run through with vermin. Parishioner who gives out the blessed bread and makes a business of it. No compassion to be expected. However, she is not more *perfect* than the famous parricide who vowed "not to be perfect," for she gives me twenty francs too many for my five-hundred-franc bill. My immediate restitution defrosts her. This act of probity on my part leads her to believe, doubtless, that I am an imbecile.

25. – Anarchistic detonations. Copious explosion at the wine merchant's where Ravachol was arrested.

The virtuous people are ill at ease in their culottes...
*Spiritus ubi vult spirat: et vocem ejus audis, sed
nescis unde veniat, aut quo vadat...*[13]

27. – "My dear Léon Bloy, what you write cannot be
read *in the salons*." Opinion of a well-bred man.

---

[13]*Spiritus ubit vult*...: Latin for "The Spirit breatheth where he will;
and thou hearest his voice, but thou knowest not whence he
cometh." John 3:8 (Douay-Rheims).

May

3. – *The Invention of the Cross!* That is, the commemoration, in the Church, of this enormous event: The Cross of Jesus miraculously found, in the ruins of Jerusalem, by Saint Helena, the mother of Constantine, in AD 327. After three centuries, nobody knew what had become of It. After three centuries, people were forced to go without It!

This object, the most precious in the world, was hidden underground. The Cross had had no part in the Resurrection, having remained in the realm of the dead. For three hundred years, nobody could provide any news of that Sign, and one totally unique day, absolutely different from all the days that had gone before it since the beginning of days, someone found it again among the rubble...

Who thinks of that?

8. – Marvelous lousiness of a Columbian billionaire or so-called, come Paris to unload a few million. This rastacouère was supposed to stuff me in his bags and carry me off to Bogota. My books on Christopher Columbus and the approach of the Centenary of the Discovery designated me for conferences in the principal cities of South America. Superb opportunity.

I learn today that my rastacouère has suddenly beat it, without saying a word. I was living for the last two weeks on the hope that this man had given me.

Full day. Georges L., a friend of thirty years, abandons me. The cross, finally erected! on Barbey d'Aurevilly's tomb, makes him feel sick. Then, an atheistic lady, whom I give heartburn to, has forbidden him to see me.

9. – Apropos of the commonplaces that I wish, one day, to collect and elaborate on in the *Exégèse*, I tell de Groux that such banal expressions, eternally repeated by imbeciles, are a prodigious affirmation of their nothingness and that, by consequence, they are *divine*.

10. – There is nothing to say, I am admirably miserable.

Talent, loved by everyone, belongs to the Father and the Son. Genius, hated by everyone, is exclusively of the Holy Spirit.

11. – Article by Charles Buet on the *Christ aux outrages*, on the front page of the *Figaro*. How perfectly fitting it is of this journal to have refused my work on the same topic only to accommodate such prose! Charles Buet! He, at least, will not calcinate the subscriber.

14. – "Old America Reconstituted" at the Porte Maillot, as a prelude to the celebration of the Centenary of

the Discovery. Ran into a friend who confirms for me that there will be no profanations. Poor good man who cannot conceive of a profanation by ridicule! The delirium of *reconstitutions* exasperates me. So well does it demonstrate the emptiness of an epoch that cannot even evaluate itself properly.

Boredom and disgust on seeing this public of whores and mountebanks. Immense masquerade throughout the world. The highly anticipated Centenary, could it be anything else? The Pope who, alone, would have the power to change the character of these manifestations, will do nothing, it is too evident. The Christophore [Christ bearer] is too much in the image of the Holy Spirit, and I know how diligent the modern Church is to distance itself from the divine Third Person.

I am the only French person, after the Count Roselly de Lorgues, to have spoken honorably in favor of Christopher Columbus, whom all the journals will speak about. Naturally, I will not be cited.

After one hour of waiting, I scram without having heard the Cantate. Besides, a longer stay becomes impossible for me when I notice the "Chat Noir," Salis and his lieutenants, having grimped up onto the caravel, where, just now, another comic is about to ape the Messenger of Salvation discovering the New World!

15. – This morning, rather long conversation with de Groux. Text: "Old America" and the inertia of Leo XIII. – If the Pope, I tell him, had the spirit of a great

Pope who would at the same time be a great saint, – having informed himself in advance of all things and considering himself to be the Mouthpiece of God, – he would ask himself, doubtless, who among his sons is most in the ways of Fire... Who knows whether he would respond that Léon Bloy is perhaps a little too much abandoned by his Father?

Enraged letter by Buet. If he had the power to do so, what refined torments would he not condemn me to, that thickheaded polygraph whom I appeared to scorn the 117th doorstop of?

20. – Anniversary of the death of *Saint* Christopher Columbus. The Protestants, who do not want any saints, do not congratulate their friends except on their birthday. And yet, the Church has named the day of the dead of the saints *Dies natalis*. Surprising confusion of ideas amongst the Protestants who take death for life and life for death. The Church celebrates merely three Nativities; that of Jesus, Mary, and Saint John the Baptist. Would this not be a liturgical and mysterious announcement that the Precursor could very well partake of the superhuman privilege of Mary, conceived without sin? The *Immaculate Conception of John*. What a thought!

21. – Traditional exegesis of the 46 years of the Construction of the Temple (John 2:20) signified by the addition of the Greek letters forming the name of Adam. The corresponding Hebraic letters produce the same result.

What is more, the four greek letters of that mysterious Name are the initials of the four cardinal points: *ἀνατολή*, east; *δύσις*, west; *ἄρκτος*, north; *μεσημβρία*, south.

Analogous to the esotericism of the famous word *ἰχθὸς* [fish].

22. – Difficult passage in Saint James: *Estote [autem] factores verbi et non auditores tantum, fallentes vosmetipsos. Quia si quis auditor est verbi et non factor: hic comparabitur viro consideranti vultum nativitatis suæ in speculo.*[14]

To examine one's natural-*born* face in a mirror, would that not be to see *death*? Is that what you wanted to say, O gentle and terrible Apostle?

24. – The most grievous bitterness of my terrifying past raises its head. Abandoned by so many friends, old and new; disappointed by so many people whom I would have never hesitated to sacrifice myself for; abandoned, it seems, by God himself, and in what a frightful manner! imprisoned, chained in obscure places and never receiving a salary; tormented, finally, without release by the most invincible poverty and menaced on all sides. What a destiny!

---

[14]*Estote factores verbi...*: Latin for "But be ye doers of the word, and not hearers only, deceiving your own selves. For if a man be a hearer of the word, and not a doer, he shall be compared to a man beholding his own countenance in a glass." James 1:22-23 (Douay-Rheims).

I offer the *Chevalière de la Mort* to Plon for a review that he has just founded. Refusal by that publisher, alleging an exclusive choice from among "the most distinguished" writers.

25. – To Emmanuel Signoret, director of the *Saint Graal*:

> *My dear Signoret,*
>
> *Buet addresses a pile of base insults at me, which leads me to believe that you must have already received from that person a pretty response for insertion.*
>
> *Being one of those to whom the "bread of deceit is sweet," according to the text by Solomon, he will not fail to claim, like everyone else, that I have received alms from him, for such is the accredited legend about a redoubtable author whom it is a matter of dishonoring by all means.*
>
> *As for Buet, the infamous* hack *who had the genius to nickle-and-dime the indigent Léon Bloy, a repeat of that noise would oblige me to [resort to] disgusting reprisals which must be avoided.*
>
> *Why would you not publish, then, instead of that individual's filth, a note thus formulated:*

> Our friend Léon Bloy, having declared, last month, his intention to refuse any public exchange with M. Charles Buet, and this latter having addressed to us, however, an offensive letter for his superior, namely the great writer whom we are happy to count as one of our own, we consider ourselves unable to publish it without prejudice to our good name. In consequence thereof, M. Buet, whose prose we did not promise forever to publish, will be content with the expression of our pacific regrets.

Saw the brochure by Darzens, *l'Amante du Christ* [The Lover of Christ], with a frontispiece by Rops. A bleeding and *joyous* crucified Christ, whose face is the spitting image of Darzens. At his feet, a naked woman who carefully rolls back the linen covering the sexual parts.

Swine! Swine!

26. – The oldest friend of mine, Victor L., of all those whom I would have thought the firmest, just stood there tranquilly this morning, the Day of Ascension, while his bitch of a wife, a low bourgeoise woman born of domestics, insulted me, and before whom he trembles. The hussy, whom I want to believe is as

faithful to her husband as to her extraction and who instinctively abhors me, rejoiced to hear of my distress, and triumphed *in the antechamber* of my supposed ruin. I could have crushed that worthless woman with a single word. The memory of a long friendship restrained me. "If I die of famine," I said to the coward, turning my back on him for good, "you will hear about it in the obituary column, perhaps."

I am abandoned in a sublime fashion by Henry Carton de Wiart, a young attorney from Brussels, who came and threw himself into my arms two years ago, whom I loaded down with autographs and counsels in exchange for several sous, and with whom I thought my friendship was ten times sure.

His papa, because he himself is a member of the bar, severely forbade him from any contact with so venenous a writer as myself. An extremely dignified letter, that my wife saw fit to honor that rascal with, went unanswered.

Superfine amalgam of Brabantine boorishness and Netherlandish beastliness. I can no longer keep count of my abandoners, but this last one merits a mention.

Letter to that Carton:

Monsieur,

Le Magasin littéraire [The Literary Magazine], which I just received a copy of, informs me that you are out of danger and even so fully restored as to write to the young people of Louvain a considerable letter, of the most habile sort, my faith! wherein I have the honor to be introduced to new generations in a luminous packet of Léon Gautier, Maurice Barrès, and several other great men.

Evidently, that ream of words was much more important than a polite response to the wife of a poor writer.

Ah! You will succeed, you will! I can feel it, and you will become a great Belgian. *God be blessed!*

While waiting, I beseech you to return to me, within 48 hours, the very complete collection of my letters, without omitting that of my wife's, dated, I believe, April 20, – the most elementary prudence not allowing me to leave such documents in the hands of a man whom prosperity places out of danger of the inconveniences of my affection and whom I no longer feel the need to esteem.

In case, – very unlikely, correct? – I should not receive that collection by guaranteed delivery, on Monday at the latest, I will address myself, that same day, to M. your father who would feel, I suppose, the importance of entering into possession of your letters, which I have already proposed the return of.

One piece of advice before I finish. It may be that I visit Brussels one of these days. If you should run into me, do not recognize me, I entreat you. It would be very awkward publicly for me to refuse the hand of a man whom I tenderly loved in the past and who, for me, from this day forward, is nothing more than a filthy bastard.

– LÉON BLOY,

P.S. another piece of advice: Barbey d'Aurevilly remarked one day that the prig Montalembert, having gotten it into his head to cite Bossuet somewhere, immediately the entire page (the page by Montalembert containing that citation) disappeared into the most vertical and eternal thin air. Be very careful, then, when citing Montaigne. – L.B.

27. – Saw the first issue of the *Revue hebdomadaire* [Weekly Review] published by that cretin Plon. Always the same stuff, always the same "great" men: Zola, Daudet, Bourget, Loti, etc.

29. – Daily office: "*Non vos relinquam orphanos, vado et venio ad vos, et gaudebit cor vestrum.*"[15]

---

[15]*Non relinquam vos orphanos...*: Latin for "I will not leave you orphans... I go away, and I come unto you... and your heart shall

These words were spoken, nineteen centuries ago. I am reminded of the chapter in *Homme* [Man] wherein Hello demonstrates that it is a dishonor to *promise* and *not keep it*. The dishonor of God! Why must I be tested to be unable to do away with such suggestions?

I have the distinct impression that everyone is in error, that everyone is mistaken, that the human spirit has fallen into the thickest darkness.

For example. It occurs to me that the famous *Microbe*, explicative of all ills, which contemporary medicine makes so great a deal of, must be and cannot be anything else than the most subtle deception of the old Enemy. What does it mean, in fact, if not to *prove* (!) that all morbid causes are *natural*, instead of SPIRITUAL, as had always been believed by men inhabited by the living God? Physiologists have seen it, this microbe. They have *seen* it with their big eyes. Ah! the good men who have gone to such efforts to arrive at not understanding that it is the *form* that the Prince of Evil himself takes *for them*, the ancient Demon who was a celestial Spirit, and that their microbe is the latest travesty of Disobedience!

30. – I go in advance of my thoughts into exile, into a great column of Silence.

---

rejoice." John 14:18, 14:28, 16:22 (Douay-Rheims).

June

1st. – Letter from a certain A.R., sublieutenant of a garrison in a distant city. This warrior is charged with expressing to me the admiration of a group of *desperate men* who want to launch a review and ask me to recommend a title, collaborators, and copy!!! But all that is naïve and of a sufficiently military allure that is not at all repugnant.

Immediate response:

My dear Lieutenant,

In so many words, you tell me that you love me. How could I resist that? My heart is well known, moreover, and people have greatly abused it, but I do not correct myself. I always gulp down affectionate protestations whole, in the hope, always disappointed, of finally meeting some sincere heart.

Could it be you? I hardly imagine. For one instant, the thought came to me to ask you a very important favor, for the sole pleasure of seeing your admiration immediately vanish into thin air, an experiment that has almost always succeeded.

But what is the point of this ferocious joke of too-probable success? You remind me that we are approaching Pentecost, and, out of pity for my soul,

*which is already sad to death, I prefer
to encourage it by some new illusion.*

*You wish to found a review? Nice! If I
had the honor of being your* friend,
*gentlemen, I would energetically
counsel you instead to give your money to the poor, to me, for example, to
help me finish my next novel which sits
unfinished on the desk, for lack of re-
sources. But that would be precisely
the fumistery of the hour, and I would
risk taking from you, as if by hand, all
your feelings for me, if I had the imprudence or malice to let you see that*
Caïn's *poverty is not entirely a fiction.*

*So, to put you completely at ease, I am
horribly happy, frightfully rich, it goes
without saying, and I will respond to
you in a good way.*

*Hey! Now that I think about it, you
have not called me "dear master";
you did not insult me with that proto-
col. It is, then, for that reason that
your letter did not displease me. Everything makes sense.*

*Let's see, you ask for what? A title for
your boys' revue. It's very simple: THE
DESPERATE MAN. Parbleu! With an epigraph of:* Léon Bloy is an angel.

*Because you expect some consolation
for a complete insuccess and because,*

consequently, victory would afflict you, – there you go, satisfied in your request.

You ask me also about collaborators. Excellent that! How is it you could have read me and supposed that I know anyone of importance, and that I have any sort of influence on whosoever it might be? Do you take me for a man of letters? Nom de Dieu!

Finally, you do not ask me for capital, that's kind of you. In recompense, perhaps I will send to you, one of these days, several of those precious lines that you compare to a diamond!

One thing alarms me though, and it is the pessimism *which you admit to be suffering from. If you are pessimists, which seems to give the lie to the rest of your message, you have come to the wrong guichet. It's with Huysmans that you need to speak.*

There is nothing in the world that I abhor so much as pessimism, which represents, at one and the same time, and to my horror, all imaginable impotences: the impotence of the mind, will, heart, reins, stomach. If I had the honor of being a commander in a time of war, I would have the pessimists shot, as one shoots spies and desert-

ers.

I respect only immeasurable courage
and will never accept defeat!

Cordially,

– *Léon Bloy.*

2. – The massive Buet, charitably alerted, renounces a
polemic.

Learned this: Mme. Maurice de Fl., from the
already distant epoch when I sometimes lunched at
her place, at *Sainte-Périne*, boasts about having had
me drink reddened water, while she drank, in my
presence and unbeknownst to myself, excellent wine
with her husband.

This last person, an irreproachable domestic
from any angle that you look at him, a pimp, and now
a rather insolent louse of letters after sucking the up-
pers of conquerors, has yet to perorate in editorial of-
fices. He affectionately obtained manuscripts and luxury editions from me, promptly *hiding* them with
care, and being resourceful just enough not to declare
so compromising a friendship as mine, while waiting
for the moment to repudiate me, like a bastard.

4. – To Henri Lavedan, author of the *Prince d'Aurec*,
and an intimate friend of the servant just mentioned:

My dear Lavedan,

Could you, exerting a generous effort of memory, recall a now ancient commercial transaction, but which was fortunate enough to have left its mark?

About four years ago, the manuscript of The Desperate Man *was purchased by you for 170 francs, paid in three installments. A first disbursement of 50 francs was effected through the graces of the affable Guiches, whose decease the journals failed to notify me about. The second time, you yourself brought 100 francs to the seller's lodging, devoid of any splendor at that time. Finally, this latter obtained from you a final contribution of 20 francs at the editorial office of the* Correspondant, *improved by your presence.*

Despite my reputation for someone who shakes people down for money, *a reputation propagated primarily by some athletes who adorably conned me, – rest assured, O victorious one who wades in another man's royalties, of my absolute disinterestedness.*

An ironic Providence has decreed the miraculous fiasco of all the apostles of silence *who had undertaken, at a contract rate, my death by hunger, and the famous legend of the* Ungrateful Beggar *has today become the most infecund refrain given that I have clear-*

*ly discovered the indisclosable secret
of how to subsist in a Godless society
without a pig's snout.*

*Why then, basely, would I accuse you
today of having previously profited
from the arch-known distress of an agonizing writer so as to acquire at a
dirt-cheap price the only asset he possessed?*

*But would it not seem monstrous to
you that in my new condition I should
forget the community of the poor and,
neglecting all pity for those dolorous
members of Christ who were formerly
my co-disciples at the school of patience, I should waste the occasion of
your prosperity by reminding you of
the duty to practice a little justice.
They would profit thereby, have no
doubt about it.*

– Your LÉON BLOY.

5. – Pentecost. *"Pater major me est,"*[16] says Jesus in
today's Gospel teaching. The *"minimus vocabitur"*[17]
of the Sermon on the Mount is mysteriously applied
to Himself, and Saint Paul says to the Corinthians that

---

[16]*Pater major me est*: Latin for "The Father is greater than I."
John 14:28 (Douay-Rheims).

[17]*Minimus vocabitur*: Latin for "[He... shall be] called the least [in
the kingdom of heaven]." Matthew 5:19 (Douay-Rheims).

Charity is the greatest of the Three.[18] So Jesus is indeed the *minimus*.

9. – Letter from my sublieutenant who transmits to me a long, glorious, and comminatory specious argument by a priest, one his friends.

Horrible heat. My soul is in contact with the void.

10. – Letter:

> *My dear Lieutenant,*
>
> *If you cannot* divine *the most obvious, most egregiously glaring thing in the world, what the devil could you and I possibly do together?*
>
> *I spontaneously offered to you – because your military demeanor pleased me – what many have desired or solicited without obtaining, and I have done as much as one can for strangers. What more can I do?*
>
> *You compare me to Veuillot, Drumont, and several other bastards whom the Holy Church reeks of.*
>
> *You compare me, above all, to your friend, the priest whose frankness you boast of, and who would like to have*

---

[18]Charity is the greatest of the Three: See 1 Corinthians 13:13.

me *"before his myopic eyes and his mug (sic)." But why? O just heavens!*

Ah! that priest who has lost nothing of his "vir"! who can knock anyone down with a slap, and who "plays at boules with a cuirassier on his left arm"!

I can do much better than that, me. I write love letters with a decameter cube made of rose granite suspended from my little finger and seventy-seven artillerymen balanced on the tip of my nose. Not to mention that each morning I violate ten thousand virgins successively, like an aperitif, in the space of 45 to 53-½ minutes. There! and I am not the prouder for it.

Your ecclesiastic is clearly devoured by the desire not to let himself be impressed. On this head, I admit my profound inferiority. I am, on the contrary, an easy target of every simple man who approaches me and appears to offer me his heart, and if I encountered someone great, I would immediately prostrate myself without thinking for one second to contemplate my biceps in a mirror and without feeling the least need to manifest my critical faculties.

He speaks about my soul's "sensual-

ism," scorns the assistance of "angels," the appetite for "mystical visions," all things that do not belong to "a man's faith," but "a female's impression arising more from a quivering of the flesh than the effort of thought."

Last year I lived for eight months in Denmark, a Lutheran country par excellence. *I can certify that such is the precise language of Protestantism, whose diabolic mission was to level everything in the human soul and which teaches that the religious impressions of a poet or a great artist* must needs *be absolutely identical to those of a seller of salted pork or a manufacturer of shoe polish. In the mouth of a Catholic priest, that is confounding.*

He is young, and that is his excuse. He has much to learn yet, and if he makes an effort to forget his "muscles" a little, and his cherished self-will, I hope that God will not refuse him his sacerdotal humility.

At his age, I too believed exclusively in my strength and I was foolishly proud of mine, which was great. After having prayed a good deal, I ended up by understanding that the complete man, the true man, *worthy of being shown by*

Pilate to the vile multitudes, must be a combination of strength and gentleness, and I have not scorned the Tears of Our Lord Jesus Christ, which have done as much for our salvation as the effusion of his Blood.

It is in those tears, alone, that I have found the almost superhuman vigor that I needed to suffer so much, to accept this most frightening existence, never to stop standing *at the foot of the Cross, in the tenebræ, in dereliction and tortures.*

But does he even know what the Cross means? that poor priest who discovered sensualism in the chapter where I speak about it, – so carnal is his spirit!

If he had the demeanor of a simple child or humble servant of God, he would have seen perhaps some mystery *in my works and in my person, vainly qualified by him as "magnificent." Then, he would not have thought of the "Jardin des plantes"; he would have not so much as noticed the N. de D., which I never use, besides, and which was a small concession, rather innocent, to the sublieutenant, who could very well be an old whore; he would not have remembered the admiration of prostitutes for his torso and his mustaches; finally, he would not have thought of any sort of antagonism or confrontation with Léon Bloy, who is old enough to be his father and who suffers, for twenty years now, for the Church.*

No, he would have understood, perhaps with emotion, that when such a man approaches you and him, in good faith, something good for your souls and spirits could have resulted from it, that the occasion was not to be lost, and that the respect for one's superiors is especially recommended to those who once were called the salt of the earth.

A cordial handshake to you, my dear officer, and to your friend whom I promise not to embrace like Marchenoir, who really could, who knows? strain his terrible muscles a bit.

— Léon Bloy.

11. – I am told the following:

The body of my beloved mother, exhumed many years after her death, in 1877, was seen by one of my brothers, *perfectly preserved*. The cadaver of our father, buried in the same year, was in the last state of putrefaction. This double circumstance suggests thoughts to me that I dare not jot down, that I do not understand myself. But I am shaken to the core, and I weep such tears as I hope for God's pity.

Saw a merchant of pawn tickets. So villainous an individual that I quit him with a violence. A second is also a thief, but less ignoble. He loans 35 francs on a value of 230, at a rate of one hundred twenty percent, and he affably undertakes to persuade me that he *loses money on it*. What a hideous world!

Plan for the dedication of a new edition of the *Brelan d'Excommuniés*:

> *"To the desolate memory of a friend of my youth who passed away so very abruptly, who did not know the glory of God, and who did not like the Sign of Redemption on tombs."*

12. – Is it not evident that I am the only man capable of writing definitive things on the Jewish question, so basely stirred up by Drumont?

To speak my contempt for the horrible traffickers of money, for the sordid and venenous kikes who have poisoned the universe, but to speak, at the same time, my profound veneration for the Race whence Redemption came (*Salus ex Judæis*), which visibly bears, like Jesus himself, the sins of the World, *which is right to wait for* ITS *Messiah*, and which was not preserved in the most abject ignominy if it were not for being invincibly the race of *Israel*, that is to say, of the Holy Spirit, whose exodus thence will be the marvel of Abjection. What a subject!

13. – A coming crisis, very likely. For several days now, I have had my heart in a vise, in these diabolic iron clamps that have tortured me since childhood.

Remember, Lord, that I had pity on You... So why these abominable troubles without issue? Why, above all, these infernal deceptions and the derisory privilege of the Word to a man of goodwill who lacks the means to make himself heard? It is the same lamentation for the last ten years and the same divine deafness. But my courage leaves me...

God is not absurd, however, and I am quite compelled to suppose myself the object of a favor of misfortune, in view of an exceptional dilatation of my patience in order to prepare me for some unknown mission. But if so, my God, how far must I descend?

14. – Began *Salvation Through the Jews*.

15. – Enormous suffering for my wife and me. For no other reason than the monotonous pace of our daily anguishes, a terrible melancholy falls on us.

I sadly explain to my poor companion that *my entire life* has been this way, which she can judge from the continual miracle needed to keep me from dying. I think, moreover, that, having married me three years ago in so visibly providential a manner, it was not enough that she should know material misery, but also this agony of the soul which is the misery of miseries and the most perfect of all torments.

I just wrote these last several lines while struggling under the darkest discouragement.

17. – A poor sum of money falls from heaven. And that is our life! Help infallibly arriving when we are on the verge of perishing, but *only then*, to give us enough time to get drunk on grief.

I continue my brochure on the Jews while shredding my entrails. Honorable work, I hope, but how difficult!

19. – Alcide G., a forty-year-old man, tells us that he *has never seen the dawn* but once, while on the train. That sad confession instills in us a certain feeling of contempt, mixed with a bit of fear.

23. – The brilliant monsieur to whom literature owes the *Prince d'Aurec* did not deign to respond to my letter of the 4th. To practice both usury and *Castigat ridendo,*[19] that is all fine and good. But to add boorishness on top of it is even better. I am no match.

Henri Lavedan undoubtedly belongs to the joyous multitude that accuses me of parasitism.

---

[19]*Castigat ridendo*: Latin for "Castigating [mores] through laughter."

25. – Dark day. I have no more strength. I collapse, physically and intellectually. If it is necessary to continue this existence of a damned man, I will die.

27. – Finished Zola's *La Débâcle*. All in all, a powerful book, to be honest, and which even haunted me for several days, – no doubt because I still shake because of that horrible war – but like all the other books by that author, *coarse* and carnal, despite the evident effort that he took, this time, to distance himself from the sewer pipe.

As always, identical processes of depiction for all imaginable tableaux, such as to revolt the lowest dogs of Naturalism. Not only that, the artist is completely absent from his work! The style of this master is that of a robust beast who eats very little in fact.

There is, somewhere, a so-called hospitable establishment run by the religious of *Wisdom* or *Holy Angels*, who take in small girls whom their parents cannot raise. They make them sign a pact by virtue of which these children must serve them until they are twenty-one years old. The parents have barely the right to see them one hour every two weeks and cannot have them back again except by paying a large sum of money. It is the Mont-de-Piété of human flesh.

29. – To Georges d'Esparbès:

My dear friend,

You said, "I will always love you," despite the horrible society that you keep and your filthy promiscuities. I even believe that you have not stopped loving me in your manner, which is not mine. But I need to see and touch.

The word "abandoned" bothers you. But, good God! what do you expect me to think when I see those who call themselves my friends gather in the hostile hand of my most despicable enemies, to turn against me the ignoble weapon destined for my extermination: Silence.

Do you not see then that silence is the conversation of dead men and that one must speak to the living, primarily when they are in agony and when the world abandons them?

If I were happy, your disappearance, which could last indefinitely even, would be but a banal act of boorishness. But you know that I am miserable and you know also, you of all people, who I am, *and for what noble things I suffer. If you had learnt of my death by hunger or despair, do you think that the feeling of having abandoned me, like everyone else, would have pleasantly perfumed your existence?*

But enough of that. I cannot help loving you, as one loves a child; I forgive you even for a little prostitution. Your soul is young and we will speak of these things in a decade or so, provided journalism, by then, has not putrefied you.

While waiting, I will do a decisive test on you. Not long ago, I scandalized some swine by proffering this assertion that there is only a single sign, just one, *by which to identify one's friends. This sign is called* Money. *I would surprise you, perhaps furiously, if I told you what it represents, in my eyes, this word which no one knows the symbolism of. Content yourself today with this preliminary lesson:*

I recognize a friend by this sign: he gives me some money.[20] *If he has none, but gives me his crucified desire instead, his flagrant, visible desire, gouging his heart's eyes out, it is absolutely as if he had given me some money and I immediately recognize him as a true friend.*

Do you understand? Maybe not. Then hear this: we are dying of hunger at my place. We have a good lodging, we

---

[20]Original footnote: This phrase is designed to fill my good little friends of the press with joy, who certainly will not fail to cite it, while *taking it out of context* with the greatest of care.

appear to be wallowing in bourgeois delights, and we are dying of hunger.

So, O my friend, some money! I will pay you back when I can. If you do not have any, but you happened to find some all the same, I will share with you the secret of financial operations that I have often performed for others: I put myself out. *I put myself out, even so far as begging, remembering that God himself was honored to be a beggar. However, if you truly cannot find any money, even after putting yourself through this ordeal, tell me, and I will believe you.*

That is it, the test is on, and I wait for you this evening.

– Your Léon Bloy.

D'Esparbès, having remained invisible for twenty months, arrives this evening and simply gives me what he has: forty francs.

July

3. – A friend sent me a money order for twenty francs, the need for which was extreme. Worthless money order, pending rectification, the postal clerk having written LÉVY *Bloy*! What to think of this Jewish name which is hostile to me at the very moment when I am glorifying the Race of the Jews?

7. – The images that one believes to have forgotten remain in the deepest recesses of the storehouses of the mind, like photographic plates held in reserve for the Day when everything must be revealed. And I think that this mysterious reserve is transmitted, with everything else, by way of natural *heredity*. Anne-Catherine Emmerich, for example, must have had extremely distant ancestors who were ocular and auricular witnesses of the scenes she recounts. *She remembers*.

     … The Prophets were witnesses who remembered the *Future*.

9. – Criminals sometimes cannot be caught, that is clear. Good people are always caught.

     To the Count Robert de Montesquiou-Fesensac [sic]:[21]

---

[21]Montesquiou-Fesensac: The Count Robert de Montesquiou (AD 1855-1921), a French count, aesthete, art critic, poet, etc. and, most famously, the "insolent dandy," on whom J.-K. Huysmans reputedly modeled Jean des Esseintes in *À Rebours*, and on

Monsieur,

Your renown for a rare mind, and es-pecially the brotherly reception that you extended to our great Paul Ver-laine, gives me reason to hope that you are not completely unaware of the name and even the works of an excom-municate who was precisely the most ardent panegyrist of the incomparable poet of Sagesse. Proud to be that pro-script, I have the impertinence to boast of enmities of the plume that my aggressive independence provoked.

The horror by riffraff for my writings and for my person is the truly princely jewel and very precious talisman that I wear on my pinky.

So why would I be afraid to inform you of this: I was the friend of Barbey d'Aurevilly for the last twenty-three years of his life. No one can boast a closer intimacy with that admirable artist than I had, and I possess sixty letters from him that are as dear to me as my soul.

One day, as holy misery furiously raged, never having had its fill of me, I saw myself compelled, in order to avert a grave peril that menaced other

---

whom Marcel Proust modeled the Baron de Charlus in *À la recherche du temps perdu.*

heads besides mine, to pawn that col-
lection which today I am trembling to
lose...

If I absolutely must, while shedding
tears that are a little more than bitter,
renounce this treasure, I would like at
least that it should fall into noble
hands, and I beg you to write to me
without delay if you would like to be-
come the possessor of it.

Forgive me for pressuring you in this
way, but I am pressured myself by the
acerbic voice of the exactor who
threatens to deprive me of my proper-
ty.

Accept, *etc.*

– LÉON BLOY.

11. – Valid and powerful anguish today, this forty-
sixth anniversary of my birth. It is the horrible last
week of the term, [when the rent is due,] and we lack
everything at home. How did I find the strength to
write this long letter:

My dear Lieutenant...

I received what you know, and I re-
ceived it most profitably, have no
doubt about it.

Would that you were a capitalist, in

fact, God permitting. But what am I saying? Your heart then would no longer be the same, for you know the inflexible law. The poor cannot effect the deliverance of their brothers, and the rich never wish to do so. Do not take this for a banal recrimination, however. I assert that there is a terrifying mystery therein which touches on whatever there is of the most profound, and ten years of biblical exegesis have enabled me to offer several plausible hypotheses that will be, one day, the matter of a strange book on Money,[22] *which I am planning [to write].*

While waiting, I work relentlessly at a brochure on the Jewish question. This brochure, which will have no more than one hundred pages to it and which gives me immense trouble, is certainly the most important thing I have written to date.

One forgets, when one vomits on the Jews, that the Savior himself, speaking to the Samaritan, spoke these words, a bit more considerable, am I not right, than M. Drumont's long-winded diatribes: "Salus ex Judæis est."[23] One

---

[22]Book on *Money: Blood of the Poor.*

[23]*Salus ex Judæis est:* Latin for "salvation is of the Jews." John 4:22 (Douay-Rheims).

appears as well to have forgotten that
all *Christian Liturgy comes from Jew-*
ish books; that this truly unique Race
was chosen to give to mankind

Patriarchs, Prophets, Evangelists, Apostles, faithful Friends
and all the first Martyrs...;
without daring to speak of the
Holy Virgin and Our Savior
himself who was the Lion of
Judas, the JEW *par excellence*
by nature – an indescribable
Jew! – and who, doubtless, had
employed an entire preliminary
eternity coveting that pedigree.

But, what! was it not necessary to follow to the end the
greedy street entertainer, orga-
nizer, and preacher of that crusade for a small bag of gold,
who does not stop preachifying
"from one day to the next" on
the small number of elect of the
All-Powerful Strongbox? – is
no one able to cite a single
Catholic protestation that was
heard when the unbelievable
effigy of that sacrilegious
Turlupin[24] was pasted all over
our recoiling walls: *depicted in*

---

[24]Turlupin: a disparaging epithet for a member of a religious sect
in France during the Middle Ages.

*knight's armor of the Holy
Sepulcher and treading with
his feet on...* MOSES!!!?

*These lines were taken for you from
my brochure. I add that, without even
mentioning the immense oracle
recorded by the Holy Spirit in Genesis
(IX, 27), or God's word of honor given
to Abraham* in æternum, *the Prophets,
both great and small, are literally saturated with the mysterious Promise of
a return which the New Testament has
not abrogated – and which regards
what is commonly referred to as the
last days.*

*That said, do not think, dear friend,
that my new work, which will soon be
completed, is a response to Drumont,
a polemic. God forbid that I should
give such importance to that individual who would disgust you greatly if
you knew him a little better, and whom
I absolutely deny, – I do not say talent: his literary mediocrity is unques-
tionable, – but* morality. *I could show
you, a certain dithyramb, of the most
incendiary enthusiasm, to the glory of
Jewish speculations, wherein* M.
Péreire is compared by him to
Napoleon! *In that already distant
epoch, the noble Drumont dared to
swindle Israel. Having failed, he de-*

clared war on it in the Church's name.

Unfortunately, it has gone a little too far. The death of the Jewish officer, killed by Morès, opened several Christians' eyes, who finally remembered the very rigorous censures of that same Church, so strangely defended by duelists and murderers.

One again, it has nothing whatsoever to do with that gentleman. But I was indignant to see vilified by the most abject order of financial inquests, that colossal question of Israel, and I wanted to speak, in turn, so as to say what no one else can or dares to say.

However glorious my conclusions may be for that elect *people, I entreat you to believe that it will hardly be easy to suspect me of having collected a stipend from M. de Rothschild or any other potentate of finance. But, if one insists, I could not care less, and I absolutely could not give a damn, resolved as before, as always, to say what has to be said, to shout it out* in lumine, super tecta,[25] *with no concern for the consequences.*

I am miffed, nonetheless, to learn that my letter "troubled [you] to the point

---

[25]*In lumina, super tecta*: Latin for "in [broad] daylight, from the rooftop."

*of making you suffer." But what were
you expecting, then? Having already
read me, you knew that I am unused to
masking my thought and you ought, I
believe, to esteem me a little more for
having said so without equivocation.
The abbot D. is your friend, and I do
not have the shadow of a motive to
suppose him unworthy of your affection. But his literary* impartiality
*shocked me. I cannot accept for one
moment that anyone has the right to
"admire me" when he admires Louis
Veuillot or Drumont. One must
choose.*

*Then again, what do you want? He
spoke a bit too much about his muscles, while expressing, with respect to
me, certain debile opinions tainted, I
thought, by that Sulpician Jansenism
which turns my stomach and which so
strongly resembles the apothegmatic
inanity of Protestants.*

*All in all, it is possible that I expressed
myself rudely, – everyone knows that I
do not have a soft voice – but it would
have been virile of M. D. to accept the
reprimand, considering that it came
from a man who is considerably his
senior, in faith as in doctrine, and
whom he declares himself an admirer
of. What to think of an admiration that*

would extend only to the external form of my thought, while rejecting my thought itself? That would put me on the same level as a vile phrasemonger.

You tell me that a "blind admiration" has nothing of the flatterer about it. I could respond, with a hellish arrogance and a reprobate's impertinence, that it is precisely that admiration that I thirst for. I have never desired anything else, and, when it is my turn to be the admirer of someone, I have admired the most generously that I could, without [expectation of] anything in return, without restriction; effacing myself, completely forgetting myself, most of all when I knew that the admired person was a poor person, admirably *deprived of his wages, a captive in dark places...*

There is always time to formulate one's little criticism, but when, for the first time, *one embraces a lamentable abandonee in whom one has divined Greatness, the moment is as poorly chosen as possible to tell him that he has scrofulous glands or a mushroom on his face.*

Admiration, it either exists or it does not. If it does, what is it then if not a sublime form of love? And love gives of itself entirely, spontaneously, if it is truly Love, that is to say, something other than the Nothing *that Saint Paul speaks of.* Omnia suffert, omnia credit, omnia sperat, omnia sustinet.[26]

It is what Ernest Hello, a great but little-known writer, deprived of wages, he too, called "intellectual Charity," which he was always refused. The prudent and reserved do not love and are incapable of admiration.

These very general reflections are precisely and rigorously not intended for your friend who may have some very high qualities of soul, but who is certainly not a humble *person, in the Christian or sacerdotal sense of that word. His response to his superiors is bad: "I have no reason to obey you, but I obey you." Seriously, what would you think of one of your subofficers who spoke to you like that? One always has a* reason *to obey, otherwise obedience would be absurd instead of reasonable, as the Apostle wants it,* rationabile obsequium.[27]

His letter to me, a letter of twelve lines to a writer whom he says he admires,

---

[26]*Omnia suffert...*: Latin for "[it] beareth all things, believeth all things, hopeth all things, endureth all things." 1 Corinthians 13:7 (Douay-Rheims).

[27]*Rationabile obsequium*: Latin for "reasonable service." Romans 12:1 (Douay-Rheims).

is simply the letter of a wounded man. Frankly, what do you want me to respond? Life is short, and I prefer to reread for the two-hundredth time the 34th chapter of Ezekiel.

The offer you make me on the subject of a publication along the lines of Pal touches me, and I ask you to thank your printer for me, but I have renounced such adventures. It was good, seven years ago. Today, I must manage my strength and reserve myself for my books. Above all, I do not want to be the pamphleteer *in perpetuity. I would perhaps be killed by misery, but not, I wish to hope, without having accomplished my destiny as generously as it was given to me to do so, by forcing myself to bear witness to the Glory of God in works capable of lasting a little longer than myself. I shake both your hands.*

— LÉON BLOY.

I have written enough of these letters, my God! If someone one day should get it into his head to publish my correspondence, when I will have ceased to suffer in this world, what lamentations! what dolorous implorations! and what cries of anger will exit the old drawers.

What singular destiny! Nobody seems better suited than myself to find the *Word* that is identical to

Money, and I spend my life searching for the one or the other. Same searching internally as externally.

People were bawling today about the execution of Ravachol, expecting him to rise again in three days. Idiotic riffraff!

12. – To the count Robert de Montesquiou-Fesenzac:

> *Inclyte et solivage Comes, Quid est quare nil mihi respondes? Quomodo tibi non est in optatis vehementibus negotium illud eximium quod suavissime – quanquam dolenter – ante oculos tuos proposui? Rescribe, quæso, ad efflagitatum[28] singularem quo lacessivit animam tuam humilis tortor.*

> *Existimatio tua præcellens in media senectute poeseos, sed potissime, nobilis urbanitas viscerum tuorum – ut dicitur – erga fratrem tuum Paul Verlaine, philomelarum in valle lacrymabili præstantissimum caput, gratis conjectionibus locum aperiebat.*

> *Reipsa, decet te turmas optimatum antecedentem inire misericordiam, lenitudinem, diligentiam accuratissimam in conspectu pauperum et blanditias humanitatis expletæ.*

---

[28]Original footnote: I know that the word *efflagitatus* is unusual except in the singular ablative. But I have the right to be original in every language.

> *Ergo nunc, recordare, obsecro, tigri-*
> *nam vocem fœneratoris et pericula*
> gemmarum *de quibus admonui te, in-*
> *stanti epistola, recentiore sabatto, in*
> *œdibus tuis viœ Franklin.*

> *Dignare, domine comes poeta, benig-*
> *niter accipere salutationem saluta-*
> *toris, – extra multitudinem salutato-*
> *rum – qui dicit tibi; salve amplius in*
> *Salvatore gentium.*[29]

> – LÉON BLOY.

13. – Exclusively polite letter from Montesquiou. Regret for being unable to acquire the collection of d'Aurevilly. Resolution, immediately executed, simply to go to his place and offer him my skill as an illuminator employed on a unique copy of his book.

Warm reception, by the look of things. This tall, pale man, thin and garrulous, who speaks in a voice that is *almost* strident, begins by telling me that it is impossible for him to accord me a single instant and talks about a rendezvous to be fixed for the following week. I obtain however that he lets me in for a few minutes, filled almost entirely, alas! by the flow of his words. I hardly had the time to inform him that I am an illuminator and that I am offering to illustrate for him, for a modest sum, a unique copy of his book, *Chauves-Souris*, I believe. That appears to sink in

---

[29]The Latinate reader is encouraged to translate as best he can. In other words, we generously leave this translation as an exercise for the reader.

with him a little, but he responds that he would need to see what I have already done in that genre. As for the collection of d'Aurevilly, he promises to find me someone who consents to become the acquirer of it, if only by *fedeicommis*. Absurd and impractical plan. Naturally, it is impossible for him to do such a thing himself, it being without precedent that a rich person should ever be able to do whatever it might be.

The author of *Chauves-Souris* is furnished and fitted out as if for a photograph of "great authors at home," and he spoke to me about my good appearance, seeming to oppose that observation to my claimed distress. I feel the prick of the thorn and I quit that earsplitting young man, little satisfied with him and with myself.

14. – National holiday of Churlishness. Expedition to Médan. Cruel trip, with claws around my heart. Introduced into that vilely opulent-looking house, I have a letter, thus worded, delivered:

> *Monsieur,*
>
> *I come a great distance – in all senses – and I entreat you to accord me a quarter of an hour of conversation, a half hour if possible, for a communication that you will appreciate the importance of. But* one on one.
>
> *Do not put too much credence in the legends of hatred, nor listen to your personal resentments. Simply tell*

*yourself that my behavior must have
for its object something completely impossible to conjecture about, and receive me, if not out of* curiosity, *at
least with the goodwill and good hu-
mor that are suitable to your strength.*

Accept, Monsieur, *the assurance of my*
unaccustomed *respect for the author
of* The Débâcle.

— *LÉON BLOY.*

"It has to do," I would have said to Emile
Zola, "with Barbey d'Aurevilly, buried for three years
now, whom you were the enemy of and who was
yours." And I would have *offered* him to assist me in
saving the precious collection. A portrait of the last of
the Goncourt brothers was in front of me, reminding
me of an abominable past. After five minutes, the domestic returns to tell me that *Monsieur cannot receive
me.* He has company and cannot be disturbed. The
funny man will not receive me. I depart then, relieved
of the terrible constriction in my heart, but submerged, drowned in disgust.

What is that soul made of? Here is a man
brimming over with good fortune and happiness, sati-
ated with triumphs, who knows that I am a poor artist,
VOLUNTARILY *poor*, that I have just made an actual trip: three quarters of an hour by train and half an
hour by walking, to try to see him, having spent for
that perhaps all my last sous – and he does not even
receive me!

He had guests, Huysmans or some other enemy of mine. Naturally, everyone everywhere will be
saying that I came only to ask for a handout. For a
moment, I am tempted to return in my tracks and demand the restitution of my letter. But what good will
it do?

I explain this to my wife who is aggrieved to
have prayed in vain for me: prayer is not to obtain,
but to *console* God (2 Maccab. VII, 6).

It appears that someone has erected a large luminous cross on Montmartre. That profanation was
all it needed. Charming fruit of [Pope] Leo XIII's re-
publicanism. Evidently, the end draws near.

15. – When I wake up in the morning, I often have,
for years and years, the impression of being one of
those unfortunate people condemned to a slow death,
who, totally broken from the tortures of the day before, are wrested from a ghastly sleep so as to endure
new torments.

To the Count Robert de Montesquiou-Fésen-
zac:

Monsieur,...

*I am wondering whether you have giv-
en any thought to the proposition I
made to you the day before yesterday.
I scarcely had time to speak with you
about it, and that was a great shame
for me.*

The proposition of my transcribing your book on sumptuous vellum, in the divine script of a Carolingian monk, and decorating each page with extraordinary foliations, is a magnificent offer, I assure you, and one fit to tempt a prince.

For in this profoundly forgotten art, I am worth, at the very least, *what I am worth in literature. And that is not at all a boast or an illusion. It is the opinion of a few extremely delicate and passionately difficult artists, whom I have much astonished.*

You told me that you would need to see a sample before any business could be transacted. I cannot provide one at this moment, but I could arrange to procure one by addressing myself to one or another of those who possess it.

Ah! of course they will tell you whatever they want about me. But if you have a deep heart and if you knew who I am, perhaps!... Here I am: ready to offer you one year of my appalling life, to create a work of art just *for you, if you wish to save me, for I am absolutely dying here. You spoke to me the other day about my "good appearance." May God, one day, inform you how that polite and maybe affectionate phrase was, for me, at that moment, of such cruel and heartrending irony!...*

I am reputed to be a cynical mendicant. It has even become a legend, propagated and accredited primarily by people with whom I had previously shared my daily bread and for whom I had "put my body in harm's way," as the good Joinville used to say. It was easy, no? to speak in this way about so redoubtable a man, who was believed to be so completely vanquished, beaten down by poverty, as his punishment for having never wished to become a prostitute of letters!

Besides, what I am asking for from you, does it resemble alms? Honestly, I do not think so. I am offering to be, for you, the artisan of a very beautiful work of art, and it so happens that your consent would save me from the most horrible torments. Is that any reason to refuse? This fancy for art, one of the loftiest that a man of your standing could have, will you refuse yourself the possession of it, knowing that at the same time it gave you real joy, that it would rescue, from an abyss of sorrows, a writer who is worth, am I not right? the effort you make, for whom you have not hidden your esteem, and who esteems you himself enough to confess to you that he is dying?

Why would you not suppose that I am absolutely dignant of being saved from this despair which you were speaking to me about, a despair courageously and heroically braved to this day and which, now, menaces me in so pressing, hard, and precise a manner?

Why would you not introduce into your life the beautiful folly, if it truly is one, of risking a chivalric action for this abandoned artist whom you met the other day for the first time, but with whom your soul has corresponded, perhaps mysteriously, since time immemorial?

Finally, I wrote this more than dolorous letter to you after returning from a distant, mad, desperate, and useless trip, – which broke my heart.

I cling to the hope that I will not have implored you in vain, and I will count the horrible hours, for I have reached the point of having tried everything, and of being reduced to hoping for a spontaneous movement of your soul, which is, like my own, in the hands of a Judge whose mercy, sometimes, appears strangely inactive or parsimonious.

Accept, etc.

– Léon Bloy.[30]

16. – A stranger sends me twenty francs in the mail,
accompanied by an explanatory letter of the most
touching kind. [Just imagine] if I dedicated *Salvation
Through the Jews* to this stranger!

Who knows? The horrifying undertaking at
Zola's – would it not, finally! be the lees of that chalice of humiliation and sorrow that God set before me,
since my youth, and which I have been drunk on
these last twenty years?

My dear Lieutenant,...

*I had no intention of referring to Wil-
lette's poster, which I have never seen,
moreover. My last letter made allusion
to* another *poster, I do not know by
whom, plastered everywhere not long
after the appearance of* La France
juive, *and which was just as I described it to you: Drumont, with his
mug of a flunky wearing eyeglasses,
pretending to be a Rhodian knight, if
you can imagine that, and, under his
conquering foot,* Moses... *– whose
name I cannot speak without shaking
for love, – Moses recognizable by his
two luminous horns, sprawling on his
back and clutching, in one claw-like*

hand, a bag from which gold pieces escape... The ignominy of that image is beyond words.

I saw it again, two years ago, at Savine's, who still must have several bundles of it. So you must believe what I say when I speak seriously, and consider me well-informed when I advance a precise fact of considerable importance.

Drumont's response with respect to the Péreire brothers is simply ridiculous. "He did not know"!!! C'mon, it makes you want to laugh, right?

Why speak to me about that little piece of s*** Taxil? Do you think you can influence me by threatening me with the opinion of cowards or the verdict of the goitrous? You know me poorly, O soldier.

The threat of contempt by everyone on earth – you hear what I am saying, no? – means absolutely Nothing to me, when it has to do with proffering, vociferating, what seems to me to be the Holy Truth, and the imminence even of the most refined torments could only pique my zeal.

Re-read my last letter: I have nothing better to say to you. My brochure will be, I believe, my greatest effort, be-

cause I will express what I had not yet dared to express, in good conscience. *You will grant me, in any case, that I do not lack cheek.*

The matter is given infinitely high importance. It is true that I mention Drumont in the initial pages, but in the same way that one jumps on a springboard. The curculionid, suddenly, does not appear again. I do not know whether you are able to follow me. *It is in God's hands from now on. One must have, for all that, a bit more than simple courage, – certain things which were previously given to me by an extraordinary being, never having been mentioned by* anyone.

Those who will try to find me on the side of the Jews will be mistaken, those who will try to find me on the side against the Jews will be mistaken, and those who will try to find me somewhere between these two extremes will be even more mistaken. I will wait for you at the reading. Only then will I know who you are.

Your letter, – allow me to say this to you like a brother, – it is a revelation of commonplace ideas. It has nothing to do with any of this. *And you are precisely seventy-eight billion myriameters away from my conception.*

        – *Your LÉON BLOY.*

17. – Reread a few pages of *Soirées de Saint-Péters-bourg* (Saint Petersburg Dialogs). Impossible to redis-cover the old savor. Perhaps I was ill-disposed. But without finding de Maistre *empty*, as the pneumatic Huysmans has declared, it is certain that I have prodi-giously moved on since the time when I passionately admired him. I will try again.

18. – I am so starving that *Salvation Through the Jews* has been interrupted for ten days.

20. Without cease, searching for money! Each morn-ing, resuming the death throes! I think that a galley slave is happier than I am. How to finish my brochure? I am adrift on the river of darkness.

26. – Exegesis. It is by Joseph, called *Savior of the world* in the Egyptian language (language of an-guish), that the chosen *Race* is offered to the Pharaoh (he who disperses or divides). It is, then, by Jesus that the children of the Promise and the children of Adop-tion would be offered to Him who is not yet known.

30. Moving house. We leave Vaugirard and the vicin-ity of the too-brutally significative rue *Cambronne*, to take refuge in Antony.

August

11. – To Gustave Guiches, called the *Cadger of Arkansas*.

> *My dear Guiches,*
>
> *I console myself, as best I can, for the loss of your friendship, by persuading myself that it is an unequivocal sign of your prosperity and that it was to your advantage to cast me overboard, in order to avert the evil hour.*
>
> *Some people, before you, and particularly the likable Fleury, already knew how to rein in their hearts to the point of accomplishing that dolorous sacrifice, with unparalleled dexterity.*
>
> *I am, moreover, quite sure to find you all again, each and every one of you, faithful and with arms outstretched, and as steadfast as rocks, on the very eve of the blessed day when success finally visits me!*
>
> *Meanwhile, the vineyards of Lot exuberate, they say, and money pours into your coffers. I possess this consoling news from M***, with whom you lived for a period of time, in the dark epoch, and who is no less crucified than me because of your abandon.*

Now, does it not seem to you, my generous friend, that after having deprived me of your affection, it is a bit severe to add insult to injury by robbing me of the small sums of money that I deprived myself of for you, when we were miserable together, the total of which amounts to no more than a hundred francs.

My commercial inferiority did not allow me to record the exact amount of diverse borrowings that you honored me with, but you know that it is more or less that, and you have too much aristocracy to contest so miserable a sum.

You will forgive me, I am certain of it, this financial reminder from our good old days of long ago, considering that I have not yet obtained the favors of capricious Fortune, and that I would, assuredly, be less necessitous of it if I had been less energetically squeezed by several elite souls who accuse me, today, of having been their torturer.

Hoping for a cordial response from you, which cannot be long in the coming, I confraternally shake your hand.

– LÉON BLOY.

P.S. It would obviously be excessive of me to remind you of the several expen-

*sive books that you also borrowed
from me, and that you have, doubtless,
long since added to your shelves.*[31]

13. – D'Esparbès informs me about the next issue of
the *Journal* and advises me to write to Séverine, capable, he thinks, of having me admitted.

Remy de Gourmont reproaches me for not yet
having used Villiers phrase about Huysmans: "Huysmans! the hands of a bishop! the hands of an infante!
Let's go! Bloy: the hands of a *hunchback!*"

De Gourmont readily sniffs at Huysmans, like
a cantharis sniffing at excrement.

14. – To Madame Séverine:

Madame,...

*You love the oppressed, well do I know
– but you do not love them perhaps the
same way that I do. You need them,
above all, fragile and pale. Your sensibility, charming moreover, and the
easily audacious enthusiasm of your
pity, are at that price, I am afraid to
say.*

---

[31]Original footnote: It goes without saying that no response ever
arrived. Gustave Guiches, who is one of our good all-around
writers and who has all sorts of courage, was promoted
Chevalier, on the July 14, 1895. CHEVALIER!!! The Academy lies in
wait for this prey.

Am I wrong to suppose that complaints of Strength, *for example, would not touch your heart, and that a rugged male overcome by the multitude would affect you infinitely little?*

If Biblical expressions please you, I am, do you not know this? one of those men of the evening *"whose hand is raised against everyone and against whom everyone's hand is raised." I have lived, apologetically, in an extreme solitude peopled by the resentments and savage desires that my execration of contemporaries gave birth to, writing or vociferating what seemed just to me, even if it killed me, and not demanding for my aggressions or defense the succor of any other secular quill.*

I will not start today, then, Madame, by insulting you, – you, whose alert prose is doubtless implored by a very large number of needy writers and mendicant vanities.

I merely wanted to tell you that I have read your fine article on the Pope, and that in my quality as an apostolic Roman Catholic, known for the prickly intransigence of his thought, I congratulate you and deeply thank you, considering myself, from now on, in your debt.

It may be that this vote of confidence is agreeable to you, coming from a man who is unlike any other, who so- licits nothing, who does not joke, and who has never been a laggard when it comes to slapping this or that power- ful person in the face.

Inhabitant as I am of the most solitary lazarets, I could not ignore your gen- erous plea, being myself on the eve of publishing, on the Jewish question, a rather strange opuscule which con- tains slaps for everyone, except those who think and act as it has pleased you to do.

In a word, I defend the circumcised for reasons that the Vicar of Jesus Christ did not deem it his duty to tell you and which are, believe me, a little nobler and deeper than the prattlings of hypocrisy or pusillanimous cupidity.

I have been paid, *moreover, from the same till as you have, but much more dearly, because of my superior notori- ety as a Catholic hired assassin, which has already earned me such abundant riches, as everyone knows.*

I hope, Madame, that you will readily accept, in all simplicity of heart, the homage of a fraternal sympathy which I rarely have the opportunity to em-

ploy.

– Léon Bloy.

Today, the 10th Sunday after Pentecost, I saw this: the Pharisee represents Jesus and the Publican the Holy Spirit. Observed that the first says *what he is not*, NON SUM,[32] while the second affirms, while asking for grace, that he *is* a sinner.

A strange light is cast on that evangel by the nearness of these two texts: *Omnis qui se* EXALTAT, *humiliabitur*[33] (Luke 18:14); *Oportet* EXALTARI *Filium hominis*[34] (John 12:34).

15. – How many times have I been struck by this idea that the first masses of the day, said at dawn or at sunrise, which so easily touch the heart, are said primarily *for domestics*! The masters do not rise so early.

There has got to be something to write about on this monstrous dereliction of the Holy Infancy of the Day. What a subject! THE MASS OF DOMESTICS.

Read several chapters of *Salvation Through the Jews* to Esparbès. Curious experiment. This ignorant fellow, as little prepared as could be for such

---

[32]Non sum: Latin for "I am not."

[33]*Omnis qui se*...: Latin for "every one that exalteth himself, shall be humbled." Luke 18:14 (Douay-Rheims).

[34]*Oportet exaltari*...: Latin for "The Son of man must be lifted up." John 12:34 (Douay-Rheims).

thoughts, nevertheless enjoyed their expression and he is pleased to cry out... It would be unprecedented to make someone swallow, by dint of art, a work so special, so profoundly religious.

> *When one speaks amorously of God, all human words resemble blinded lions looking for a water well in the desert.* (Salvation Through the Jews.)

22. – A letter from Zurich, insufficiently stamped, which I am required to pay fifty centimes for. I had them, by a miracle. *Negative* response from Montesquiou to my cry of despair on July 15. But how negative, and who could say? Even the handwriting is nonexistent, indecipherable, like the nothingness that is the habitacle of that soul.

Esurivi, et non dedistis mihi manducare: sitivi, et non dedistis mihi potum...[35] "These works are simple," said Hello, "but the Columns of Heaven tremble."

26. – To Georges d'Esparbès:

> *I am not content with myself, my dear d'Esparbès. You told me, yesterday, an admirable thing and I did not know how to express my emotion to you which was very powerful. It endures still. It took hold of me in the great*

---

[35]*Esurivi, et non...*: Latin for "I was hungry and you gave me not to eat: I was thirsty, and you gave me not to drink." Matthew 25:42 (Douay-Rheims).

calm of the night and I felt its presence in all the folds of the tenebræs.

That pit of Chaos that swallowed up a battlefront, that gob of earth that avidly inhaled, in a single gulp, the horse riders and foot soldiers, the cannons and bugles, the drums, children of thunder, and all that hullabaloo of the melee around the flags; that sudden swallowing, by Death, of a multitude in conflict with Glory; and that hollow of the Globe whence painfully remounts, – like a slow spider on the pale thread of fright, from the abyss – the aphonic clamor of majesty, a dying insect's shiver, almost inaudible already, which was the Dominical Orison of the liturgy of the Potentate, sobbing now, in the back rows, with the people in agony, in the intestines of the abyss!...

It is prodigious, that, my friend, and I would consider myself criminal if I did not express it to you as forcefully as I can.

It is a strict duty and the most noble charity in the world to fill an obviously superior man with a feeling of his proper strength. I know this, me, who almost never obtains anything of that alm.

> *In good conscience and in all honesty,*
> *my dear d'Esparbès, I do not know of*
> *any contemporary capable of invent-*
> *ing such a poem. I am obsessed by it.*

> *– Your* LÉON BLOY.

27. – In the *Mercure de France*, long article about me. Œuvre by a little Swiss-German who generously stuffed himself at my table, last winter. One could not be more vilely malevolent, and it is difficult to be stupider. This effort of his deserves some sort of payment:

> *Most assuredly, my dear monsieur*
> *William Ritter, it was within your*
> *rights not to see in me anything other*
> *than an unjust, arrogant, scatological*
> *pamphleteer, a fierce stirrer-upper of*
> *the most abject sentiments, exclusively*
> *committed, or nearly so, to the menial*
> *tasks of a cesspool emptier, etc. Such*
> *are your amicable expressions. But*
> *you forgot to include one gracious epi-*
> *thet, that of the* ungrateful *beggar, a*
> *regrettable omission that will, have no*
> *doubt about it, sadden some very no-*
> *ble hearts.*

> *It was equally within your rights, and*
> *this is incontestable, not to adore my*
> *books and even to give me some ad-*
> *vice, such as that of writing for "noble*
> *young women"!!! What am I saying?*

No law demanded that you accept a
compromising *friendship, it is true,*
which I offered to you out of the good-
ness of my heart.

One always has the right to possess
vile sentiments and to express his
opinions uningeniously.

But to betray the most... imprudent
hospitality, to the point of including, in
hateful terms, the names of my family
in the divulgation of a poverty that I
perhaps have the right to be proud of,
having preferred it to the profitable
prostitution of my literary enemies, –
that, my very dear monsieur, is simply
a villainy. I am ignorant of the Swiss
language; but in French, there exists
only one word to qualify precisely a
pigswill of that barrel.

You lack even, and it is frightening to
say so, a corner grocer's instinct of
justice, who, in the absence of nobility,
would have warned you of the material
prejudice *that such an indecent re-*
portage could cause me.

In consequence, I entreat you immedi-
ately to return to me the two dedica-
tions which, at the request of a com-
mon friend, I had the stupidity to write
for you. I want to prevent you, in the
future, from falsely taking advantage

*of a friendship or of an esteem that I
refuse to extend to you from now on.*

*Having become my declared enemy,
you will disgust me infinitely less.*

– LÉON BLOY.

28. – "We have no need for rabid dogs." Response from Fernand Xau to whom my collaboration was proposed.

29. – I am close to finishing *Salvation Through the Jews*, horribly difficult work which required me to elaborate under circumstances where the writing of a memorandum of fumistery[36] would have been discouraging even for a hero.

The difficulty is so great that I fell into a profound despondency for one hour this morning. Example. The 23rd chapter of Ezekiel to be explained thus: that *Oolla* is the Synagogue and *Ooliba* is the Church, but how to say that? So I must assume the air of a prophet and announce that the Church will treat the Holy Spirit just as the Synagogue treated Jesus. Terrible! And that's not all. I need to return to the "cursed Fig Tree" and the *excrements* that revive it, so that the

[36]Fumistery: a kind of exaggerated or elaborate deception that goes to great lengths to pull the wool down over somebody's unwary eyes, in the style of Candid Camera; it was practiced by various writers and performers at the Hydropaths Club and later the Chat Noir cabaret and journal during the Belle Epoque. See *Ten Years a Bohemian* by Emile Goudeau, published by Sunny Lou Publishing, 2021.

Salvation through the Jews might be the consequence of a new fructification of that symbolic tree. Etc. All the art in the world is useless, I must have ideas and facts. My work will be in vain and absurd if my conclusion is not perfect, and that is why I am so very anxious.

31. – I found my conclusion. I will finally be able to escape, then, this brochure which keeps me captive for two long months now.

I suppose that, from here on out, there are no more friends to be hoped for, for me, in what is called the Catholic world.

Some fine little dramas are playing out around us. It is frightening to think of the things that one does not know, of the venenous beasts hiding [in obscure places] and whose vicinity is near.

September

1st. – Completion of *Salvation Through the Jews*.

Very unexpected visit by an artist from Michigan or Illinois. This American crossed the Pacific, traveled through Asia, then directed his trajectory towards me from the summit of the Great Pyramid. Unfortunately, he speaks only English. Our conversation is rather painful.

2. – Reread several pages of Balzac (*Peau de Chagrin*), almost with boredom. The weakness in style of that great man appears extreme to me, and my recent scriptural preoccupations make me see, cruelly, the *nothingness* of that intelligence which is completely external, which never went any further than the superficies.

It is clear that a vast chasm has just opened up before me and that I see myself profoundly separated from the strongest impressions of my youth.

4. – More of the *Peau de Chagrin*. Balzac wins back my heart a little. His form is forever null; his thought is too often debile. But he possesses the mysterious gift of *life* and it appears that that suffices. No matter, I can no longer rediscover the Balzac of my youth.

6. – De Groux declares to me that he "is ashamed to

carry a watch while I am starving." And he hands me fifty francs.

7. – Heard this in a café: "I always bend over for money."

Recounted by de Gourmont. A journalist goes to interview a professor of theology at Saint-Sulpice *about the Holy Ghost*. Response: "Its time is passed"!!!

8. – De Gourmont tells me about his anger with Huysmans who wrote him a ridiculous preface for the *Latin mystique*. Oh! we understand each other very well.

10. – To Henry de Groux.

Dear friend,...

With inexpressible stupefaction, I learn that, tired of being a great artist, you are on the verge of accepting a job as a [floor] polisher with an art dealer who offers you the dazzling wage of five francs a day.

You have failed to understand that, as such, you would be the willing dupe of a pretty little trick that the amiable S. would profit by, who makes a pretense of looking down on you and who, in cahoots with the thrice-hateful dealer of secondhand goods, would make you sweat blood so that he can entertain the chlorotic whores of his choosing.

Really, I am suffocating with rage to see you so disarmed, the unwitting dupe of every riffraff, when a firm attitude would surely make you triumph.

For it is glaringly obvious that you are, at this moment, the ONLY painter and that people need you. How to make you see it?

You are worth fifty thousand francs a year, at least, and it is because there is unlimited confidence in your foolishness as a man of genius that they offer you, knowing full well that you haven't two sous to rub together, a job more suited to a fille du tube *at one hundred sous a job.*

You would consent to that, you, the greatest artist I know at the present hour! No, tell me it is not so. Someone told me a joke.

Your only friend, perhaps, the uncouth man who tells you the truth because he loves you.

– LÉON BLOY.

12. – Read an article by the filthy Lepelletier on Barbey d'Aurevilly, whom he proclaims to be a great
man, three years after having dragged his name
through the mud, the same day of his interment.

20. – "M. Adrien Demay, bookseller, 21, rue de
Châteaudun, Paris, just put on sale a new book by
LÉON BLOY, the audacious writer whose name alone
strikes fear in the entire press corps:

SALVATION THROUGH THE JEWS

*The author, openly hostile to anti-
Semites whom he demonstrates the intellectual non-existence of, is not
afraid to take sides with the race of Israel, in the name of higher interests,
and he goes so far as to claim that the*
salvation of the human race is in solidarity with the destiny of the Jews.

This book wherein LÉON BLOY, *so
well-known for his extraordinary powers of eloquence, appears to have surpassed himself, will be regarded, without a doubt, as the most decisive response to the furious aggressions of a
party whom the Catholic church itself
condemned the rage of."* (Publisher's
Prospectus.)

Article by Remy de Gourmont in the *Figaro*.
Very capably executed. He had forewarned me of its
irony. There is none. The subject appears to have

grabbed him.

Demay informs me that Georges L., a friend of thirty years who so disgustingly abandoned me, came, in my absence, insidiously to counsel him on *moderation*. Who deputed this little Judas?

Dedication among others:

For you, my very dear friend, Georges d'Esparbès, this book written in the cave of the equitable Molossians, so that you might have, if possible, the vision of that flaming Sword that turns, which is mentioned in the BIBLE.

21. – Received *Au Ciel!* a volume of eucharistic poetry by Jean Casier, a Belgian lyrical poet. Idiot.

24. – Dolorous day. Our life resembles a poor boat riddled with holes that cannot stay afloat for one single hour at sea.

My publisher has not sold one copy.

26. – The *Gils Blas* takes me back. Their money is as good as any other, and all the journals pay the same. The poor have no right to be disgusted.

October

3. – The necessity of finding topics for articles that can interest both myself and the *Gil Blas* exasperates me! This swine of a journal, and this journal of swine, is brimming this morning with such praises for Renan, who just died, that I botch the beautiful news item provoked by that bastard. The "End of a Charming Promenade" is most certainly an execrable long-winded piece that I will never be able to live down.

6. – Honestly, I still cannot believe that I am condemned to this ignominious collaboration with the *Gil Blas*.

8. – To Alfred Vallette, director of the *Mercure de France*, accompanied by a copy of "*Le Secret de Renan*."

> *My dear Vallette,*
>
> *I had promised you the beginning of my* Exégèse des Lieux Communs, *and today you see me afflicted by being unable to keep my word, for I am an* exact *man and very proud of this virtue that only my friends know about.*
>
> *You will not have my copy then, this time, but, most fortunately, I have*

something much better to offer you.

Here attached is an old, rather short article, by Ernest Hello, the great Un-known Writer, on the god of cowards who has just been buried equitably, like an old rotting cow.

This article published by the Revue du Monde Catholique, *on November 10, 1863, appears to me a strong and cu-rious thing to reproduce, on the day after the funeral orations for that Ju-das...* Maccabee.

It was not enchased, I believe, in any of that poor, great man's books – books, moreover, which were pro-foundly ignored – and I think that the Mercure *will not be dishonored by its insertion.*

Please accept, etc.

– LÉON BLOY.[37]

9. – Heard speak of Georges L., my friend of thirty years. There is nothing more to say, he has complete-ly and irrevocably abandoned me. His mind is made up. He obstinately maintains that a cross existed on d'Aurevilly's tomb, all these *thirty-three* or *thirty-five months* during which no human eye could perceive it. A

[37] Original footnote: Hello's article, "*Le Secret de Renan*" [Renan's Secret], was published, with this letter, in the *Mercure de France*, November 1892.

lady told him so, and that suffices for him. He ac-
knowledges owing me a great deal; he does not deny
that, without me, he would be exactly less than nothing, but such is life that the best of friends have a falling out in the end, alas! We end in senility.

10. – Cross of Saint Paul. 1 Cor. XIII, 13. "Nunc
autem manent, fides, spes, charitas; tria hæc : *major
autem horum est charitas.*"[38]

FIDES **CHARITAS** SPES

12. – Ah! They make me work hard for my daily
bread, the people of the *Gils Blas!*

Here it is, fifteen years now that I am [stand-
ing] in boiling oil, before the *Latin Gate*, and it is
through this gate, however, that the triumphant must
pass.

15. – Good article by Bernard Lazare on *Salvation
Through the Jews*. This Lazare appears to be the *only*
one to have seen that the basis of my doctrine is "the
adoration of the Poor."

---

[38]*Nunc autem manent...*: Latin for "And now there remain faith,
hope, and charity, these three: but the greatest of these is
charity." 1 Corinthians 13:13 (Doauy-Rheims).

16. – Continuation of agreeable marvels. An exquisite
letter arrives from a reader in Indre, Henry Hornbostel, perfectly unknown by me until today, who cul-
tivates his admiration for my prose as if it were an infinitely rare plant, for the maintenance of which it
would be expedient not to spare any prodigality.

Lunched in Berny, at Yvanhoé Rambosson's,
with d'Esparbès and Alcide Guérin. At desert, I share
military anecdotes, memories from 1870. D'Esparbès,
all beaming in glory, thinks that such tales, in the *Gil
Blas*, would consolidate my situation by showing me
to be something else besides the pamphleteer of leg-
ends. Maybe.

17. – To Henry Hornbostel:

Dear Monsieur,...

*I am deeply touched by the extraordi-
nary way in which you express your
admiration for me. I have so many enemies, and I am so habituated to a
perfect injustice with the most atrocious maneuvers of hatred, that testimonies of sympathy which are made to
me, I do not know why, for some time
now, always cause me an extreme surprise.*

*I began my literary life too late, and I
have lived too much outside the world,*

sequestered in thoughts that it despises, so as not to have, with respect to it, the disadvantage of an incorrigible naïvety of soul, which my enemies have abused with marvelous cruelty, I urge you to believe.

Despite the faculties of a vociferator that people are generally in agreement to recognize in me, I have presented myself to this sad world, terribly unarmed, as a facile dupe, with a mark on his back in advance. I have given myself to habile enemies who have not given themselves to me, and I have given all my soul in exchange for hypocritical protestations. When I learned from my mistake, it was already too late, and my indignant complaints passed naturally for the height of ingratitude.

It is easy, is it not? to conceive of the frightening situation of a man deprived of fortune, an indigent among indigents, overwhelmed, left to die for despair, for lack of absolute Justice, as incapable of resignation as of calculation, and face to face with a society of ruffians or empoisoners, against whom he feels irresistibly called on to utter the divine Clamor...

You have read The Desperate Man. *Well then! tell yourself that the somber*

Marchenoir is I, and that I have not recounted half my hell.

You know, doubtless, that I was interdicted by the entire press, alone against everyone for years, without encountering, unless it were by pity, a single being courageous enough to defend me. The most intrepid among those who are revolted by iniquity, which I have greatly suffered from, those even who are generally regarded as temerarious or daredevils, have trembled or tremble still.

Ah! Life has not been sweet to me!...

For the last three weeks, however, a reprieve was declared. The Gil Blas, *at risk of dying in its own liquid, has imagined infusing itself with human blood. This recourse arrived just in time. Having to preserve other people's existences besides my own, I have repressed my disgust and put myself to the task that devours irreparable time...*

For the grace of God! I want to hope that this provisory journalism will not distance from me those who love me, as you do, for "my talent and my character."

Here attached are three journal articles already published. I think that you

will feel the embarrassment of a stal-
lion of my sort, yoked to this vehicle of
prostitution and stupidity. I write what
I can, as sincerely and as nobly as it is
given to me, but with prudences that
hardly encourage me, and in such hor-
rible vicinities!

Accept, etc.

– LÉON BLOY.

Read in the *Figaro* the preface to Bourget's
next book: *Promised Land.*

Oh! The imbecility and pedantism of that
preface!

18. – To Bernard Lazare, *ut reviviscat*:

I am so used to not expecting any sort
of justice from my contemporaries,
and the mere effort of introducing me
[to the public] presupposes so rare an
instance of heroism, that your article
gave me, I dare say, a sudden shiver.

I had addressed the volume to you
without ulterior motive, nor calcula-
tion, simply because it gave me plea-
sure to do so, because your nickname
of "God's adjutant" was agreeable to
me, and because, knowing you to be

*devoid of riches although circumcised,
I had reason to believe that no one
would suspect me of wishing to sell a
dedication.*

*You had responded with a beautiful,
truly generous article, – a very un-Is-
raelite thing to do, which you yourself
acknowledge. I send to you then, in
addition to my dedication, a warm embrace with both hands, which are not
yet, I urge you to believe, on the verge
of falling into putridity, much as some
individuals, deserving of a thrashing,
would like to be persuaded.*

*You knew enough to see that the Poor
was the basis of my thought, the
adored captive of my solitary donjon.
That, Monsieur, is infinitely honorable
for your soul.*

*The fact is that I have nothing else to
say. Jews and Christians, carnal readers of a frighteningly symbolic Book,
all live, for forty centuries now, on the
illusion of a magnificent and omnipo-
tent God. I think, on the contrary, that
one must quit everything, sell everything, in order to give alms to this
Lord who possesses nothing, who can
do nothing, who is infirm in all his
members, who feels very ill, who is
stretched out on the dungheaps of the
Orient and the Occident, and who*

*cries with anguish, for eternities,
while waiting for the Carillon of the
Seventh Day.*

*It is for that reason, Monsieur, that I
execrate the triumphant and delicate.*

*If the Jews were unjustly oppressed,
they would still interest me because
there would have been a Pharaoh to
cover in insults; but, happily, they
were oppressed the most justly in the
world, being themselves the most equitable and abject oppressors ever seen.
Marvelous occasion for me for an œc-
umenical insolence.*

*I love them then for having procured it
for me and, in that sense, you are a
thousand times correct to call me a*
philosemite.

Accept, etc.

– Léon Bloy.

20. – The *Eunuch*, my article on Bourget, appears this
morning. The epigraph is an attention grabber:

*Paul Bourget: "You really detest me
then, Bloy, don't you?" Léon Bloy:
"No, my friend, I despise you." [From
a conversation] at Barbey d'Aurevilly's place, in 1882.*

I still remember it, and Bourget must remember it, although it was ten years ago. He was so furious!

Everyone counsels me now to fall on Maurice Barrès. Why not? Renan's daughter!!!

22. – Let us read this cantankerous person, given that our profession demands it. Impossible to flush out anything other than the little mechanism of the *Me*. Narcissistic ass-licking to foment the loutishness of schoolboys. Curious imagination, if one must absolutely like something; ignoble soul, certainly, but how ignoble! Who could say?

23. – Eruption of excrement. "The Bad Poor," an article against me in the *Gil Blas* of all places. It states that I am a "hysterical, filthy, launcher of stink balls into salons; a sad, intermittent, and insipid fella, but invariably abject; a Diogenes of brothels and a cynical puppet, embodying in himself all the vices, all the compromissions, all the base behaviors; and finally, a *lubricious*, parasitic, sanctimonious *hypocrite*."

Work of a poor devil descended, through domestics, from an old family of Périgord, and now in the service of Bourget, who takes shots at me. Nom de plume: *a woman's name*. Quite a pointless precaution, I would really be sorry to cause him (or her) the least trouble.

26. – Response. I observe, with moderation, that all this is quite boring because simple folks will readily believe that I refused to sleep with that *lady*. I end by announcing to the public that I will discuss, in my next article, Maurice Barrès.

27. – Huysmans says that he *dictated* all my books to me. Gustave Guiches himself, the quiet cadger, would have given me some helpful counsels.

31. – Steps taken by Richepin, sent by Barrès to the *Gil Blas'* administration, to obtain that my new article be refused. Insuccess by the ambassador who consoles himself by considering the irreproachable volley [of invective] that his excellent friend will very probably receive.

November

1st. – Bells [ringing] on the night of the dead. Bells that ring for a long time because of their parentage with the Ghost who must resuscitate all the dead. Why couldn't Paradise be defined like this: A place where all the church bells ring forever?

8. – Read *Promised Land* by Bourget. Unforgiving tedium. The mediocrity of this author is so infallible that I do not even come across any of the remarkable stupidities that I expected.

If only it were rinse water, one could nourish the pigs with it! But it is toilet water, after washing the bidet!

11. – Publication of *The Abyssinian*, the first of my military tales. Conclusive attempt. I will leave my literary contemporaries then – provisorily – to eat a bit of Prussian. This will change me, and I will become perhaps durable at the *Gil*.

A stable where one might have regular meals. A paradise for an old bag of bones scorned by the knacker. Such is my lot.

14. – New attempt at reading *Promised Land*. It is clear that Bourget has given it his greatest effort of an indigent spirit. But how vile a soul shows through!

The poor, bizarre fellow is hypnotized by such commonplaces as this: "Children do not ask to come into the world."

15. – I devise the story of an old gendarme who, not wishing to know anything else than his duty, which is to arrest all malefactors, undertakes the arrestation of fifty thousand Germans.

20. – Saw, in the journals, the horrible business of Bismarck, confessing his iniquities before the entire world. That dreadful old man assuming, in this way, the extermination of a million men!

24. – To a young writer who will not keep his promises:

> *My dear friend,...*
>
> *Pardon me for writing you a letter, a very rapid one moreover, without any sort of need, merely to please myself.*
>
> *I have read your book in a single sitting,* with extreme satisfaction. *You must believe me. I have never flattered anyone, you know that, and I tell you my honest thoughts. It is Maupassant, perhaps, but, then again, a very superior Maupassant,* on the edge of the abyss, *inspirited with the most bitter*

Flaubert.

The newlyweds D. have paid me a visit, like phantoms who had never before seen my contempt for the world, and who have filled me with the most salutary horror...

Of course, your form still leaves something to be desired. You are hesitant still before the definitive word, the implacable word that one never retracts, which can set occult powers into motion. However, what a wonderful hand you already have to capture people's heart!

And this is what surprises me, given that you tell me you have not suffered. You do not know this perhaps, but I will tell you that it is enormous to have received so much gratis.

There is, particularly in the last tale, a sort of presentiment, how can I say? something like the act of leaning over the balcony in order to see what is beyond, *infinitely beyond the story itself. The redemption of the Poor Man by the Prostitute! Ah! if only you knew where that leads to!*

A very cordial hand shake.

— LÉON BLOY.

December

2. – From Paris to Mamers. I am the immediate neighbor of a poor tubercular woman who goes to die in her home town, and whom I wrap in my blanket so as not to see her freeze to death along the way. This unfortunate woman makes her way on *charity*, and the good hearts that expedite her to the cemetery of her natal village have, naturally, offered her a homicidal 3rd class seat. I suppose the Christian intention is to hasten the end of her sufferings.

Read, in a Mamertine café, "The Obstacle," the fourth of my military tales. What joy to contemplate my phrases at forty leagues from Paris.

5. – The *Art Moderne*, in Brussels, has just published the following article, refused, it goes without saying, by the ponces at the *Gil Blas*, with the most impetuous indignation.

The Archconfraternity that it speaks of is nothing but Anarchy, explosive and militant Anarchy, which made a bloody paté, last month, at the police station on the rue des Bons Enfants.

THE ARCHCONFRATERNITY OF
THE GOOD DEATH

*In momento, in ictu oculi,
in novissima tuba.*[39]

*People are going to think, of course,
that I am on the verge of uttering a
homily. Would that they might calm
down. I would simply like, after so
much of the world, to reassure, if only
little, a public struck with inquietude,
by conferring on it in my turn some inestimable advice.*

*But, before anything, I want to make
an observation, an amusing thing, that
at the precise moment when Dynamite
made a pastiche, once again, of True
Anger, they had not yet completely finished paraphrasing, here and there, in
the churches draped with night, the
several canonical words that I auda-
ciously stamp this chat with, and
which are the very essential rubric of
the melancholic and redoubtable November of the Dead.*

*"At that very moment, in the blink of
an eye," and even in the fiftieth part of
the interminable span of the blink of
an eye, one is reduced to gruel, osten-
sibly and irreparably swept away by*

---

[39]*In momento...:* Latin for "In a moment, in the twinkling of an eye,
at the last trumpet." 1 Corinthians 15:52 (Douay-Rheims).

*the villainous, but incontestably deci-
sive blast of Anarchy.*

*So why then would I be forbidden from
designating in no uncertain terms the
anonymous companions of the* Propa-
ganda, *by bestowing on their sympathetic troupe the well-deserved denom-
ination of* ARCHCONFRATERNITY OF THE
GOOD DEATH?

*Ah! well do I know that this appella-
tion has served too often already. It
would be inexcusable of me to ignore
that a mass of Christians has long
since usurped it.*

*No one can tell me that a large num-
ber of devout people, more or less
promised an evisceration and a calci-
nation, have not many times formed a
coalition with a view to escaping, by
reciprocal suffrages, the inconvenience of appearing inadvisedly before
God, with a dirty conscience. But the
anarchists, informed of the inexistence
of this God, have fortunately found the
presentable expedient that was needed
to envisage, in our epoch, the necessity of dying with less fright.*

* * *

In 1871, Louis Veuillot who was not

masking his thought any more than his visage, and who was willfully lambasting his adversaries, was made aware one fine day of the inclemency of the populo. *He was made to understand that it could very well happen that he would be killed at home.*

He immediately responded, in a famous article, that the accomplishment of that menace would satisfy his wishes, by sparing him in a certain way from the disgusting agony that he, doubtless, bitterly foresaw and that the disloyal inaction of his assassins did not allow him to evade.

Let us imitate this great man who died a dotard and whose strong soul liquifacted, ten years in advance, at the thought of the mechanical bed and the "ridiculous vessels presented by lachrymose affections."

This rude male would have envied us the electrifying consolations of dynamite. To be dissipated in one second, as if by thunder, while dismaying the multitudes, and terminating – just like Romulus – an existence ordinarily filled with filth and troubles; to obtain even, by the example of the most illustrious citizens, a funeral at the expense of the State and a panegyric by a President of Council, declaring that "you found death at the moment when you were accomplishing your duty, like a fallen soldier in the battlefield, defending the flag*"; to receive the "last farewell" of the municipal Council and the Prefecture of Police, and to leave the world with that impression that you were the holocaust sacrificed for something infinitely great!... Ah! the* Good Death *and the enviable destiny!*

For there is no doubt about it, it is for sacred and noble things that we have all *been invited to the expressive contradances of Anarchy: Property, Money, the right to enjoy, the right to be cowards and imbeciles, and the facultative privilege, above all, of having no pity for the poor, – from Christopher Columbus who discovered sixty nations and doubled the size of the World without having ever received the shadow of a salary, to the least of our teeth-clacking vagabonds, who does not even know where to find a morsel of bread and who would, with all his heart, make an alm of his useless eyes to the fish in the river.*

* * *

An individual recalls, several days ago

in the Gil Blas, *the curious story of crates of dynamite stolen from the little train station of La Chapelle, in Paris, last July, and which the police were unable to recover.*

According to that informer, the precious material, thus hijacked, can amount to 150 kilos, and the charge of the bomb detonated on rue des Bons Enfants was only, in the words of an expert, from 7 to 8 kilos.

So there would be, supposing that the anarchists were assisted by Providence, one nice little explosion per week, throughout the winter. What a delicious thought! Do you not find that this archconfraternity of dynamiters is about to become particularly interesting, and that because of it we are going to find ourselves in the rather glorious position of scorning, for example, the eventual return of that ignoble cholera, which had nothing more to offer us than a dirty and stinking death?

My God! we will simply have to get used to it, just as we get used to bugs or scabies, and if we fail to get used to it, we will need, necessarily, to die of fear.

We will be able to contemplate, then,

if we take the time to lift ourselves a little higher than base ideas, the marvelous fructification of the seeds of bourgeois hypocrisy and philosophical atheism, after half a dozen lusters.

The sensualists, practically innumerable, who do not consider themselves riffraff, had dreamt of accommodating themselves to the divine Absolute and instituting, for the entire duration of the centuries, a moral middle ground. But the Absolute refused to subscribe, and the expiry of practical jokes having arrived, it is Panic, in a full sweat, that one hears knocking at the door...

* * *

Do you wish to know what a raggetytaggety and rawboned prophet wrote, several years ago, whose name I do not have the right to mention, – if you know, you know – extremely obscure as it is. That atrocious page of writing, although lacking a certain eloquence, is rather curious to read, at this moment in time:

> "Ah! you teach us that we are on earth to amuse ourselves. Well! let us go amuse ourselves, we others, dying of hunger and dressed in rags.

You never see those who are weeping, and you think of nothing but diverting yourself. But those who have wept while watching you, for thousands of years, will one day divert them-selves when it is their turn and, – given Justice is decidedly ab-sent, – they will come, at any rate, to inaugurate the simu-lacrum, using you for their en-tertainment.

"Given that we are criminals and the damned, we will pro-mote ourselves to the dignity of perfect demons, in order to ex-terminate you ineffably.

"From now on, no more prayers muttered at street cor-ners, by shivering, hungry beg-gars, while you pass. There will be no more claims or harsh recriminations. It is finished, all that. We will grow silent...

"You keep the money, the bread, the wine, the trees, and the flowers. You keep all the joys of life and the inalterable serenity of your consciences. We will no longer ask for any-thing, we will no longer desire all those things that we have desired and asked for in vain, for so many centuries. Our complete despair will publicly proclaim, from this moment on, *against ourselves*, the definitive prescription that adjudges them to you.

"Only, be on your guard!... We keep the *fire*, while supplicating you to not be too surprised by the next fricassee. Your palaces and your hotels will burn very nicely, when it pleases us, for we have attentively listened to the lessons given by your chemistry professors, and we have invented small devices that you will marvel at.

"As for your persons, they will be made to acclimatize their dying breath under the heelless sole of our threadbare slippers, at several hundred paces from your fuming intestines; and we will find perhaps a large enough number of swine or errant dogs to console, with a bit of love, your chaste companions and very innocent virgins whom your precious loins have begotten...

"After that, if God's existence

is not a perfect joke, which the example of your *virtues* predisposes us to believe, let him exterminate us when it is his turn, let him damn us without remedy, and let it all be finished! Hell, probably, will not be more atrocious than the life that you have made for us.

"But in that case we will be forced to confess before all his angels that we were his instruments for consuming you, for he must have had enough of your faces! He must be, at least, as disgusted as we are, this hypothetical Lord; he has, doubtless, vomited you out one hundred times, and, if you subsist, it is because apparently he is in the habit of returning to his vomit!?"

Such is the canticle of the modern poor, from whom the fortunate on earth, – not satisfied with possessing everything, – have imprudently snatched the belief in God. It is the *Stabat* of desperate men.

They have remained standing at the foot of the Cross since the bloody Mass of Good Fri-

day, – in the middle of shadows, stenches, derelictions,
thorns, nails, tears, and ago-
nies. For generations they have
whispered impassioned prayers
into the ear of the divine Host,
and, all of a sudden, – it is revealed to them, with a spurt of
electrical science, this dusty
gibbet where the teeth of beasts
have devoured their Re-
deemer... Damn! and then they
will go amuse themselves![40]

* * *

*I promised, at the start, several pieces
of advice, and I believe them to be so
excellent... and so perfectly useless,
that I have kept them for the very end.
Here they are, then:*

*1ˢᵗ Solemn translation of Renan's rot-
ted corpse by a group of cesspool
cleaners to the most distant national
sewage works;*

*2ⁿᵈ Erection, at the top of the Tour Eif-
fel, of a colossal Cross in solid gold,
costing several tens of millions of
francs at the City of Paris' expense;*

---

[40]Original footnote: *The Desperate Man*, Soirat edition, chap.
LXVIII.

3rd Obligation, for all Frenchmen, to listen to Mass every Sunday and to take communion at least four times a year, under pain of death;

4th Abolition of universal suffrage, etc.

I stop here for I sense, all too well, just how much all this is a matter of "take it or leave it," and also how premature such advice is, which will not fail to appear all the more amusing as the moment draws infinitely near when the very children of the people will write, on the crumbling walls of Sodom, these simple words: CATHOLICISM OR THE PETARD!

Choose then, once and for all, unless you are one of the dead.

— LÉON BLOY.

13. – Consulted the *Liturgical Year* by Dom Guéranger, for Christmastide. Little benefit. The rare insights or liturgical documents are drowned in a moral jumble of devout phrases. One really needs to be famished or dying of thirst to find any savor there.

17. – Finally! I'm spared the ignominious examination of my copy. Delivered today the seventh of my military tales. One has to believe that a certain segment of the population cannot get enough of me, and

that a little confidence is born because the humiliation of a trial reading to the fetid and murky administrators of the *Gil* has clearly been spared me.

18. – I thought I knew the extent of d'Esparbès' ignorance. How wrong I was. From a religious point of view, it is staggering. This evening, at 6:35, *he still did not know that the Church believes in the Virgin Mary!!!* And his unintelligence is even more surprising than his stupidity. Invincible obturation and diabolical sentimentality.

Something very bitter enters me when I try to explain to him that he has a duty to have his child baptized, – a baby boy, several weeks old, silent and sad like all youngsters who are about to die, – I encounter the insurmountable obstacle of his refusal.

"He's *my* son!" he tells me, matter-of-factly like a slave merchant who does not brook reply. Ancient paternity, then! O the ferocity of sentimental writers!...

19. – D'Esparbès again. Read the interminably long, imperial, singsongy *A Regiment*, published today, in a supplement of the *Journal*. He wanted to depict a Catholic priest, a village curate on the battlefield in 1814. Alas! What a priest! A horrible jabberbox, a kind of Puritan or Covenanter who vomits, from atop a wagon, Biblical passages translated into French by Osterwald and inconceivably tailored to Napoleon, while men are being massacred around him, – instead

of assisting them in their agony!...

The poor d'Esparbès believes that a good Catholic priest must be like that. I recall having read a completely analogous scene in *The Puritans* by Walter Scott, whom he certainly does not know. I will let him know.

27. – A creditor who demands money from me.

My dear monsieur Maur...

Your letter touches me deeply. Were it not for the terrible New Year's Eve that is upon us, I would not let an hour go by without rendering you the financial service that you do me the honor of soliciting. I would readily comply, with all the more heartfelt joy, as I would have the hope of ameliorating if ever so slightly the bitterness that my poor, little literary successes fill your soul with. Rest assured, however, that this recomfort will hardly be long in coming, and that, in the first days of the coming new year, you will receive a new installment of my affection.

Your devoted,

LÉON BLOY.

29. – Ran into d'Esparbès at the *Gil*. Already ill-dis-

posed for the villainous reception by one of the three loutish administrators of that lupanar, I speak to him in no uncertain terms about his last tale which greatly displeased me. I meet the stubbornness of a zebra. He insists, at all costs, that his tale is excessively good.

30. – To d'Esparbès:

My dear friend...

I was suffering a little, yesterday evening. I was stronger with you than I would have wished to be, and I ask you for your pardon. It's the least that a man of goodwill can do.

However, I cannot, without injustice, and without falsity, modify my judgment on what afflicts you.

I am certain that you are mistaken.

My admiration for you is great, and I believe that I have expressed this to you, in no uncertain terms, on multiple occasions. Have I shown myself to be stingy with the praise, when it came to glorifying what I esteem most in you, as a fellow human: military sensibility and French sensibility? I would not hold anything back, believe me, if I had to speak publicly about your work.

Why then, in return, would you not

*have a little more confidence in me? I
tell you simply, with* love, *that you are
mistaken; I tell you, and I give you my
reasons and my experience, coolly,
without exaltation or prejudice. Why
would you refuse to believe a man who
loves you, who is perhaps the* only
*person who loves you in the dreadful
literary world, and who* knows better
than you do? *Why would you want to
weaken and profoundly alter our
friendship by condemning me to con-
firm in you a defect of pride in tatters,
or a writer's vanity that I was infinitely far from suspecting.*

*Come on, d'Esparbès, ignorant and
marvelously gifted d'Esparbès, remember that you are a man, and respond to me nobly.*

Your friend,

— LÉON BLOY.

31. – An unsavory end to the year. It was only by a
hair that I did not slap to within an inch of his life the
administrator Albiot, litigious and capricious politi-
cian, whose congenital boorishness shouts, at times,
as if from the rooftop, with a little too much magnificence.

I am in terrible need of reminding myself that
I am not alone in the world.

1893

Nonne qui oderunt te, Domine, oderam? et super inimicos tuos tabescebam? Perfecto odio oderam illos, et inimici facti sunt mihi.[41] – Psalm, CXXXVIII, 21-22.

---

[41]*Nonne qui oderunt...*: Latin for "Have I not hated them, O Lord, that hated thee: and pined away because of thy enemies? I have hated them with a perfect hatred: and they are become enemies to me." Psalm 38:21-22 (Douay-Rheims).

January

1st. – Sinister New Year's Day.

2. – Worshipers of the Father seem to be handed over to the sins of Pride, Envy, Anger, and Sloth. Those of the Son, to the sins of Avarice and Gluttony. Those of the Holy Spirit, to the one sin of Lust.

It is from among the lustful that the Paraclete will gather his flock.

The pious memory of the dead is the only remedy against Lust. The empire of the Dead belongs to the Holy Spirit which the mythological Pluto symbolized.

A joyous reporter told me of his plan to interview me and *inquire about me*, supposing me a candidate for the Academy. Such happy wit in the world!

Ignoble scene with my editor in chief, who cruelly suffers for being a eunuch and will not forgive me for it.

5. – To d'Esparbès:

> *My dear friend,*
>
> *Would you not have received the letter that I wrote to you, Friday, December 30, and which might appear rather important? One of the great sorrows of*

*my life, have no doubt about it, would
be to learn that you are like others.
But that, I refuse to believe it, as long
as you have not proven it to me yourself, and I very affectionately and very
fraternally shake your hand.*

— LÉON BLOY.

*P.S. – Here, for me, is the title of your
volume:* The Song of Eagles. *I confess,
however, that it would need less lyrical panache in order to make your
work popular in the casernes. Perhaps
you have found something better.*

To Georges L., the friend of thirty
years, of whom it was said:

*As long as Georges L. had not odious-
ly left the oldest and surest of all his
friends, the poor writer who loved him
like a brother for a quarter of a century, he could believe himself authorized
to retain, under diverse pretexts, the
rather numerous books of Léon Bloy
which ornament his library. It was,
then, but a simple abuse of the privi-
leges of friendship. Today, it would
constitute an abuse of trust.*

*Therefore, Léon Bloy, believes himself
to be quite certain that Georges L. will
not put off that necessary restitution to
the day after tomorrow.*

– Léon Bloy.

I imagine stuffing an exploration unit of Prussians into the frightful house of that mad painter whose atelier I visited, near Elseneur, two years ago.

10. – A letter, finally! from d'Esparbès who assures me of his never-ending friendship. I still believe him a little. But how negligent and superficial the poor fellow is!

11. – To Georges L., the friend of thirty years:

> *Georges L., evidently incapable of humiliating himself in any other way than by post, said, a little bit everywhere, but particularly to Henry de Groux, who preferred my testimony, and to Victor L., whose cowardice was unparalleled, that I myself had abandoned him!!!*
>
> *This vile calumny gives me ample right to consider his recent letter as a lie.*
>
> *Georges L. had been given a mission whose fulfillment had to do with the salvation of his soul.* He had been given the mission of being a faithful friend to Léon Bloy.
>
> *Having deserted his post, it was in-*

*evitable that he should hand himself
most dreadfully over to atheists and
Satanists.*

May God have pity on him!

— Léon Bloy.

12. – Ah! the *Gil Blas* livestock! Of course! I earn my keep.

14. – Caught sight of Gustave Guiches at the lupanar. I looked that strange fellow in the face. The expression in his evasive eyes is abominable. Elegance of a Cadurcian landlord. Allure of a wet cat. He always has the air of having been thrashed with his own stakes by a rough tenant farmer.

17. – It seems to me that the pamphleteer in me is dying. I give birth, however, to "The Expiation of Jocrisse,"[42] a yellow-press article on the occasion of Huysmans, who becomes a little too pontifical since his nauseating compilations about the Devil.

Exercise that gives me a moment's rest from the military tales.

18. – Read *Latin mystique* which I promised to review

---

[42]The Expiation of Jocrisse: see *On Huysmans' Tomb*, published by Sunny Lou Publishing, 2021.

in the *Mercure de France*. A reading more tiresome than agreeable. De Gourmont has merely wit and a nervous sensibility, but he does not dispense them except in dribs and drabs. Far more would have been needed here. I will write my article *over him,* not without difficulty, I fear. It is true that the preface by Huysmans is execrable. At least, de Gourmont is a Latinist, while Huysmans never was. Why then that preface which the beneficiary [even] blushes for? They must have killed someone together.

30. – The *Gil Blas* and its editor in chief!... My God! Save me from this ignoble servitude.

Letter to de Groux who is going to marry and who counts on me, naturally. I confess my financial distress, the feeble splendor of my cloths, and I implore a notice sufficiently in advance of his wedding day.

February

2. – Marriage of Henry de Groux to Enghien. After the preliminary little joke at city hall, the church. There, profound emotion for me. De Groux and his fiancée have absolutely decided on the last class, the marriage of the poorest. That appears so great to me that I cannot hold back the tears. I tell de Groux: "It's more beautiful, that, than the *Christ aux outrages!*"

4. – Reading of Moritz Busch's *Bismarck*. Ignoble book. The author wanted to glorify the Chancellor, but he did so so vilely, so stupidly, that the heavy volume is the most scathing pamphlet ever written against that false great man, whose mediocrity jumps out at you on every page. How abject the German spirit must be that such a book, wherein the war is recounted day by day, never gives a sense of greatness!

10. – Finished my great paper on *Latin mystique*. Proposed Title: "The Language of God." Will de Gourmont understand that that was the *true* title of his book, if his book had been genuinely Christian? I doubt it.

By way of recreation, and in order to switch things up, read *Par le Glaive*, a Romantic drama by Richepin, of an impetuous mediocrity, it seems to me.

20. – Extremely sad letter from de Groux. He feels seriously threatened and fears for his life. I respond that it depends on him to recover his perfect health, if he wants to obey the extraordinary physician whom, "by exceptional privilege and because he was my friend," someone had found for him.

I reproach him for always saying *we*, ever since he got married, instead of *I*, when he writes to me, – as if he were a bishop! Whenever his letters arrive, each time, it feels as though I am receiving a Papal brief.

22. – Ran into Maurice de Fleury at the *Gil Blas*, one of my most agile abandoners, who, unable to avoid me, has the audacity to address me using the informal "tu."

Without budging, I stare at the coward, in silence, and he takes flight.

Disgust strangles me.

24. – To a stranger:

Dear monsieur,

I would clearly be an individual little deserving of interest if I did not respond to your friendly letter by informing you of the very great pleasure it gave me. I am not used to receiving such homage, and the justice that I have spent my life demanding for a few others has been refused to me with remarkable energy. Some even have done whatever they could to ensure that I might die of starvation, – so incompatible is this world with beings who seek out only God, and for whom the Absolute is a necessity.

I readily send to you, then, the "key" to The Desperate Man, *which you have asked me for, asking you to keep it. Many others possess it, written in my hand, and I certainly! do not see any danger in giving you a copy of it. One small error in your letter:* Pillory *for* Pal. *You do not know about* Pal, *then, that unfortunate hebdomadary pamphlet which lived only for four weeks, and which died because of my misery? I am ready to offer a copy of it to you, if you are willing to receive it.*

The Desperate Man *which you have had so much trouble procuring a copy of, you say, is without a doubt the Soirat edition. There exists another that just appeared,* unbeknownst to me and without my authorization *(by Stock), very defective, moreover. Living on my labor, day in and day out, and having no other means to defend myself against pirates, I am forced to endure the prejudice that results from this brigandage.*

To wrap things up, my dear reader, your envelope, very commercial and postmarked in Bordeaux, made me suppose – will you forgive me for saying so? – that you could be a wine merchant.

"He is asking you for the key to your book," my wife said to me, laughing, "ask him for the key to his cave."

I share this pleasantry with you for what it is worth and affectionately shake your hand.

– Léon Bloy.

March

2. – De Gourmont, you disenchant me!...

Impossible, I think, to bring up lofty matters with this man. Spiritual, assuredly, and gifted with some intellectual generosity, one might believe, he does not love the Absolute and declares that he does not perceive any object worthy of his enthusiasm. With respect to my tales, he reproaches me for my *durity* towards the Germans, whom he does not judge inferior to the French. Evidently, the superiority of *race* does not exist for him any more than the *actual presence* of God in human affairs. He speaks about the Slavs who will overrun the Germans and Latins, and the Chinese who will overrun the entire world. Opinion whose extreme banality both surprises me and disconcerts me.

My wife then says to him: "You are for evolution and Léon Bloy is for *miracles*." A precise delimitation which is over his head.

In the end, it will amount to not much more, I fear, than any old friendship. Too bad!

De Gourmont has been too fond of Huysmans. He has retained, not only the majority of his points of view, but also some of his *mannerisms*.

When one knows just what nothingness Huysmans is the tabernacle of, it is enough to instill fear.

6. – A circular:

Antony, March 6, 1893.

Monsieur Editor in Chief,

Living far from Paris, in a profound solitude, I solicit the publication in your journal of a protestation, tardy no doubt, but necessary and of a nature to interest all my confreres, whatever their personal feelings for me might be.

I understand that an edition of one of my books, The Desperate Man, *was just published, unbeknownst to me and against my formal will, by the publishing house Tresse et Stock.*

This edition, anterior to the only one the public is aware of, was supposed to have been thrown into the dustbin in 1886, – M. Stock not having dared to publish it at that time and the mere thought of exhibiting a copy of it making him die of fright.

Certain threats that now no longer appear to have any effect on his soul, had made him renounce the idea at the last moment.

No contract *authorized him, moreover, to move forward with a publication which he considered so dangerous and which had to remain, consequently, in the form of a completely defunct project.*

I am told, today, that this surprising publisher, about three weeks ago, decided to unpack his paper, presently on sale just about everywhere. This industrial operation, I repeat, was done without my knowledge, in contempt of every equity, and in a superb disdain for what constitutes the most elementary rights of an author.

I add that M. Stock's edition, as clandestine as it is pirated, not being in conformance with the approved edition, which was carefully *expurgated and launched by me, in 1887 (through the publisher Alphonse Soirat, Paris), – I felt it my duty, before any other step should be taken, publicly to disavow that publisher's speculation,* which an overly permissive law toward unscrupulous individuals forbids me, unfortunately, from qualifying.

I hope, Monsieur Editor in Chief, that you will not refuse the insertion of these several lines, and I urge you to accept the assurance of my perfect consideration.

– Léon Bloy.[43]

---

[43]Original footnote: Published in the *Evénement* and the *Eclair*.

7. – I will try to write a story with the hateful Bismarck in it. Return of a sadness that habitually martyrs me, especially when I need to write for the *Gil Blas*, which I am so little sure of and which I am so ashamed to be a part of. What a hard and abject captivity! My wife comes to console me, telling me of her very imminent profession as a tertiary of Saint Francis.

8. – A large Lyonnaise review, *The Catholic University*, speaking of *Salvation Through the Jews*, accuses me of restoring the "heresy of Vintras" and "of arriving at a frankly heterodox conclusion."

10. – Another tirade about *Salvation Through the Jews*. This time I am not called a heretic, but the text "Salus ex Judæis," poorly translated or badly interpreted by me, is not *as mysterious* as I am pleased to suppose. Moreover, I myself do not even seem to understand the meaning of my book.

Salus A Judæis, QUIA *Salus EX Judæis*, I could respond to any other doctor [of divinity]. But I know this person all too well. He is by and large an insignificant Netherlandish pettifogger, a recently *naturalized Belgian!!!* to please his papa. He honored me with a sort of friendship when he was twenty years old, when he had not yet become the ornament of his fatherland (See May 26, 1892).

14. – I soon hope to be delivered of this defiling collaboration with the *Gil Blas*.

19. – The Holy Spirit never stops recruiting, *for the deliverance of Jesus on the cross*, an innumerable army that must be the human race. The Crusades, composed of knights and churls, mysteriously prefigures this universal and definitive coalition.

24. – I cannot open the Holy Book without an infinite sweetness coming over me, a marvelous suavity, an intoxication that brushes me up against the stars!... I am, at that moment, how many billions of leagues away from the *Gil Blas*?

30. – To the Director of the *Catholic University* in Lyon.

> *Monsieur the Director,*
>
> *It was only a long time after its publication that I was able to read the article by* "Calamus" *on* Salvation Through the Jews, *in the bibliographical section of your February 15 issue.*
>
> *It would clearly! be in bad taste for me to contest others' right to criticize or blame, which right I have so broadly exercised myself that many people,*

*more or less sincere, more or less in-
formed, believe me to be exclusively a
pamphleteer.*

*So it would, in my eyes, be very natu-
ral for your collaborator not to like
my work, and I would find it perfectly
legitimate for him to condemn it liter-
arily, even with an extreme durity.
God forfend that I should suppose that
the person in question who hides behind the pseudonym of* Calamus
*should be deprived of the necessary
authority to judge so inconsequential
a writer as myself.*

*But does it not seem to you, Monsieur
the Director, that the right of criticism
is, on this occasion, singularly exceed-
ed? If* M. Calamus, *or any other
masked individual, had written, apropos of my book, that I was a fraud, for
example, or that I have vile morals, it
is likely that you would not have inserted such dangerous calumnies,
which French laws authorize the victim to demand a severe compensation
for.*

*Am I to believe that, by benefiting
from the atheism of these same laws,
you have accepted,* sciens et prudens,
*that one of your editors should without
evidence accuse me of the most enormous crime that a Christian could*

commit?

I am speaking of the crime of heresy, immeasurably graver, in the eyes of the Church, than all other prevarications or injustices. Since February 15, every reader of your review can believe that I am a restorer of the heresy of Vintras and that I announce, in the most explicit terms, an imminent "incarnation of the Paraclete."

This vile heresy, quite anterior to the miserable Vintras, has always horrified me, and my book does not mention a word about it. I cannot explain, then, the exorbitant accusation of which I am the object except by what typographers call, I believe, a mastic.[44] *Certain lines and words, designed to figure into another article, will have unwittingly slipped into that of* M. Calamus. *Otherwise, how else to conceive of the frightening thoughtlessness of a man who expresses himself with a certain apparent gravity and who clearly must not dispense with reading attentively the works that he deigns to judge?*

Whatever the case might be, the prejudice is enormous, and I urge you to insert this letter into your next issue. I

---

[44]Mastic: an inversion of lines, words, or characters in a typographical composition.

dare to hope, Monsieur the Director, that you will not refuse this necessary reparation to a Catholic writer whose person, to this day, has not contested orthodoxy.

Accept, etc....

– Léon Bloy.

Published by the *Gil Blas*:

A solemn letter, written in Franco-German patois, addressed from Dresden to the administration of the Gil Blas, *informs me that MM. the Prussian or Saxon officers, patriotically indignant by my military tales, are after my hide.*

"When we believe the moment to have arrived," they say, "we will see what your man of letter's mettle is in the presence of a Prussian saber."

There would be, perhaps, – even in Germany – a certain restraint not to recall that Prussian saber, *which I saw, in Sarthe and in Loiret, much more heroicly employed in the presence of women and the wounded than at the sight of fusiliers or franc-tireurs.*

Nonetheless, here is my response, and

it is very simple:

I inhabit Antony (Seine), 53, route d'Orléans. My house has a door on it and a few windows that all open very easily...

I will see these warriors coming with a satisfaction that I am unable to express. I will, moreover, as of today, place a considerable order for disinfectants.

However, as I want to suppose them stupider than malicious, I charitably counsel them – before bringing their excessively large snouts before me – to inform themselves, with care and attention, about a certain Marchenoir who hides in the skin of Léon Bloy and who, in 1870, had the kindness to kill more than a few Prussians, among whom were found, I believe, some Saxons.

– LÉON BLOY.

April

3. – Visited the crematorium at Père La Chaise. It is, I think, the most impious and atrocious thing of the century. By means of several sous, I am shown everything. They open even, for the joy of my eyes, the execrable furnace where the dead are incinerated. The physical horror is only tolerable because I arrive at the end of an operation. All that I perceive, in short, is a skull in the process of being consumed [by the flames] and the indiscernible remains...

It appears, in addition to those who are voluntarily incinerated, that they odiously burn the severed remains of the poor devils who died in hospital and whom nobody claims. Of course, I will speak one day about this infamy which summons all the tempests of God [against it].

Saw also the *Columbarium*. It is admirable how impiety is condemned to being so grotesque!

8. – The lack of money in my life is such a great mystery that, even when I do not have any, it seems like it is *diminishing*. A lack of money is the form taken by my *captivity*.

15. – Received the *Australian Courier* from Sydney which reproduces, in French, one of my tales, but not without mutilations. It appears that my literary form scandalizes the galley slaves, – liberated or not – of

New South Wales. If only these convicts paid me for the reproduction, at the very least!

20. – Another insertion in the *Gil Blas*:

> *It seems clear that our affable van-quishers are more apt to fence with the pen than with the saber.*
>
> *While I wait at home for the effect of their death threats, these gentlemen continue to rain down on the adminis-tration of the* Gil Blas *comminatory letters, with the intent of* forcing *this journal to refuse me a hospitality that I dishonor by employing it against the filthiest enemies of France.*
>
> *Here is the latest message that for the rest of my life I would reproach myself for attenuating the cretinism of:*

> Berlin, April 11, 1893.
>
> To the very honored adminis-trators of the *Gil Blas*, in Paris.
>
> Messieurs! Nothing other than the inphamyes [sic] can make the French heart jump! To ad-dress them immediately to the very honorable Herrn Dr. Busch is punishable temerity. The employee Bloy must be re-jected. We know that you de-

test this "insulter for hire," as our very great Bismarck calls him. It is for this reason that we grant you the pleasure of publishing the lines here below.

If this thing is not righted, we will publish everywhere that the *Gil Blas* sells military documents stolen by Bloy to the reater. So, at this price, it is plausible to be exact, curious, and important!

Here is the Report that you must entrust to the primter, without the leest little change, or if not, we will lodge a complaint in Paris.

> *Monsieur Léon Bloy has never been a part of our Editorial staff. He was simply a Writer of articles. From now on, he is no longer here. The malicious provocations, we sincerely deplore them.*
>
> — BERNH-KHRAMER.
>
> *Secretary to Dr. M. Busch.*

I had, entirely naturally, addressed my

tale, "Bismarck at the Court of Louis XIV," to the honorable doctor Moritz Busch, the Chancellor's historian. It was my duty, no? and I would have failed at the most elementary of proprieties by not doing anything for the great man's anniversary. Such is the result of my overzealous attempt.

It is so rich though that I have to believe it a farce. The doctor Busch is obviously a cretin, and he has written an enormous tome just to prove it – 500 pages of 40 lines each, to estab-lish, unconsciously, *that his patron is a MEDIOCRE person and an ap-palling scoundrel!*

But he must know a little French, as much as a Saxon pedant can pick up; and however stupid his book might be, I refuse to believe that he could have dictated to his secre-tary, or presumed secretary, so imbe-cilic a letter.

Instead, I prefer to suppose, until fuller information is available, that the incoherent babble transcribed earlier is the painful labor of one of those excellent Prussian officers who spoke about cutting open my belly, and I imagine, without too much ef-fort, that this fully astute person has prudently borrowed the signature of

> *some random individual to escape the*
> *prolonged flogging that his imperti-*
> *nence deserves.*

— LÉON BLOY.[45]

21. – Glabrous response by the Lyonnaise Director of
the *Catholic University*. That smoker of Pascal candles refuses the insertion of my letter from March 30.
I could make him. But to what end?

22. – Stumbled upon a Capuchin father today whom
I do not know. Afflicting and grotesque confessor. To
be sure, I have run into many execrable ones before,
but I do not remember having been expedited with
such velocity before. I was baffled on hearing him
rattle off his stereotypical exhortation, which I could
not grasp the meaning of, so quickly did the words,
one after the other, exit his mouth. This religious
struck me as belonging to the breed of ratters. *In mo-*
mento, in ictu oculi,[46] he breaks your back, the sinner.

25. – One has to be a sot to believe in luck! As I was

[45]Original footnote: Is it necessary to observe that this quarrel by
Germans was a mere mystification orchestrated in concert with
one of my friends living in Germany, aimed at learning what the
administrators of the *Gil Blas*, the millionaire dotard Desfossés
and his domestic Albiot, could swallow? Discouraging result: the
two greedy pigs asked for more!

[46]*In momento, in ictu occuli*: Latin for "in a moment, in the
twinkling of an eye." 1 Corinthians 15:52 (Douay-Rheims).

returning from bringing to the place of ill repute the manuscript of *The Alms of the Poor*, the best thing, perhaps, that I have submitted to the *Gil Blas*, I ran into Coppée in the street, and look at me! being greeted by that academician.

My faith! yes, the alm of the poor! I didn't need it, but he gave it to me all the same, that largess with the tip of a hat; then he walked away, his heart gently buoyed, saying to himself: "I have just made someone happy! Excellent François! It is true that he did not see me from a distance, that I practically ran into him, and that it would have been difficult for me to feign distraction. No matter, it is so good to be generous, and I would be quite the scoundrel if gratitude was not stifling me!"

The heart of Coppée! Ah! I will never know a more craven or indigent one. – Knock, knock: Who's there? cries Jupiter's envoy. – *Everyone's friend!* responds Amphitryon's valet, trembling.

Affable and earthy Coppée! You do not know, my good fellow, that I have a small account to settle with you, that I *continue* to wait for your response to a certain letter loutishly disdained by you, in May, 1890; that a poet much greater than you waits for it *six feet under;* and that I am, in a way, the most solvent of contemporaries.

26. – Received Verlaine's small book: *My Prisons*. Literature of a drunkard. Poor, great Verlaine![47]

[47]*My Prisons*: See *My Hospitals & My Prisons*, by Paul Verlaine, published by Sunny Lou Publishing, 2020.

30. – Four abandoners in a single day! Those there, they came to fill their belly at my table every Sunday for six months.

May

1st. – The geldings of the *Gil* ask me, *like a personal favor* for which I would be magnificently compensated, whether I would accept being amputated by one third of my salary. Have a nice day.

6. – Scene in the street. Several dignant young fellows accuse me of having intentionally troubled their sister's soul. Response:

I was unaware that mademoiselle your sister is in love with me, but if she is, that, messieurs, would do her the greatest honor!

7. – My beloved wife says to me:

"Everything is in turmoil, everything changes, everything perishes, except God. And, by his will, the most humble images of Himself or those who have loved him *abide* and appear immutable to us. While generations hasten, and our thoughts or affections continuously change, an innumerable host of holy figures throughout all the churches in the world stand immobile, in perpetual Adoration."

9. – Heard a more-than-mediocre conference by Laurent Tailhade on the Magi. He mocks Péladan and Huysmans. But he lauds Guaita, Papus, etc. and he admires Simon the Magician (!) and other Gnostics.

It's not very clear to me how he rises above his ridiculous adversaries.

19. – Discourse by Zola to students. To be preserved. That idiot replaces God with *work*.

25. – Read *The Legend of the Eagle*, by d'Esparbès. Pointless and tedious reading. His stories are, sometimes, amusing and appear beautiful enough even when read in isolation in a journal; but collected in a volume, they are monotonous and infantile. It is always the same story. Then he stupidly refused to leave out his bad piece: "A Regiment," which I had strongly advised him to cut.

30. – Yesterday evening, around 10 o'clock, in our absence, an attack and besiegement of our house by a group of bums who claim to be offended.

One might have believed that it was, finally, the sudden downpour of those Saxon patriots who menaced me in March. The fortress, defended by a young girl and a child of two, was not about to be surprised and was able, quite easily, to resist the attack until the arrival of several neighbors, – these messieurs having neglected to equip themselves with a catapult or magonel capable of staving in the front door at first blow. But the noise was horrible, and the besieged could very easily have died of fright.

While waiting for an equitable retribution,

which I take sole charge over, the functionaries whom it concerns are informed of the presence of the anonymous malefactors, and measures, likely efficacious, will be taken against them.

But what a sense of smell they had, those enraged swine, to come in the absence of Marchenoir!

June

3. – Saw, at the Champ de Mars, two pastels by de Groux. It's the same hallucinogenic color, the same dream of mad intensity. His *Tribu errante* is muddled, and the principal figure in his *Fille de Pharaon* is treated like an accessory. But these things give insight into the obsession, and that doubtless comes from the painter's transparent soul. If he succeeded at reining himself in, what a terrifying landscape artist he would be!

Everything else at the exposition, seen in passing, was execrable. To be noted, a tableau by Frappa, showing Coquelin Cadet, Silvestre, Coppée, etc. in religious costume, as prelates or monks. The infamy of that glazier is unspeakable.

Received the volume on Villiers de l'Isle-Adam by Pontavice de Heussey. I cast my eyes upon it and, immediately, I am overwhelmed by an unbearable bitterness. The author, a very poor man, appears to have been inspired by Huysmans, the appropriator of the great writer's agony, and the author must have been shamefully misled on all the essential points. The impression of horror is so strong that my wife hides the book from me. Later, I will tell perhaps the *real* drama.

7. – I partake in the glory of Joseph, so that God might "open his lips" and so that *He who can explain dreams* might be released from his prison.

10. – Received *Fin des Dieux* [End of the Gods], by Henri Mazel. Not to be read.

11. – Alcide Guérin, who has just seen Tailhade, tells me that this bizarre individual is planning on holding a conference on me, in October, and that he wants to speak with me, one of these days, so as to say nothing that might be disagreeable to me.

17. – Ollendorff, sounded by a friend, refuses to accept the collection of my military tales (*Sueur de Sang*). The publisher of Maupassant, he could not be mine, at the hour even when that author, shamefully calumniated by me, agonizes. Clown!

20. – Dentu, less honorable clearly than Ollendorff, willingly consents, Camille Lemonnier having, it is true, warmly recommended me.

25. – Holy Scriptures. The more I understand, the more I bury myself in the tenebræ. Said to Alcide Guérin, a faithful friend: "You are made for silence and joy. I am made for noise and sorrow."

26. – To the same:

I have precious little time to write you

this morning, my friend. I feel compelled to do so, however. I will tell you what I told you yesterday. You must follow me because I have need of you and because you have need of me. You must follow me from now on, *because I am always on the move and you would remain, in the end, too far behind.*

God knows what He is doing and it is not for nothing that He has brought us so particularly close together. One of the most enormous regrets in my life would be to lose you.

Recently I felt that you were not where you ought to be, and it was necessary to tell you this, lest I should be a false friend. But, at the same time, I saw, the most luminously in the world, your true path.

If you have confidence in me, be then very docile, very faithful to your generous resolution. Read, this evening, several lines from the Holy Book, and you will not delay in knowing what my counsel was worth.

Once again, you would lose yourself on the side of war and on the side of torments, when you are so clearly, in my eyes, a man made for peace and joy.

Joy! Let yourself rush into this river, my very dear friend, you who re- mained faithful to me in the days of terrible tribulation. Do not doubt what I told you and persuade yourself that the writer *in me is nothing but an acci- dent of my substance, that I have something more...*

SOMETHING MORE, *in truth, and that I can receive strange lights in order to guide you.*

– Your LÉON BLOY.

28. – Oh the tiresome letter by Wagner which serves as a preface to the translation of his operatic poems! Reading it killed me. The so-called frenetic is a dull and vile German professor. His Christianity, certified by Villiers, is a monstrous joke, and I feel the need to shout down that glory that stinks already like a cadav- er.

30. – Perfect vexations at the *Gil Blas*. The swines tri- umph. My God! when then will I be delivered of this revolting livelihood?

July

2. – Extreme emotion, at church. Psalm 41 seems to me to express, more than any other, my distress; and I invoke my Father of the Lilies, in the divine spirit of this prayer.

This feeling of universal hatred which I am the object of, no matter what I do! *There are people who think they love me but who actually hate me.*

5. – *Judaic antiquities* by Josephus. For the hundredth time, I notice, in this historian, the scant sublime preoccupation not to displease anyone. "I leave it to everyone to think what he pleases." Such is his usual saying. One might think it were Coppée.

What a singular person, however, this Josephus who appears to have been a sort of prophet, and what a frightening tourbillon this Jewish people, rolling in the abysses of its own chastisement!

6. – I learn about the hideous death of Maupassant. Several days of noise in the journals, then the eternal oblivion. He's one of those who have done me the most harm.

9. – Idolatry is to prefer the Visible to the Invisible.

Adultery. It is still said, sometimes, that the

lover of a married woman suffers from sharing. What hypocrisy! It is the opposite that is true. It is precisely this sharing that is the great ragout. The man sitting down to the meat is an ineffable swine.

14. – Began the series *Histoires désobligeantes* at the *Gil Blas*.

I suffer terribly for this literary corvee and I would really like it if God did not inflict it on me for too much longer. It is frightening to think that the existence of several depend on me alone, and that I have no other resource than my imagination!

After the military series, which has done me honor, I no longer know where I am going.

22. – The final pages of *Sueur de Sang* are at the printer's. I asked myself who, among the living or the dead, could possibly be universally enough, unjustly enough, and cravenly enough decried that I might dedicate my book to him. I have found no one better than Bazaine.

*Dedication of Sueur de Sang
(1870-71)*

To the defamed memory of

François-Achille BAZAINE

Marshal of the Empire

Who bore the sins of all France

And was condemned

By an appalling injustice

On the testimony of all the craven

And all the disobedient

*Whom he had the feebleness or heroic
generosity*

Not to chastise and condemn.

The publisher does not wish to go beyond the word
France. Obviously that can still work. Perhaps it is
even better like that. In any case, no one will say that
I neglect the means of ensuring the complete insuccess of my books.

25. – Read *Fantôme* by Remy de Gourmont. Nothing
to write home about. As much wit or talent as one can
have. But what an obsession with German philoso-
phards, in palpable imitation of Villiers, a jumble of
carnal ideas and the misguided need for irony, bordering on sacrilege.

27. – I am told that my new collection of tales is a
success. It is curious, really, that I am always condemned to *tours de force* that are not to my liking,
which I judge myself incapable of, and which, nonetheless, succeed. Before *Sueur de Sang*, I did not consider myself a storyteller.

There is, in the new tale brought this evening

to the *Gil Blas*, a phrase, well-constructed for all that, on the *Bourgeois*. I am informed that the administrator Desfossés, the doddering millionaire, previously mentioned, might be indignant for it, taking it for a personal insult! I strike it then, but what stinking stupidity!

29. – Saw de Gourmont, very mediocre, this evening. With respect to Scripture, I get him to declare that *he does not contest the letter, but the spirit of it*. I renounce explaining to him that it is THE SAME THING.

August

8. – Vague project of a *gallery* of scribblers of feeble caliber. Title: *The Plutarch of Abortions*: Bourget, Loti, etc.

9. – A photographer, of exceptional inferiority, gives me three different proofs of my portrait. The first two make me look incredibly like de Goncourt! The third like Rochefort!!!

11. – Immeasurably ridiculous letter from a very young Emmanuel Signoret: "May the azure be with you." It is in this way that he expresses himself.

22. – *Literary Esteem*, long article in the *Gil Blas* by Camille Lemonnier. I find this in it: "... the hyperbolic and grandiose Léon Bloy, the most classically Latin genius of French letters, for three centuries now, I proclaim it."

I spontaneously respond:

My dear Lemonnier,

My book, Sueur de Sang, *is at the printer's and about to be published, and you are naturally one of the first to whom I will send a copy. It would clearly be foolish of me to write fancy*

*phrases to you. We are merchants, you
and I, alas! merchants sometimes of
little worth, but we don't need to exchange our cheap rubbish with each
other.*

*It happens, however, – God knows
what he is doing, – that you were designated efficaciously to help me when
no one else would help me, and to be,
in sum, the benefactor of an individual
reputed to be far beneath the basest of
riffraff. Do you not think, dear friend,
that that gives me some rights over
you?*

*My pretty fate is known to you. You
know that everyone believes that anything and everything is permissible
against me and that, in the eyes of the
many, who are very nearly the spawn
of scoundrels, in the beginning of the
Gospel according to Saint John, it is I
who am to be vomited.*

*The wisemen explain that. I bear, they
say, chastisement for having shouted
down my contemporaries. It could be
that simple folk, ordinarily more clair-
voyant that wisemen, had different
ideas, that they conjectured something
else, and that the only crime of never
having consented to lick their boots
appeared to them insufficient to explain the universal proscription of a*

writer.

One day, I hazarded this: "In my life, if I had not attacked anyone, the execration that the multitude gratify me with would be the same. It is the Absolute *that they reprove in me, the Absolute, detested by the world because it implies the violation of orders and the intransigence of lamentations."*

They have employed "the great pamphleteer" epithet against me often enough! When messieurs the journalists are forced to name me, to break, for one moment, the concerted silence *which they believe so mortal, they have nothing else to say but that, and they say it as loudly as they can. What a recourse! A pamphleteer! Ah! I am something else, however, and they know it quite well. But when I was that, it was out of indignation and love, and my cries, I let them out in my despair, because of a ransacked Ideal!*

Also, what rage, O Lemonnier, to discover in me a storyteller, an artist who, each week, imposes himself on the attention of a multitudinous public and whom they cannot accuse of continuing as the pamphleteer, without their seeming ridiculous!

How many generous souls there are

who would like to see me dead! But they will never exterminate me! They really thought they could get rid of me through famine and sorrow. Alone against everyone, I have endured what no man can endure, and still I LIVE, more than ever. *What a prodigious failure and what a magisterial fiasco for those frivolous gentlemen who condemned me to the rubbish heap!*

Here is the favor, then, that I wish to ask of you. On the occasion of this new book, so very unlike those that preceded it, to say, in the Gil Blas, *which will not dare to refuse me this publicity, or in any other resounding journal,* EVERYTHING *that you think about me; to shout it out very loudly, in the unanimous silence of the craven, in the plenitude of your strength and of your authority as a highly-respected author. What beautiful justice!*

I very affectionately shake your hand.

– LÉON BLOY.

27. – The curate of B. interests us. He really seems like someone who believes in God.

31. – Response by Lemonnier:

> *I await your book. I will read it passionately... And then, yes, have no doubt, I will roar my admiration, just as, with everything else about you, one must roar.*

September

3. – To Paul Adam:

My dear Paul Adam,

Despite the "dear master" that you unjustly wither me with, your letter, received at the Gil Blas, *has, I assure you, deeply touched me. I was a little sad, as often, in this brothel, and your words have recomforted me. Consider, then, in me, a man, not very happy, who has become your debtor.*

I would like to be even more so. Why would I not admit it? You know that few writers have been deprived of caresses as much as I have. Others have even done everything in their power to kill me. Yet, I am generally accorded superior gifts. I have [been granted] that kindness. Some even go so far as to grant me genius. But everyone would sooner have the skin torn off their backsides than to inform the public about it.

A few resounding slaps in the face of some connoisseurs of fecal matter are not enough to explain the unanimous detestation of me by the band of crooks. There are more profound reasons at work, which I have said and will continue to say. They want nothing to do with a person who proffers the Absolute, not even through a golden bugle. You are, I believe, one of the few people who can understand...

I do not have your temperament. Pity cannot mitigate in me the anger, because my *anger is the daughter of an infinite presentiment. I am gnawed on by the need for Justice, as by a dragon famished after the Deluge.*

My anger is the effervescence of my compassion.

So, do you want to, or can you, make me an alm of a little of that justice that I so ardently desire for so many others? You will receive my book tomorrow.

My situation as the enemy *forbids me all imploration of articles, and you are, – after my old friend, Lemonnier, – the only one from whom I might wish to ask for such a service. Where, then, would I find the third?*

There is of course de Gourmont who could work, and who will work perhaps. But he is a solitary among pink glaciers, who only does what it pleases him to do.

It is up to you then, Paul Adam. I add

that I am the father of a family, if that
should be of interest to you.

Your friend,

— LÉON BLOY.

8. – I learn of the death of the hateful Buddhist Charcot. It appears that, on the night of his agony, the patients at the Salpêtrière[48] jumped up and down like little demons.

10. – A copy of *Sueur de Sang* for de Groux. Dedication: "While waiting for God."

13. – Card from Georges Bazaine and his brothers, "thanking me for honoring the memory of their uncle."

Response, while sending them the complete dedication:

Messieurs,

Here is the complete dedication of Sueur de Sang. *This dedication, which was cropped from the word "France" on down by my editor, who thought it was too dangerous, was published in its entirety by the* Mercure de France *in its September issue.*

---

[48]Salpêtrière: a hospital for the mentally ill, among others.

I am immensely happy, messieurs, to have had the occasion to protest against one of the most appalling iniquities of the century, whatever the consequences might be for me of an act that cowards find audacious. Thus have I always done, thus will I always do.

I have the honor of being the most feared writer and, by consequence, the most calumniated of this period. Was it not natural that I should piously turn, with all my heart, to the most unfortunate of men, and that the memory of your uncle should be honored, before everyone, by an artist whom the microbes of the quill have sought, for ten years now, to overwhelm through poverty as a form of chastisement for having fearlessly demasked contemporaneous stupidity and turpitude.

Rest assured, messieurs, of my most vivid condolences.

– Léon Bloy.

24. – Laurent Tailhade, Henry C., and de Groux spend the entire day with me. Tailhade makes me read, twice in a row, "*Le Réveil de Alain Chartier*," my new and as yet unpublished "*histoire désobligeante*," and I do not know how many other things.

I have never before enjoyed feeling my strength and acting in so certain a manner on intelligences. It is a very great happiness, a veritable intoxication, I confess, and the mysterious prefiguration of future Joys.

26. – Saw Rodin, who had expressed a desire to meet me. His face astonishes me. One cannot have a physiognomy less suited to his art. This great sculptor, whose work exudes strength, appears to be just a regular bloke. One could imagine him to be a pharmacist or an office manager [by his demeanor]. He receives me, however, in an affable manner and shows me around his atelier for an hour.

It seems to me that I will always depart from a sculptor's atelier as from a subterranean quarry, with the bizarre impression of having been in the vicinity of ossuaries and dark pits.

27. – Read, in the *Journal*, a defense of the French Press, by Bergerat!!! who reproaches Zola for not having praised that trollop enough at the London congress. I cut out several lines wherein it is stated that the *conspiration of silence no longer exists for anyone;* I glue this precious fragment onto a piece of white paper and I send it to the said Bergerat with the apostil of "Ah! this is quite good! LÉON BLOY."

What is a "scatologue"?

It is an author who *does not prostitute himself.*

But a novelist who sees a print run of one hundred thousand copies is never a scatologue.

October

2. – *Vitraux* [Stained Glass], by Tailhade. Absence of
naïvety and lack of color, it is the height of disgrace
for stained glass.

3. – To Paul Adam:

> *My dear Paul Adam,*
>
> *Not receiving a copy of* Entretiens, *I
> did not read until much later what you
> wrote about me, and I offer you, as
> soon as possible, an expression of my
> gratitude such as it is.*
>
> *You must believe it, Paul Adam. I am
> neither a journalist, nor a writer, nor
> a pamphleteer, nor a thinker, nor an
> artist, nor a student, nor even a patri-
> ot, – as you quite simply suppose, –
> nor anything else, if not the* Catholic
> Léon Bloy, *of faithful memory.*
>
> *You do not love war! You do not love
> anything then! It is terrible, you know,
> not to love anything. One is like the
> Devil, and who could say just how
> boring that is?*
>
> *It is distressing and astonishing that a
> spirit such as your own, one of the
> rare few that are alive today, should*

*renounce the Wonder in order to enter
into the service of a declamatory commonplace.*

*My phrases, my dear and poor phras-
es which you speak of, are but an appearance, like war itself, like everything that exists in the crepuscule of
sensible life, which you take for broad
daylight.*

Your friend,

– LÉON BLOY.

13. – After communion:

My God! You are with me, at home with me, and in
me. I see you, I feel you, you speak to me, I speak to
you, and, nevertheless it is impossible for me *to have
an idea of you*. Have pity!

To a perfect droll:

*M. Maurice de Fleury is, since 1889,
the depositary of a manuscript by
Léon Bloy, – Pal, with an illumination
in frontispiece by the hand of the same
author.*

*This manuscript having been given by
the said Léon Bloy to a friend who
died four years ago, – and what a
filthy death it was!!! – M. Maurice de
Fleury must understand that it is of the*

strictest equity that he restitute the object in question, in tact, *as promptly as possible.*

Consequently, Léon Bloy waits for the manuscript to be returned to him within one week, – if not: war.

– LÉON BLOY.

14. – Admirable stupidity of Zola, who prepares us for a novel about Lourdes and whom an imbecile from the *Journal* interviews:

> *"If I were to see an incontestable miracle, it would greatly upset me.* I would not believe it, *it would create a duel between my senses and my reason, I would lose my equilibrium.* That would be DANGEROUS for me!!!*"*

17. – To the President of the Artistic, Literary and Scientific Circle of Anvers:

> *Monsieur,*
>
> *I write to you in haste, from a café where I receive your letter unexpectedly.*
>
> *I consent to giving talks in Belgium and Holland. I commit to being sublime, i.e., to presenting myself as equal to the first person who comes along. It*

is not just anyone who can do that. It is a gift that God does not lavish.

Such dazzling promises are worth something, isn't that right? Consequently, here are my conditions:

1ˢᵗ. First class travel;

2ⁿᵈ. 300 francs, at the very least, per talk, all expenses paid;

3ʳᵈ. Six talks, at the very least, guaranteed in advance;

4ᵗʰ. An immediate *advance of 500 francs;*

5ᵗʰ. Finally, a formal assurance that I will not, under any circumstances, be forced to shake the hand of M. Henry Carton de Wiart;

Once these five articles are consented to by you, I am, Monsieur, at your complete disposal.

– LÉON BLOY.

To the intimate friend of one of my abandoners:

Monsieur,

I had the honor of meeting you most recently. You had held out your hand to me, which I was not expecting, I urge you to believe it. Therefore, you are a friend, am I right?

Do you want to explain to me, then, the hateful, venenous, and absolutely incomprehensible letter from M. Léon Deschamps, director of the Plume, *to Laurent Tailhade? In that letter, M. Deschamps, your friend and the friend of Scholl, claims to reject* a request for pecuniary assistance to be accorded to Léon Bloy, *– the which Bloy asks for nothing, even though he had been* robbed *of eight hundred francs.*

I think, Monsieur, that having received your amicable handshake, I have the duty to inform you of the danger that he runs, M. Léon Deschamps, the friend of Scholl and the overzealous servant of everyone except the proud, *by persisting in this loutish joke.*

Yours, etc.

– LÉON BLOY.

19. – Change of domicile. We are relocating to Paris. Antony has no more mystery to it after fourteen months, and I leave this village of brigands with shouts of joy.

22. – To Henri Mazel, the director of *l'Ermitage:*

Monsieur,

I avow to you that the article by your collaborator Saint-Antoine would have been more agreeable to me, and would have appeared more literary, *if it had treated of my book instead of focusing obstinately and exclusively on the dedication.*

It is true that your collaborator did not have the duty to be agreeable to me. I am too independent myself to contest with others the points of view that suit them.

Will you permit me, however, to respond with several lines of surprising moderation?

1ˢᵗ. Saint-Antoine, who is determined to offer me lessons in bravado *and history, could have told himself that the excision he asks me to give an accounting of was perhaps imposed on me by my editor. It would be easy for me to prove it, by producing a letter by this latter person. It was necessary to submit to his demand or renounce the publication of* Sueur de Sang.

Why would I have sacrificed my book, given the requested deletion removed nothing, in short, from the overall meaning of the dedication? The suspicion of lacking boldness greatly sur-

prises Marchenoir.

2nd. Saint-Antoine puts seventeen (!) questions to me, which he believes to be damning, about Bazaine, whose supposed betrayal is an opportunistic, Orléanist, and MacMahonian legend, which educated people or merely the attentive *ones have abandoned, long since, to the* populo.

The following response seems more than sufficient to me. Here it is:

"For the lack itself of any other proof, Bazaine's innocence would be demonstrated, superabundantly, by the appalling vulgarity of his accusers and JUDGES."

While entreating you, Monsieur, to be so kind as to publish this letter in the next issue of l'Ermitage, *Marchenoir offers you, with all his heart, the expression of confraternal sentiments.*

— Léon Bloy.[49]

High mass at Saint-Pierre de Montrouge, a

---

[49]Original footnote: Published in November, with this addition: "Saint-Antoine limits himself to calling out, in response to the above-mentioned letter, that the sad end of General d'Andlau, to whom allusion is doubtless made, nowise destroys the condemnation, ratified by history, of Bazaine as a traitor."

Ratified by history! What history?

church whose architecture fills me with Merovingian thoughts. A memorable event, really extraordinary. At the end of mass, a solemn *Te Deum* in honor of the Russians, I suppose, and, immediately afterwards, singing, no less solemn, of *Libera*, for Marshal MacMahon who just passed away.

De Groux proposes the following idea to me: the disappearance of my book from bookstore shelves, would it not happen to be a consequence of the Franco-Russian delirium? One reads, in fact, in the preface even, this affirmation, judged, doubtless, hardly hospitable:

> *France is so preeminently the first among nations that all others, no matter which, must consider themselves honorably served when they are permitted to eat the bread of her dogs.*

24. – Celebration at the Opéra; exceptional ham acting for the amusement of the Russian navy. Always the Russians! For several days now, impossible to cross the boulevard. Public drunkenness, ever so slightly dishonorable. I would like, by means of some very powerful electric projection, the following words to appear in the dark sky:

FRANCE HAS NO NEED OF ANYONE.

27. – My second [letter], to a perfect droll, as a follow-up to the business begun on the 13th of this

month:

> *M. Maurice de Fleury can cop all the attitudes that he pleases. Those postures will change nothing with respect to the well-known fact about him, which no joke can make disappear.*

> *In November '89, M. Maurice de Fleury and his wife abruptly stopped seeing Léon Bloy. Two letters by the latter were left unanswered. Léon Bloy understood, then and there, that any other attempt would be pointless, that they had simply and ignobly abandoned him because de Fleury needed to act as a valet or to prostitute himself to the* Figaro, *and that his friendship [with Léon Bloy] was becoming compromising to him.*

> *M. Maurice de Fleury told everyone that Léon Bloy had been his parasite because this latter, always obsessed with ridiculous invitations, came once a week, on Mondays, to eat several leftovers from Sunday, at the Sainte-Périne asylum. Mme. de Fleury has since recounted to various people that they chose, expressly for Bloy, the worst morsels, and that they served him red-colored water to drink, while she herself, as did her husband, drank a real,* so-called medicinal *wine. Naturally, she made this villainy out to be*

*an honor, like a spiritual trait or a
meritorious act. Pointless to add that
they do not say one word about the
dinners and authentic merrymaking
paid for by Léon Bloy out of his own
pocket.*

*Léon Bloy, accustomed however to
submit to all sorts of betrayals and vil-
lainies, found this all the richer given
that Maurice de Fleury had appeared
to warm up to him, unreservedly, like a
true friend. The* pamphleteer *has information from him of the most curious
kind, on Daudet, Mendès, Her-vieux,
Bonnetain, de Goncourt, etc. even* on
himself. *One does not make such con-
fidences to a man whom one does not
love with all his heart, and this man,
so perfectly abandoned and calumniated, immediately after declares that
he does not understand.*

*Léon Bloy, who could have nothing
but slaps to offer to M. de Fleury, will
not visit him. He energetically refuses,
astonished that the manuscript was
not remitted to his messenger. He does
not wish to see an individual who is, in
his eyes, a literary fool and a dirty domestic. But he absolutely must have
the manuscript back.*

*Léon Bloy takes this occasion to renew
to M. de Fleury the assurance of his*

disgust, by reminding him that Marchenoir is quick to slap, has a ravenous hunger, and possesses an infinitely short fuse.

– LÉON BLOY.

30. – Saw the Sagot bookstore catalog, wherein figure, in considerable number, books that had belonged to Tailhade and that he sold. Almost all mine are listed and so highly thought of that the seller *left all the dedications* in them. He is, perhaps, a bit *mufle* [loutish], that author of *Pays du Mufle*.

31. – Recovered the *Pal* manuscript finally. The "perfect droll" not responding to my request, I had to resign to bring things to an end myself, to take the object from his home myself, despite my excessive repugnance, – having decided to take possession of it in a violent fashion, if necessary. In the event of a scandal, I had three witnesses accompanying me, among them Marius Tournadre!...

Irreproachable gentility by my ex-Amphitryon. By way of compensation, I promised him a copious thrashing the first day I find him *out and about*.

On descending the stairs, Tournadre said this:

"Another one I won't be able to *smack!*"

November

1st. – Chatted this evening, for several hours, with mimes and puppets, in a boulevard café...

Will you forgive me, my God, for this wastage of precious hours on the Day of the Dead?

6. – To someone from Marseille:

Dear Monsieur,

I send back to you the proof of identity *that I received this morning and which could be useful to you. I am content knowing that your principles, conduct,* manners, *mores, and health are good, that your physical appearance is agreeable, and that you are at one and the same time a bachelor and a lawyer. All that I need to know now is whether you are rich or poor.*

I suppose that you are, naturally, a Catholic of rare fervor, given that you were able to swallow me. So there is nothing that might get in the way of amical relations being established between us.

I like the tone of your letter and I do not hate making myself a few clients as I get older. Up until now, that ex-

periment has seldom succeeded. A certain number of individuals who emitted flames in the beginning soon evaporated when they saw that my books were not lying, that I truly am a man who suffers. The sensible fear of being, one day or another, utilized, *sent them running.*

It goes without saying that these generous abandoners have spread the word, here and there, that I tried to rob them. I would wager that the writer who gave you my address, and who has "such fear of me," is one of my ancient "huge devotees." But what difference does it make?...

Are you reading my Histoires désobligeantes, *published every Friday in the* Gil Blas? *I strive to do a good job of it, even though I am wretchedly paid, because I would have no other reason to exist as a writer if I were to lack a conscience, in the example of so many literary cooks. I have treated the bastards of the quill too roughly to have the right to loosen my collar for a single instant, and they make me feel it, moreover, rather keenly...*

I hope, monsieur, that you will have the charity of not immediately suspecting me of beastly pride. But I write, – at what price! – in order to say some-

thing. I write for the small number of people who love me, or who say they love me, and I want that not to be in vain.

Amicably,

– LÉON BLOY.

7. – To Victor Havard, publisher:

Monsieur,

I entreat you to put at my disposition the Belluaires et Porchers *manuscript, which I will take or have taken off your hands. But why did you write to me that you do not see in it any chance of success, and that this is the reason for your refusal? Did you forget that I am no longer a little child?*

It would have been better, I believe, to have come out with it honestly, – as you did the first time, – that you were forbidden *to publish me.*

I would really like to accept, as you desire, the assurances of your sincere devotion, *but I'll be damned if I can guess the secret of making it work for me.*

With profound respect,

– LÉON BLOY.

12. – Feast Day of the Dedication of Churches. Gospel story of Zacchaeus. That publican received Jesus in his house which appears to be a *bad place* – like the *Gil Blas*, – and the Lord affirms that salvation is accorded to that residence which then becomes, in the eyes of the Church, the archetype of the House of God.

24. – Paid a visit to the Great Rabbi, to whom I had sent, several days earlier, a copy of *Salvation Through the Jews*. Vainly, I attempt to make him see the importance of my conclusion. More vainly still, I explain the violence of certain pages with the intention of *exhausting the objection*, a famous method, recommended by Saint Thomas Aquinas. He persists, stubbornly, in seeing nothing but the *letter* of these violences and being disinterested in the conclusion, which he did not even bother to inquire about. Finally, he counters me with the most abject commonplace: Appeasement, conciliation, etc. This successor of Aaron asserts to me that THERE IS GOOD IN ALL RELIGIONS!!!!!

To be sure, there are people as stupid and as cowardly among the Jews as there are among the Catholics.

26. – The most terrible punishment for criminal spouses, would it not be to engender a monster? That is precisely the story of Adam and Eve, who engen-

dered the Son of God. – *Ego sum vermis et non homo: opprobrium hominum et abjectio plebis.*[50]

XXIVth Sunday after Pentecost. The admirable Liturgy of this day asks God "to excite the will of the faithful." As I was saying to my dear Jeanne that the human Will signifies, doubtless, the Holy Spirit, just as Substance is related to the Father and Knowledge to the Son, according to Saint Augustine, she pointed out to me, in turn, that the *Fiat voluntas tua*[51] of the Lord's Prayer can, then, be translated thus: *Que l'Esprit-Saint soit au Ciel et sur la Terre!*[52]

We deplore, once again, the impossibility of being understood, even by our most intimate friends. My wife, raised in the palpable tenebræ of the Lutheran world, long before she knew me, was tormented by a desire, by the violent need, no longer to *protest*, and to enter finally into [the realm of] the Absolute, and she asked with a simple faith to be entirely separated from the world. Was not her wish answered, in an entirely perfect manner, by marrying me?

"If you only knew the jouissance that God gives and the delicious taste of the Holy Spirit!" said Ruysbroeck the Admirable.

---

[50]*Ego sum vermis...*: Latin for "I am a worm, and no man; a reproach of men, and the outcast of the people." Psalm 21:7 (Douay-Rheims).

[51]*Fiat voluntas tua*: Latin for "Thy will be done." Matthew 6:10 (Douay-Rheims).

[52]*Que l'Esprit Saint...*: French for "May the Holy Spirit be present in Heaven and on Earth!"

30. – I ask the Apostle Saint Andrew, whom the Lord loved "like a perfume," *in odorem suavitatis*,[53] for the grace of no longer being an abominable bastard.

---

[53]*In odorem suavitatis*: Latin for "an odour of sweetness." Ephesians 5:2 (Douay-Rheims).

December

2. – If you shut your door for just one night, be afraid upon waking to find one of your brethren dead on the sill for cold and famine.

6. – Distrust people who promise you millions and oblige you to pay for their drinks.

8. – We are so deep in the tenebræ, my wife tells me, that the only presentiment of a mystery for us is the light.

10. – The journals inform me that someone threw a bomb into the middle of the legislative Chamber. Fifty people were hurt, the worst off being a priest, the abbot Lemire, a new deputy, who would have done better to care for souls. I confess to feeling nothing but perfect indifference at the telling of this catastrophe.

Léopold Lacour joins us for lunch. He proffers that these explosions, assiduously renewed, will end by compelling the bourgeois to practice a bit of justice. Idea of a lighthouse keeper.

This Lacour is not disgusting, but one finds him a bit loud.

18. – To Eugène Demolder, in Brussels:

Monsieur,

*I write to you on the advice of my ex-
cellent and very dear friend de Groux,
who told me that I cannot do better. I
had already conceived the idea of it,
for several weeks now, and it is a circumstance very foreign to my first im-
pulsion which motivates me today, I
have to admit.*

*No matter. Whatever the case might
be, I want to profit by it, by telling
you, in all candor, that having read,
last month, the Contes d'Yperdamme*
[Tales of Yperdamme], *on the express
recommendation of the same de
Groux, this reading gave me a very
great joy that I reproach myself for
not having expressed it to you sooner.*

"The Massacre of the Innocents,"
"The Miraculous Sin," "Mary Magdalene," *and, above all,* "The Malbertus
Nocturne" *procured for me a kind of
religious intoxication and an intoxication of art, which I must, in good conscience, thank you for from the bottom
of my heart.*

*These things, monsieur, are in my
opinion quite superior to the majority
of contemporary Belgian productions,
scholastic and provincial* forgeries *of*

French art, which have left me, sometimes, on the verge of disgust or vomiting.

Accustomed, for a long time, to saying or writing whatever pleases me, I cannot wait to publish on this head, my feelings...

I will get to the point now, of infinitely less importance, which is this. A publicity agency communicates the attached document to me: "Le Passé de la vieille fille," by Léon Bloy, inserted in the Patriot *of Brussels, on December 3.*

This veridical tale was published on October 20 in the Gil Blas, *signed by my name in fact, under the already well-known rubric of* Histoires désobligeantes, *BUT with this title: "LE PASSÉ DU MONSIEUR," – a title desired by me, exclusively and absolutely.*

It is a rule that the reproduction of all my tales is forbidden, and it is solely by the negligence of the printer that the afore-named, in the original, does not carry that mention which one can read at the end of each of the others, immediately below my signature.

Does it not seem to you, as it does to me, that the choice of this morsel, which, by itself, *is not expressly and* typographically *protected against theft, demonstrates with evidence an intent to despoil me, every time one believes himself able to do so without consequences. Your* Patriot *reminds me of those dives where the most constant vigilance is indispensable so as not to lose one's hat or umbrella.*

However, I could console myself for this mischief. I have the inveterate habit of being cheated. The so-called latest edition of The Desperate Man *was published, last April, by Stock,* without prior contract, without authorization of any sort, and without their even bothering to inform me about it, *published even with modifications and ALTERATIONS!!! That is a little too much, don't you think? compared to the* Patriot *which seems to me to belong only to the lowest order of scoundrels.*

I could still, at a pinch, try to heal myself with a semblance of collaboration with that paper at the Court of Miracles, although such a promiscuity profoundly wounds me. But I confess, the travesty of my labors exasperates me and I refuse, with the most indomitable energy, to appear to espouse the stupidity of my plagiarizers.

Everyone knows that I am the most

contemptible of men. It is no longer permissible to ignore that ingratitude, cupidity, drunkenness, bawdiness, calumny, blackmail, and the filthiest pimping are my regular practices. All this was written by citizens of high merit who have always carefully kept themselves outside the range of Marchenoir's offal. Shall I dare to mention that these testimonies efficaciously consoled me for many troubles and helped develop an aesthetic sense in me?

My reputation as a writer, *however, was respected, I do not know by what miracle. None of my austere dispensers of justice wanted or dared to claim that the art of writing had been denied to me. It is therefore quite natural that I should retain this sole good and not allow literary helminths to propagate in my intestines.*

If I do not raise any protest, tomorrow undoubtedly another paper, Brabantian or Luxembourgian, would present to its public The Aggrieved, *a novel by Léon Bloy, or* The Whist of Excommunicants, *by the same author, from cuttings or reworkings deemed acceptable or necessary. And I would never see the end of it.*

There you have it then, my protest. I

will speak more loudly if one requires it. If it is absolutely necessary, I will do violence to my pacific nature and I will depart, not without affliction, from my customary gentleness. In the meantime, I will make an effort to display whatever I can of urbanity, courtesy, and reverence.

Will you, monsieur, be so kind as to offer, on my behalf, this letter to some periodical in Brussels that is independent enough to publish it? I would address it directly to such or such a one that was always perfect for me, if I were not afraid of encountering some great mishap, not to mention that I would have lost the opportunity of asking you for a favor. I am told that this is the secret to winning you over.

Accept, etc.

– LÉON BLOY.[54]

25. – Complaint:

(*Gil Blas*)

For several days now, the famous fumist, Marius Tournadre, occupies the public with one does not know what

---

[54]Original footnote: Published by the *l'Art Moderne* of Brussels, February 18.

*ridiculous disagreement with Baron
Alphonse de Rothschild, and the name
of our collaborator Léon Bloy, mentioned by a great number of journals,
inexplicably finds himself embroiled in
this farce.*

*Léon Bloy, justly revolted, urges us to
publish this: that he declares himself
an absolute stranger to M. Tournadre's intrigues, whom he never authorized, in any manner, to abuse his
name in this fashion, and that he energetically denies any solidarity with
this hoaxer.*

One must always distrust men who are penni-
less and who are Godless, someone once told me.

31. – Gospel reading on Saint Sylvester's Day: "*Estote similes hominibus expectantibus Dominum suum,
quando revertatur a nuptiis.*"[55]

I really want it, O Saint Luke, and I will wait,
upon your word, for my Lord to come back from the
Nuptials, because you tell me that it is then that "He
will make me sit down at His table and serve me."

---

[55]*Estote similes...*: Latin for "And you yourselves like to men
who wait for their lord, when he shall return from the wedding."
Luke 12:36 (Douay-Rheims).

1894

Deus non patietur vos tentari supra id quod potestis.[56] – 1 Corinthians X, 13.

---

[56]*Deus non patietur...*: Latin for "God... who will not suffer you to be tempted above that which you are able." 1 Corinthians 10:13 (Douay-Rheims).

January

23. – The Church today remembers Jesus' Prayer in the Garden:

Pater mi, si non potest hic calix transire nisi bibam illum, fiat voluntas tua...[57]

I repeat this terrifying prayer, as best I can, which makes me tremble, and I feel something of the mysterious Fear of the Master: *Cœpit pavere.*[58]

My God! what will I need to endure still?

25. – Always more tales to invent! The idea comes to me of adapting the story of Naundorff to a bourgeois family.

So I reread the popular short story of the individual, and this reading disconcerts me. How to approach a poem of such sorrow?

It is impossible for me to think of this dreamlike and prodigious man without being intimately touched in my soul. The figure of Louis XVII, wandering and renounced by all the earth, is it not the most astonishing *symbol?*

I think that there is certainly SOMEONE very

---

[57]*Pater mi...*: Latin for "My Father, if this chalice may not pass away, but I must drink it, thy will be done." Matthew 26:42 (Douay-Rheims).

[58]*Cœpit pavere*: Latin for "Began to fear." Mark 14:33 (Douay-Rheims).

poor, very unknown, and very great, who suffers in the same way, *at this very moment*, and that one must be afraid of not recognizing Him when one encounters Him.

27. – The sentimental imbecility of Protestantism, vaguely complicated by the filth of Spiritism, what is more invincible?

To discuss it, one must descend into a swamp. The words expended in vain *come back* immediately, like an ebb tide of fetid mud, onto the heart of the man who uttered them.

The three Concupiscences that Saint John speaks of:

Concupiscentia carnis. – One sins like a brute.

Concupiscentia oculorum. – One sins like a man.

Superbia vitæ. – One sins like a God.

28. – Sexagesima. The liturgy of this day, so particularly allotted to Saint Paul, inspires some reflections in us, especially the Gospel.

The "Sower": the Father; and "his Seed": the Word his Son, who falls, at first, along the "way," *secus Viam*, in other words, upon Himself, *from one end to the other*; – then, upon the "rock": the Church; – then, amidst the "thorns," which are *sollicitudines, divitiæ et voluptates*[59]: the Crown itself of Jesus; – finally into the "good Earth": Canaan, that of the Paraclete.

After dinner, very long quarrel about music, with respect to Meyerbeer and Wagner: one of our guests exalting the first, whom de Groux shouts down in honor of *Parsifal*. I intervene to formulate precise maledictions against all music not directly having the praise of God as its sole object. I say that the most beautiful music, even at church, appears beautiful only because it is the occasion to appreciate the *real* music, the divine harmony that lies at the heart of Perfect Silence.

30. – The central idea of my last tale, "*Propos digestifs*," being that no one can be assured of his *identity* and that each one of us probably occupies another person's place. Jeanne asked me how such disorder could exist in God's Work.

"And the Fall?" I replied... "Nothing is fulfilled. We all have to wait, because we are in *Chaos*," in the great chaos that separates the Bad Rich from the glorious Poor. It is reserved for us, then, veritably to assist at the Genesis, to be witnesses of the Creation, from the *Fiat Lux* until the birth of Adam, etc.

---

[59]Sollicitudines...: Latin for "solicitudes, riches, and sensual pleasures."

February

3. – "Monsieur, you have tried to turn me away from my duties."

"And you, madame, have you not tried to turn me away from mine?"

4. – One never knows whom one is the nearest relative of.

7. – Sent to Roinard the following, for the strange book that he wants to publish in collaboration with everyone, *Portraits du prochain siècle* [Portraits of the Next Century]:

ERNEST HELLO

There will likely never be a more troubling reality than the physical resemblance between Ernest Hello and Henry de Groux.

It was necessary for the equilibrium of one knows not what globes crawling across the bottom of abysses, that the painter of Tourments *should resemble that Provocateur of Thunder.*

For the very rare few who knew Hello, it is frightening to contemplate him thus, after his death, in the most burn-

ing cave of Hell. For the painting by Henry de Groux appears to be of that terrible Place.

Seen from a distance, Ernest Hello reminds one of the Paralytic beside the Pool of Bethesda, healed by a word of Our Savior, and he always seemed like he was carrying his bed around with him.[60]

That filthy cot has become, by a greater miracle, the legacy of his spitting image, who dismantled it to make a colossal trestle out of it.

Such is the mystery that I propose to the dreamers of the "next century."

All men are disinterred, and Hello's tomb, – his real tomb – *has to be EMPTY.*

– LÉON BLOY.

8. – Atrocious difficulty at times to find, each week, the subject of a new tale... I place an *empty* sack on my table and I draw my nourishment from it.

Léopold Lacour declares his feelings of esteem and admiration for me. He defends me, he says, against everyone, and finishes by proposing a pact. If some particularly serious malicious gossip should

---

[60]Original footnote: Unintelligible phrase for people who do not know that Hello was slightly hunchbacked.

threaten to divide us, whoever of the two has any anxiety about it will immediately go and tell the other person everything. Foolishness passes the time in life, said Villiers.

11. – Attempted, conscientiously, to listen to a preacher of Lent. I am struck by this evidence that the means God has taken to establish his Church, the Apostolic Predication, is precisely what is the weakest today, the most mediocre. *Sal terræ evanescit.*[61]

12. – Birth of my son André, at the *Angelus* of noon.

The midwife being Protestant, his baptism can never happen too quickly.

14. – One must not scorn presentiments. They are to the imperfect what the discernment of Relics is to the Saints. Jeanne's words.

16. – To my friend, the lieutenant:

> ... *One must pray. Everything else is vain and stupid. One must pray to endure the horror of this world, one must pray to be pure, one must pray to obtain the strength to* wait.
>
> *There is neither despair, nor bitter*

---

[61] *Sal terræ evanescit*: Latin for "The salt of the earth vanishes."

sadness for the man who prays a lot. It is I who say it. If only you knew how much right I have to say it, and with what authority I speak to you!

You are familiar with life's banal miseries, but you are ignorant of true Sorrow. You have not received the real blow that pierces the heart. Perhaps you never will, for very few receive it, though many claim to have.

The number is infinite of man-children who believe that they suffer beyond measure, and who suffer, in reality, very little. The number is infinite of those who imagine themselves in possession of the Faith, but whose faith would not move a grain of dust. As for Hope and Love, what words have been more prostituted?

Faith, Hope, Charity, and Sorrow, which is their substrate, are diamonds, and diamonds are rare, as you know. They cost very dear, do not forget it.

They cost the Prayer that is, in itself, an inestimable joy which it is necessary to conquer. It is rudimentary and formidable.

It has to do with praying simply, foolishly, but with a powerful will. It is indispensable to pray for a long time, patiently, without listening to disgust or fatigue, until emotion comes, which feels like a brand in the heart. Then one can go in peace and endure it does not matter what...

You tell me you see only my "hand" in some of my tales, but that in others you see my "heart."

You read me poorly then, dear friend. I put my heart into all that I write. But I write for a frivolous journal where I cannot always express myself openly. I am, on the contrary, forced to hide myself.

Reread, for example, "La Taie d'Argent," or "Une Recrue," and with a little attention you will find some nourishment there for you. I put something of my heart into each one of these stories which are often enough, believe me, allegories.

I give the impression of speaking to the crowd to amuse it. In reality, I am speaking to several exceptional souls who discern my thought and apperceive it under its veil. You should be among them, my dear André. The apparent farce that the Gil *published, yesterday: "On n'est pas parfait" [No One's Perfect], came out of a fervent communion in which I had asked for Light, in the name of the dolorous*

Crown of Jesus Christ.

– Your Léon Bloy.

18. – Faith is the knowledge of our limits.

22. – "Monsieur Bloy, you ought to write pamph-
lets!..." Counsel, confidently given, by a simple man
who sometimes reads the journals when piquet or
manille allow.

March

1st. – The *Mercure* publishes an article by de Gourmont in which it is said that Jesus lacked *logic* in his words!!!!

2. – Someone points out to me a financial scheme, the success of which could be very profitable for me. My old salary would be restored. It is very uncertain, but God knows how much I would prefer not to have to write for the *Gil Blas* anymore! That odious journal – which pays me so miserably, – consumes my life, week after week. I will be fifty years old soon and I have the best part of my work as yet to do.

4. – Inconceivable blindness of the Jewish historian Josephus, who talks nonstop about God, but who never sees Jesus Christ in the extraordinary punishment of Jerusalem.

Idea of a work of imagination or criticism on this subject. Considering that at the time of the taking of Jerusalem, by Titus, in AD 70, the majority of actors or witnesses of the Passion were very probably still alive.

7. – There is no such thing as chance, because chance is the Providence of imbeciles, and Justice wants imbeciles to be without Providence.

Card from a stranger who tells me that, having been unaware of my name until now, and having only recently, fifteen or so days ago, learned about me by chance, his admiration for me has won him over to me.

Response:

Léon Bloy, several times having been deceived by fetid rascals or appalling imbeciles who claimed to admire him, invites M. X***, whose card he just received, to give a fuller account of himself, but in writing. M. X*** says that he came across Léon Bloy's books "by chance." The word chance *does not exist in the dictionary of this rather impatient writer, who would like to know whether he had any objectionable intentions.*

– *LÉON BLOY.*

8. – Appearance of the first fascicule of *Vendanges*, – drawing by Henry de Groux, text by Léon Bloy. A large, magnificent brochure in folio, which will cover us in glory and money, – if the enterprise, miraculously, does not abort.

Here is my first song:

THE ABANDONED VINEYARD

ELOI, ELOI, LAMMA SABACTHANI?[62]

People, formerly, collapsed on the tiles when these Hebrew words were read in the illuminated evangelistary during the office of the second day of the Sorrowful Week.

They had as much sorrow as a person could have, because all men, then, were children and the stronger the men were, the more they seemed like very small children.

They would truly die to learn that Jesus was abandoned by his adorable Father, on his Cross and in his Languors.

The Languors of God! The Dereliction of God! That was what, above all, broke people's heart!

* * *

But how far we have come from those elementary times, and how reasonable and learned we have become since we stopped weeping for love under an explained *firmament!*

The pale paintbrush of electric projections, from now on, precisely delin-

---

[62]*Eloi, Eloi...*: Hebrew for "My God, my God, why hast though foresaken me." Mark 15:34 (Douay-Rheims).

*eates the Ignominy of the Savior of
Souls.*

*That livid ray illuminates the spent
Sun which no longer gave any light,
and whose very place was so profoundly forgotten that those who weep
had renounced looking for it.*

*And there he is! the poor God who can
no longer bear being abandoned, who
can no longer bear always dying, but
who dies, most definitely, of scientific
Opprobrium, without having been suc-
cored!*

*The filthy beasts may approach. They
will be less offensive than that pallid
phosphorescence of rotting refuse that
encourages them.*

* * *

EGO SUM RESURRECTIO ET VITA.[63] *Are
these really your Words, Lord?*

*Now look at your last friends, and the
poor even, who are in flight. Your Cal-
vary, in the end, becomes too dreadful,
and if people who have turned to dust
could come back to life, don't you
think that they would run away too,*

---

[63]*Ego sum resurrectio*...: Latin for "I am the resurrection and the
life." John 11:25 (Douay-Rhems).

from your Person, while letting out cries?

In the past, suffering Redeemer, you were the Father of the poor. You called yourself their Head, and they called themselves your Members because they hoped for your Glory.

But that really is too much, and if you continue to languish for just one more century, we will need to call you the Father of the Dead.

* * *

Someone appears, however, Someone who is all in tears.

It is not the Mother. It is not the Evangelist. It not the Golden Lover, the magnificent Fiancée, that Madeleine of the flames whose tears are as "hard" as Hell's crystals.

It is neither a Martyr, nor a Virgin, nor a Confessor. And it is assuredly even less one of those murdered Innocents who play, for two thousand years now, with their palms and their crowns, beneath the Altar of Heaven.

That one there is a Stranger among all strangers. He is the solitary Unknown One who waits for nobody and whom nobody waits for.

*Would it be He whom Jesus has so of-
ten called out to in his Languor? The
mysterious Liberator who must decrucify him?*

*But if so, good God! he has taken his
sweet time to come!*

* * *

*Ah! without a doubt, when Christianity
was thoroughly sublime, and when the
burning Blood of Jesus Christ ran in
the veins of its first Saints, like an impetuous molten metal racing through
the bronze aqueducts; – when little
children and prepubescent girls borrowed "the voice of cataracts" to
sing; – when an army of affable lions
and an entire empire of executioners
were on hand; – when Christians
strolled amidst the tortures, as in a delicious garden, and when the sound of
their torments made the city walls of
Asia sweat with the sweat of horror; –
yes, without a doubt, in those olden
days, there could be no question of un-
nailing the Savior of the world.*

* * *

The centuries eventually came to lie down timidly at the foot of the Cross. And when the Church had finally placed the feet of its throne on the four corners of the earth, the Middle Ages, crenelated with basilicas, hoped for nothing better than to suffer.

What was needed was the present date of redemption and the cyclone of turpitudes that blew from Protestantism.

But, once again, how late it is! And how miserable that supposed Liberator appears, that Elijah of mud stains and the rabble, who presents himself in tears at the lugubrious moment of the End of ends.

If that there is the Consoler, he is seen so far beneath misfortune itself that the appalling Misery of Christ looks immediately like magnificence in comparison.

* * *

After all, he has his Cross, the Lord who dies does. He has his Church, – now draped in insults, it is true.

He had his worshippers who were skinned alive for love of him. A large number of others, at the mere sight of him, have obtained for themselves the stigmatization of his Wounds...

He is the Solomon of ignominies, and as much as the universe wants nothing more to do with him, the sad and mangy universe is filled with his Face.

The other has nothing, absolutely nothing. *Not even the look of a desperate man, not even the attention of the venomous beasts that now swarm over Golgotha.*

Well then! So much the better! SURGE, ILLUMINARE, JERUSALEM![64] *To deliver the King of the poor, what was needed perhaps was Someone who was even poorer than him, but who arrived...* too late.

* * *

It is the Worker of the last second of the eleventh hour.

It is he who believed that the Day could never end, and who even comes after that abominable vermin that was afraid to arrive too early.

If the Master of the Vineyard remuner-

---

[64] *Surge, illuminare...:* Latin for "Arise, be enlightened, O Jerusalem." Isaiah 60:1 (Douay-Rheims).

*ates the workers of the "eleventh
hour" as much as the workers who
bore the weight of day on their shoul-
ders, what will become of that impossible companion who presents himself
when the mercenaries have stopped
being paid, when everyone has left,
and when the wells of Night have been
opened?...*

*The Vineyard itself must needs be giv-
en to him, the pale and abandoned
Vineyard, the poor VINEYARD of the
Lord who is dying.*

9. – New letter from that invoker of *chance* whom I
responded to the day before yesterday. He says he is
an anarchist and a litterateur, but in what language,
and sporting what turkey's caruncle! I wanted to
know whether I was dealing with an imbecile. Now I
am sure of it. He is a perfect imbecile.

11. – Roman history. Modern criticism, with Niebuhr
leading has declared, against the authority of Titus
Livius, that the early days of Rome, such as the old
historian recounts them, must be called the *mythical
epoch*, and our own Michelet has made himself the
popularizer of that doctrine.

But what if all these savants were mistaken,
and Titus Livius were right!

All that ancient world is, moreover, terrifying. What a mystery it is, the silence of God among the Gentiles, for so many centuries!

22. – Ever and always writing for this ignoble *Gil!* Fatigue and disgust bordering on despair.

25. – Interview of Zola published, this morning, by the same *Gil*, wherein that brute calls himself a *lion*.

April

3. – Someone communicates to me about an article in the Chicago *Tribune*: "Shocking Story current on the Parisian boulevards." It appears that the merchants of salted pork have taken seriously and hold, from now on, for historic document, a sort of joke, [which] appeared in the *Gil Blas*, last January 19, under the title of "He Who Had Sold the Head of Napoleon 1st." I was imagining a Parisian hooligan who, in 1870, would have handed over this Relic to Emperor Wilhelm, ravished by the acquisition. Weak epigram which had the effect of a startling revelation for the serious men of Illinois. What success!

5. – Yesterday evening, Laurent Tailhade, dining at Foyot's with his mistress, received a pretty bomb. Some journalists, ill-treated by him, express their joy.

7. – De Groux, a much more avid reader of the journals than I am, comes to speak with me about a villainy by the swine of the quill, ganging up on Tailhade, whose condition is grave and who can even die from it. He is detested, and they are rejoicing everywhere because of that unfortunate man's distress, whose crime is to have written, against his contemporaries, several verses inspired by my humble prose. Little by little, – kindled by de Groux, who represents to me, energetically, that I do not have the right to be disinterested in a man against whom everyone had

unleashed on, – I decide to write an article to defend him or avenge him, even though I am almost certain to lose my daily bread because of it.[65]

8. – Pointless dispatch announcing to me a vain letter that does not arrive. Such is the pace of this imbecilic world.

Response to a Protestant who wants to get me on board: "I refuse all discussion, and I have no need for it, as I believe only in *obedience*. Jesus commanded me to obey the Pope and that is enough for me."

9. – Very nice letter from Rachilde, sending me the detailed account of a famous evening in which Tailhade assumed, once and for all, the execration of journalists, by whom he is, today, so cravenly insulted.

Good document for my dangerous column.

10. – Delivery to the *Gil Blas* of "The Poet's Hallali." Such is the title of the monitory. Epigraph: "Oh! The Swine! The Swine! The Swine!" The administrator Albiot declares the peril, but does not refuse my ginger, and promises me the protection of his pinion. That's all I need.

---

[65]Original footnote: This day cost me the death of two of my children and more than two years of diabolic misery, not to mention insults by the entire press who turned against me, – insults that I have always considered very precious.

11. – Signature, along with Léopold Lacour and André H., to the extravagant and lucrative contract that assures each of us a Rothschildian opulence in the case of success of the most improbable enterprise in modern times...

13. – "The Poet's Hallali" came out yesterday. The stinking *Venerable*, Edmond Lepelletier, considering himself offended, sends to me, in the evening, two subtle louts who arrange, *naturally*, not to find me at home. What a shame! it would have been agreeable to me to have received them properly.[66]

On the matutinal announcement of a visit by these two paladins, I sent, around noon, this dispatch to the *Gil Blas*:

> *I have yet to see anyone come, and my personal affairs do not permit me to be, all day long, at the disposition of witnesses of the* first person to come along. *Dueling is, in my opinion, a ridiculous and filthy business, invented by saltimbanques. I will gladly replace it by kicks to the pants... of others.*
>
> *– Léon Bloy.*

That explains everything.

---

[66]Original footnote: See the complete story of this affair in my brochure, *Léon Bloy devant les cochons*, published two months later (Paris, Chamuel, publisher).

14. – The *Gil* begins the publication of *Lourdes*. The atrocious boredom of that defecation [...].

15. – Léopold Lacour comes to tell me that everything is going poorly for me at the *Gil*. My refusal to go to blows necessitating a heroic expenditure by my editor in chief, according to the rites of journalism, [would provoke] general indignation and have me expelled from that lupanar. Lacour, having seen these rascals, yesterday evening, took it upon himself to come and ask me, at least, for an unambiguous and definitive response. What was the point in saying to him that my response was known, in advance, for ten years now, – but they want it in writing and signed.

Overcome with lassitude and disgust, I write that I cannot do tomorrow what I could not do the day before. – "Let monsieur Lepelletier attack me personally, all he wants, my contempt protects him!..." Such was my last word on the subject.

16. – Blessed and profitable day! I cease to belong to the editorial staff at the *Gil*. I am let go, once again, as villainously as possible, on the occasion of one of the most noble articles I have ever written.

The petulant loutishness of Albiot and the venenous idiocy of Desfossés, – the two administrators who *executed me*, – have infinitely surpassed my secret hopes. Albiot, between the fear of sudden slaps and the nobler fright of displeasing the dotard he uses, assumes a position, – after removing himself to behind a desk, – of completely renouncing me. That incontestable scoundrel even dares to mention *Christian charity(!!!)* which forbids injury. Desfossés, himself, has nothing but the inarticulate chuckles of a person exasperated by goiters.

As it was natural, for the good of my poor soul, that I should lose so filthy a daily bread, could I expect a more efficacious recomfort than the spectacle of so sumptuous an ignominy?

Cries of joy, transports of happiness in my house! Carillon of hearts! Let us prepare the table for the joyous celebration of Misery!

17. – Léopold Lacour, figuring that I am lost, spontaneously abandons me, with an unbelievable noblesse.

20. – Roinard suggests to me an apologetic brochure. So be it. I will write, then, sixty pages under this title: *Léon Bloy devant les cochons* [Léon Bloy Before the Swine]. The good Roinard, whom I met only today, and whom I did not know was so taken with me, believes he can find me a publisher. He hopes even to collect some money for me.

21. – Letters by strangers, congratulating me for having exited the cesspit, but not offering me one centime.

Filthy frenzy by some worthy friends of Lepelletier, who, seeing me disarmed, launch their hearts at me with both hands. I collect all that caca with pleasure.

23. – Edmond Lepelletier's son protests against his father's villainy.

I begin my brochure, *Léon Bloy devant les cochons*.

27. – To Tailhade, inpatient at the Hôpital de la Charité:

> *My dear Tailhade,*
>
> *I just read, in the* Journal, *the interview by Jules Huret, curious to inform the public about the "state of soul of a bombing victim."*
>
> *My stupor is enormous. Was that slave unfaithful? If not, how could you have failed to mention me, me, the* only one *who has defended you and at what a price! having spontaneously sacrificed my daily bread and that of my family – when I am, because of you, inundated with filth by that same press that insulted you?*
>
> *That, Tailhade, would be terrible. Have you not considered that your tes-*

timony at this moment, when everyone abandons me like a leper, could be infinitely useful and precious to me, and will I need, in the brochure that I now prepare, to include you among those who have abandoned me because of Laurent Tailhade?

No, right? That would be too abominable. Huret is a whore, right? It goes without saying; and I expect to read tomorrow in the Journal, *a vehement rectification.*

Your friend,

– LÉON BLOY.

28. – Response by Tailhade, who confesses not to have spoken about me and asks my pardon, protesting that "neither his heart nor his will are for nothing." (!) He promises me I do not know what apologetic conference held at the start of next winter. Let's go! He is one of those men whom one must constantly keep an eye on, with an oyster knife in hand. New letter:

My dear Tailhade,

You beg my pardon *before I have even had the time to feel really offended. Yesterday, I felt only some chagrin, an atrocious chagrin. The* Journal *has come before my eyes, in a moment when I was trying to recover, after*

*several moments, from abominable er-
rands, from the recourses of a reprobate, to which state my expulsion from
the* Gil Glas *[sic], several days ago,
has condemned me. Think about it, my
friend, that not only have I lost my
only source of income, but I am covered with a thick ignominy, being deprived of all means to defend myself
and no one having, thus far, spoken up
for me.*

*You must be familiar with the ignoble
schemes of journalism to know how
much of a* simulacrum *it was, that depressing duel, that they pretend to de-
base me with. The interview by Huret,
in the* Journal, *a widely read paper,
was the unique occasion and it will
never materialize again.*

*When I saw the title, I could barely
hold back a cry of joy, from the bottom
of my distress. – At last! I said to myself, a little justice! Ah! I did not doubt
your energy...*

*My deception was inexpressible. Your
silence, have no doubt about it, filled
my enemies, who are also your enemies, with a joy proportionate to my
mourning. They can triumph now:
"That Bloy is so abject that even the
person he immolated himself for dis-
owns him." What would you say if,*

*this morning, some columnist ex-
pressed that gracious thought?*

*De Groux, whom I saw yesterday
evening, was floored, not having
thought, in his wildest dreams.... believing that he had fallen into a chasm.
What could we do, if not latch on
strongly to the idea that the reporter
had been unfaithful and dishonored
you in that way, in order to please?*

*You write to me saying that he was not
[unfaithful]... Then, what? You add
that "your heart had nothing to do in
this omission." O Tailhade, your po-
liteness is as hard as hell!*

Ah! If I had been in your place, my
heart *would not have allowed me to
remain quiet. It would have leapt out
of me! I would not have* spoken *about
the poor writer having accepted the
worst sufferings for me. I would have*
shouted *his accursed name, I would
have bawled it, I would have spit it out
twenty times, like clots of blood into
the face of the coward who would
have come to enquire about my "state
of soul," and I would have demanded
his very faithful transcription, under
pain of death!*

Now, I ask you, what good can an
apology *do for me that comes too late*

*and which one makes efforts to stifle,
or a conference set far into the future,
which no one will mention?*

*Huret having been exact, there is no
room to rectify whatever it might be,
at the* Journal. *There is absolutely only
one thing to do, but at once. To profit
from the situation of the "man of the
hour," which is yours for over one
month now, in order to obtain the insertion of a special article in a daily of
large circulation, wherein you would
do for the wounded Léon Bloy what I
did for the wounded Laurent Tailhade.
It would be easy for you to explain
that you did not wish to risk denatur-
ing that defense by exposing it to the
dubitable transcription of an interviewer. Such is, I repeat, the only
thing to be done, and to be done immediately. But will you do it?*

Your friend,

– LÉON BLOY.

De Groux brings me, this evening, thirty
francs more or less, which he procured, I wish to believe, by assassinating someone.

New response from Tailhade, still more miserable than the preceding one. – "Ah! when the hounds
need to be brought to the chase!..." groaned, habitually, an old relative who raised me. De Groux's indignation is at its limit. If, in one week, Tailhade has not

done what I demand, I will let him have it at the end of my brochure.

Léon Bloy devant les cochons! It will be the most beautiful of all.

May

1st. – We have about twenty francs left, to keep us until the Last Judgment.

4. – Lines by Henry de Groux to be published in *Portraits du prochain siècle*.

LÉON BLOY

Bloy has said that I look like Hello.

So be it. I will try, then, to say what Ernest Hello would have *written* about his friend Léon Bloy.

Bloy has but one line, and that line is his contour. That line, – it is the ABSOLUTE.

The Absolute in thought, the Absolute in word, the Absolute in deed.

Such Absoluteness that everything in him is identical.

When he vomits on a contemporary, it is infinitely and exactly as if he were chanting the Glory of God.

It is why the glory of this world is refused to him.

And I consent to be grilled alive if

anyone can prove to me that Hello would have had anything else to say.

– Henry de Groux.

10. – Considering that Tailhade, wounded principally in the head, could very well no longer possess his perfect balance, I renounce, once and for all, to lay into him in my brochure, but I demand a letter of formal adhesion, absolute and immediate. De Groux takes it upon himself to obtain it from him.

12. – Confused memory of a dream. I saw myself amongst of the dead, filled with a feeling of the greatest tenderness for the dead, for the multitude of the dead, and I keep the impression that I ought to be saved or delivered by a dead person very profoundly unknown to me.

17. – Letter from Tailhade, asking me for a vignette, (!) "one of my beautiful illuminations," for a publication that he is planning... Poor devil! death, really, would have been better for him. "I gave myself arms that speak," he wrote to me, "*back when I was smug*, a laurel branch (Laurent), flanked by this device: *Viret semper laurus*."[67] A peruker's banality in those arms and device, which I was ignorant of, fills me with tender feelings.

---

[67]Viret semper laurus: Latin for "The laurel always flourishes."

24. – I am forced to read two dispatches from a scandalously rich woman, whom someone had tried to interest in my destiny.

The first one shows somewhat benevolent dispositions, but with the reserve that she believes she knows that I am not "real." (!) The second is an outpouring of filth. She declares that she couldn't "give a damn" about me and my little family, and insinuates some dark accusation of "hypocrisy." It is fortunate that I am not condemned to owe anything to such a jezebel!

30. – "You have no notion of duration," I said to my dear de Groux, "and it is extremely serious. The hours are not similar to each other, nor the days. There exists between each hour of the day, and each day of the week, an absolute, essential, divine difference."

For example. According to Genesis, Monday belongs to the Light; Tuesday, to the Sky; Wednesday, to the Earth, to the Sea, and to Vegetable Life; Thursday, to the Stars; Friday, to Fish, Reptiles, and Winged Creatures; Saturday, to Beasts and to Man; Sunday, to the Lord's Rest.

I am persuaded that an analogous picture could be established for each of the hours of the day or night, for each of the months of the year, and for each of the years of a century.

So, when you have decided, – with more or less wisdom, – that such a thing ought to be accomplished for you, on such a day or at such an hour, that day and that hour receive, from the mysterious power of your will, a certain character of opportunity that immediately makes the other days and other hours destitute of what could make them favorable to the success of your design.

So, one is nearly certain to fail if one lacks *exactitude*, that is to say, if one inverts the role of the hours or the days, – because then it would require that God act miraculously, so that success might be obtained whatever the case.

June

1st. – *Miraculously*, Chamuel consents to publish *Léon Bloy devant les cochons*. The discovery of this publisher is a masterwork of perseverance and audacity on the part of Roinard alone, something that no one but this Gaul would have dared to attempt. The prodigy is justified, moreover, by the sign outside the establishment: *Bookstore of the Marvelous!*

2. – Someone sends me a Belgian Catholic review. One of the Messieurs of that paper informs the elite intelligences, for whom he works exclusively, of my profound misfortune. It appears that I "mix with riffraff" and that "the formidable stylist Bloy is no longer, at the present hour, but the entrepreneur of a sewage disposal business for all human base acts *and even other things*."

I cite, word for word, in my brochure, an insignificant Brussels pimp who says the same things, in the same style. It could be they get drunk together.

5. – Reread a few stories by Edgar Allan Poe, whom I used to be quite passionate about. And it would seem that I am, no doubt, still. Incontestable beauties that resemble, sometimes, splendor. But it is the splendor of ebony, as they say. What a dark genius! What a tenebrous imagination! God is absent from it, as He is from hell.

6. – Spoke with de Groux about a project for a book.

The words of Saint Paul, *Videmus nunc per speculum in œnigmate*,[68] would be the skylight for plunging into the real *Chasm*, which is the human soul.

The frightful immensity of the abysses of heaven is an illusion, an external reflection of our own abysses, apperceived "in a mirror." It has to do with *turning our vision inward* and practicing a sublime astronomy in the infinity of our hearts, for which God wanted to die.

No man can *see* anything but what is in himself. If we see the Milky Way, it exists, *actually*, in our soul.

8. – Tried to reread *The Future Eve* by Villiers. Too much human science and too little divine science. It is the same impression that I have for Edgar Allan Poe. These poets did not pray, and their sometimes eloquent contempt is nothing but the bitterness of their terrestrial impatience. They are too much of the earth, like idols.

11. – Confession at Saint Sulpice. I address myself to the first priest that comes along, whose face I do not see even and who expedites me as if turning on a light

---

[68] *Videmus nunc per...:* Latin for "We see now through a glass in a dark manner." 1 Corinthians 13:12 (Douay-Rheims).

switch. While hearing my rapid confessions, *he was counting his money!* He was doing his cashbox. It is the first time that such a thing has happened to me.

The Angels themselves, could they say what Confession is?

The internal word of God to the soul: *The more you have betrayed me, the more confidence I put in you!*

18. – Our life is appalling...

Events don't mean anything, my wife tells me, it is all about feelings. The worst catastrophes do not make us suffer if God has given us internal joy, because everything that is outside the soul is pure illusion.

19. – To Monsieur Clémenceau:

Monsieur,

I have the honor of sending to you a copy of my brochure: Léon Bloy devant les cochons. *This little book, which could only seem excessive to the handful of puppets called out by their miserable names, will fall, infallibly, into the abyss of silence. The promoter of the absolute and justice, which people detest in me, must not expect from the eunuchs of publicity anything else than suffocation or a strangling.*

In that case, why then would I not simply and virilely call on you, who had the honor once of standing nearly alone against everyone, *of being insulted, vilipended, cursed by the multitude, – whom, I presume, must have execrated in you something that transcended it?*

Why would you not take up the defense of a man whose Destiny, to a certain degree, so perfectly resembles your own, – of a solitary and redoubted writer, who could have prostituted himself like any other, but who, proudly, out of love, fifteen years ago, chose to marry the most terrible poverty?

Why finally would you yourself not speak, in the plenary independence of your most gallant disdain, to the enormous stupor of the silentiaries *of the Late Roman Empire who believe themselves so sure, am I not right? that no man would dare to raise his voice in defense of such a proscript?*

Please find herein, Monsieur, the expression of my most profound sympathy,

– LÉON BLOY.[69]

---

[69]Original footnote: Without response and without effect. Had I not written to the same person, a month earlier, that "I am

21. – Decisive word by my editor Chamuel: "The bi-
cycle kills the book."

22. – A Christian woman said this to me: "One must
have a husband in order to be a virgin."

To which I respond with all the Church: "Inte-
gral virginity is in proportion to the supernatural desire of maternity. It is by force of being the Mother of
God that Mary is perfectly Virgin."

To a young Scandinavian Catholic, in love
with a converted Jew:

> *I do not congratulate you on your
> choice, poor girl... Since the begin-
> ning, the Jewish race has been separat-
> ed from other human races, so pro-
> foundly separated and kept in reserve
> for ulterior Designs that mixing with
> the Jews has always been regarded,
> among every nation, as a sort of sacri-
> lege.*

> *If you desire to become the wife of a
> Jew, even a converted one, you expose
> yourself to a frightening malediction,
> and I tell you this on God's behalf, –
> despite the advice of all the cowardly
> or imbecilic priests whom you might
> consult.*

eternally ignorant about politics"?

25. – The going on sale of my *Swine*, and the assassination of Carnot, stabbed yesterday evening, in
Lyon...

Continuation of my destiny. Bad luck is obstinate to the point of not shrinking before the assassination of a President of the Republic, in order to deprive
me of a possible success.

26. – I ring for a long time at Tailhade's place, the
concierge assuring me that he is home and providing
me with indubitable proof. Determined to push the
experiment to the limit, I go wandering about under
Odéon, and I return one hour later.

New carillon. In the end, a half-naked woman
half-opens the door and declares to me that he went
out. I conclude from this that he must be in the *pays
du Mufle*.[70] [71]

This man could not find the means to visit me,
five weeks after he left the hospital.

To a friend, an entrepreneur of masonry, who

---

[70]*Pays du Mufle*: French for "Land of the Boor," the title of
Tailhade's first book of poetry.

[71]Original footnote: One of Laurent Tailhade's most vile insulters,
when he was agonizing from his wound and when, alone against
everyone, I took up his defense, was Edmond Lepelletier.

Recently, Tailhade was calling him "dear and venerated Master"
in his columns, laboriously imitative of me, which everyone could
read.

inexplicably distanced himself:

> *My dear friend,*
>
> *The brochure that you receive, togeth-
> er with this letter, will instruct you ex-
> actly in what manner I had to leave
> the* Gil Blas, *in case you do not al-
> ready know.*
>
> *Will you be able to find for me, in any
> office or building site whatsoever, any
> sort of job? The moment has come to
> forget that I am an artist, a writer, and
> to remind myself that I need to feed my
> family. The privations that one en-
> dures, for two months now, can no
> longer be supported.*
>
> *I would accept, then, it does not mat-
> ter what job, were it the employment
> of a* manual laborer, *rather than to see
> those who have been entrusted to me
> perish.*
>
> *I understood, more than a year ago,
> that you no longer desired to see us,
> and I resigned myself, as best I could,
> to that injustice towards some very
> poor folk who had never offended you.*
>
> *But I hope that you will find your soul
> again so as to render me this last fa-
> vor which ought to be easy for you.
> Keep in mind that it would be a verita-
> ble cruelty not to respond to me, that*

> *the three sous that are franked to this*
> *letter represent a great effort, and that*
> *your response can never come too*
> *soon.*
>
> – *LÉON BLOY.*

27. – The sending of a copy of my *Swine* to Remy de Gourmont: "A souvenir from someone who takes pleasure in dying of starvation."

Standing for one hour on the terrace of the first café I came across, to see a feverish and mad multitude defile, in fictive mourning for Carnot, and in contestable jubilation for the election of Casimir Périer, who was just made President. Ignoble crowd.

28. – Response from my friend of the day before yesterday. Polite and cold. He declares himself "sorry" to be unable to help to me. I am completely ignorant of just how much the existence of certain men is saturated with *desolation*.

Nothing was more beautiful than the fervor of that man, who came to me like a brother, three years ago, and I will never know, doubtless, the reasons for his decision to flee from me. Poverty is like the Devil. When it has taken a man captive, it surrounds him with excrements.

30. – Time is the *Incarnation* of Eternity. Jeanne's

idea.

Completed the second poem of *Vendanges:*

THE FIANCÉE'S CORTEGE[72]

The Woman who mischievously troubles the soul of a cesspool emptier and who does not give herself, immediately thereafter, to that cesspool emptier, will be judged by a tribunal of prostitutes and homicides. Such is the law, verified by nineteen centuries of Christianity.

You make us die of desire and despair, O hanging Garden of Voluptuousness, upheld by all the columns of society.

You are high and erratic like the sea, and you riddle with torments the unfortunate men who "received their soul in vain."

Horrible Virgin with the inaccessible womb, Pourer of poison, Cupbearer of

---

[72]Original footnote: Unpublished. The first poem, "The *Abandoned* Vineyard," published in March, had obtained the insuccess fitting for a kind of publication that cannot claim the approbation of any bordello. One will understand that such a result was naturally encouraging to me.

De Groux, whose magnificent drawing was supposed to once again illustrate my text, was counting, it is true, for this new *commercial* attempt, on the "word of honor" of an individual who disappeared.

death, sublime Brute!... the little stars that rotate at the back of sky are closer to us than you are, much closer, and it is frightening to think about the morose multitude of black swine that form your cortege and who could have remained men if you had had a heart big enough to become, really truly, a hussy!

But you are a wise virgin, *who does not let her lamp go out, and you are always ready for the delectations and transports of the Bridegroom who comes unannounced. You have soiled neither your dress, – nearly nonexistent, it is true, – nor your very pure flesh, and it is all the same to you, is it not? if all the dead who are behind you, if all those poor dead men without a* de profundis, *hold their shadowy hands out to supplicate you.*

So greatly do you believe, atrocious Wench, that the firmament adores you, that the mechanism of the skies moves for you, and that you do not owe anything to Vermin.

But, take care, they are patient, the little convives of the putrefaction of pretty women; they are utterly patient and utterly immortal – and they have gnawed on the head of Gods!

* * *

But once again, we are troubled, we others, fragile humans, we are troubled in a dreadful manner, and this trouble is among the things that Jesus bore in his Agony.

That inexpressible bitterness, of disappointed concupiscence, is the very lees of the Chalice that he had to drink. For it is the most hideous of tortures. It is the torment that cannot be magnified, of all things it is the one that best effaces the Form of man because it is the only form that he cannot *choose.*

Beings made in the Image of the God who suffers, and whose souls could have been like torrents toward a Pacific Ocean of light, have lost, because of you, imbecile Idol, that original Resemblance that configured them for eternal Reason.

Scrambling down ten thousand steps, they have become more foolish than you, to accompany you, on their four feet, as far as that black water, – over there, beneath the ragged moon.

Those there are the living, the so-called living of this earth.

But you are filled with the dead.

Who will count them, after so many centuries? Are you not, from time immemorial, the commonplace of the most banal misery of the children of men?

Female shearer of enfeebled Samson, Exterminatrice of innocents, Prophetess of tormenters;

Putrid Virgin, inclement Virgin, infidel Virgin;

Mirror of injustice and Throne of folly;

Vessel of matter, Vessel of shame, Vessel of blasphemy;

Tuberose of asphyxias, Tower of hunger, Donjon of tears and gratings;

Gate of subterranean places;

Funereal star;

Agony of Agonists, and Consolatrice of those who are not afflicted;

O Our Lady of Recoverance for all those who will never be Christians;

Regina Tenebrarum et locorum Tristitiæ;[73] *It is you who carry, invisibly,*

---

[73]*Regina Tenebrarum...:* Latin for "Queen of the Tenebræ and Sad Places."

*o'er all the earth, the severed Head of
the Precursor, which the erotomania
of the old tetrarch gave you in payment!*

* * *

*You are called, precisely, the Young
Lady of the World, of this "world" for
which the Savior declared that he "did
not pray"* (non pro mundo rogo).

*You are, in fact, the swinish Pucelle,
saturated with perfumes, on whom our
priests are edified, who communes
regularly in her parish, whom no man
has contaminated and who kneels, ele-
gantly, to receive the Body of her God
in the latrines of her heart!*

*Do you think, my love, that all these
dead, all these lamentable dead, without eyes and deprived of entrails, are
so incorrigible for your beauty that
they do not stop whinnying after you,
from the depths of the earth, and that
the promises of a young coquette are,
for her, the authentic and indissoluble
betrothals to her Putrefaction?*

*They call out to you, these putrified
dead. Implacably, they hold on to the
cedula of your smiles, your glances,
your amorous postures, and the black*

swine who woo you in the Hall of Night are inhabile at supplanting them. Whether you like it or not, they must possess you, these uncuckoldable bridegrooms, for there is no promise that need not be infallibly fulfilled, in the end of ends!

And regard! – O almighty God! – regard! The nuptial pit is right beside you!

"We will be punished," Jeanne tells me, "for what we did not do and what we could have done.

"We will be recompensed for what we did not do and what we could have done."

July

1st. – Prince Ourousof sent me some money. Letter to thank him from the bottom of my heart.

Funeral apotheosis of Carnot. Convoy of trucks to the Panthéon. Immense crowd. The morose puppet of the Guignol of potentates, having been assassinated in the same fashion as Henry IV, attracts grandeur, just as he would a fly, – in his agony, – and, in one stroke, cuts a figure like the martyr King.

2. – Our dear little Véronique! We seriously ask ourselves whether this child of three has not received some gift that might determine in her a mysterious faculty of *vision*. How many times have we not surprised her speaking to invisible beings whom she amorously holds her little arms out to!

Often, she calls out "Mary," in a very loud voice. There is also I do not know what being, real or imaginary, whom she denominates extremely strangely and whom she appears, from time to time, to verify the presence of.

I do not think about it without emotion. The Supernatural has held so enormous a place in my exceptional life, and I bear, on every point of my soul, such deep stigmata of a Sorrow that seemed immeasurable, that I would not be surprised to find, in this little creature come from me, some *luminous* trace of my past.

3. – To Henry de Groux:

> *My dear friend,*
>
> *Here is all that I could manage, thus far, for your illustration project of our friend Roinard's* Portraits du prochain siècle. *The small book reads quite well, and I think that the attached notes, inspired by this review, are not jarring. I will consider myself satisfied, therefore, if they can suggest some sketches to you...*
>
> *First page of the* Argument. *From top to bottom, comical poets congratulating each other, shaking each others' hands, embracing each other in groups of two or three, some crowned with laurel, others aureoled, still others emitting rays from their forehead or their nostrils, etc.*
>
> *Second page of the said* Argument. *An impossible tree whose top sweeps the sky of the page and whose base pushes roots beneath Roinard's text. The "sounder of swine" wallow in its shade. Through its branches, a sun and moon appear, as in the illustrations of an almanac.*
>
> Stéphane Mallarmé. *– A drawing in the margin, everything that might ap-*

pear symbolic about what is impene-trable. Bolted doors, garnished with triple bars; enclosing walls surmount-ed by broken glass; "boxes" carefully padlocked; a monstrous lock securing a tiny place; an old maid hermetically buttoned up and guarded by two drag-ons; etc., etc.

ALFRED DE VIGNY. – A small "ivory tower," in the darkest night.

BAUDELAIRE. – A few sketches of hell; on "a splendid throne," a pot of hair dye with the brush.

EDGAR ALLAN POE. – A mouth sur-mounted by "a mustache of serpents." An "aerolithe" falling into Mallar-mé's hat.

GÉRARD DE NERVAL. – Hands carrying the "precursor's laurel." Dreams and Life playing at dominos. Ruins of a "bazaar."

HUYSMANS. – A moving figure seated on a chamber pot, sac au dos, *between Là-Bas and Là-Haut.*

LAUTRÉAMONT. – Henry de Groux invit-ing a monster to enter his atelier.

FLAUBERT. – Vomiting on the next cen-tury.

THE GONCOURT. – Two secondhand

goods dealers united by one membrane.

BECQUE. – A flight of Crows above an "old lion in its thicket." The doddering lion given over to medications.

VALLÈS. – A scoundrel throwing Homer into the latrines. Another scoundrel pissing on "the Tablets of the Law."

ERNEST RENAN. – Plato vexed in front of a door on which it is written: Someone inside.

TAINE. – An entrepreneur of masonry crushed by his "edifice."

TOLSTOY. – Christ chased from the temple by merchants of Russian books.

BALZAC. – An immense eye, nothing but an eye.

VEUILLOT. – An atrocious gob, a pair of battledores, Mme. de Sévigné and the Imitation of Jesus Christ.

BARBEY D'AUREVILLY. – A woman veiled in black, breaking a cross above a tomb half-drowned in its shadow, where only these words can be read: Saint-Savior. To the right and left, other tombs on which one sees Hebraic characters.

ERNEST HELLO. – *An empty casket on a trestle.*[74]

VILLIERS DE L'ISLE-ADAM. – *The fall of the Chimera into the abysses.*

IBSEN. – *A gorilla writing the word* Fatality.

BJÖRNSON – *A bear studying the Ursa constellation.*

STENDHAL. – *Winged heads of death, flying above a pig's heart.*

TRISTAN CORBIÈRE. – *A shark at the brothel.*

JULES LAFORGUE. – *Moon, kazoos, puppets, wooden horses, dime stores.*

ARTHUR RIMBAUD. – *A little runt relieving himself at the foot of the Himalayas.*

PAUL VERLAINE. – *An angel who drowns in the mud. Church portal and public house shop front.*

Ouf! The rest later. It goes without saying, my dear Henry, that you must *permit yourself everything. What you could not draw, you must write it, quite simply. The more foolish it seems, the more beautiful it will be.*

Your,

---

[74]Original footnote: See above, February 7, 1894.

– Léon Bloy.

4. – Response from the Belgian lawyer-journalist, Jules Destrée, to the sending of my brochure.

That response, as stupid as I could have imagined. Jules Destrée advises me, reprimands me, and protects me.

5. – At the end of a sinister meal, we decide that, from now on, nobody will be admitted to our table without the preliminary Sign of the Cross.

6. – I think that I must never have success through my books, not because of external circumstances, but for *essential* reasons. It is important, perhaps, to my destiny, that I should never have literary triumph and that money, if I am ever to possess it one day, does not come to me in this manner. The best packaged book for the general din, and the most capable of exciting public curiosity, will *necessarily* and immediately become unsellable if it has my name on it. That was verified with *Sueur de Sang*, and it is verified even more so with my *Swine*.

7. – Read a book, horribly written, on Freemasonry in England, but filled with a salutary and refreshing execration for the English race! For fifteen or twenty years, I am of the same opinion, the same vision. I

continue to *see* a victorious army of a million men, around London: – Would that all those who love Mary, *bleeding Mary*, and the white Vicar of Christ *come* to us, and that then twenty thousand pieces of the most powerful artillery might blast on the damned city, without lassitude and without pardon, until only an immense pile of dust remains.

England is to the world what the Devil is to man. An idea to be developed in my book on Napoleon.

8. – Apropos of Saint Elizabeth, queen of Hungary:

Any woman who does not put the Supernatural into her life and into all the practices of her life, is a prostitute, – virtually or effectively.

9. – Book of Job. *Elegit suspendium anima mea.*[75] Is it not Jesus himself who speaks?

17. – Letter from Henry de Groux, dismal. The first faces he saw, on arriving at A., a beach in the neighborhood of Boulogne, were those of *drowned people*. Within an hour of his arrival, two girls, friends of the family he came from, were being brought in from the sea, barely alive, and a third was not found until a day later... Response:

---

[75]*Elegit suspendium...*: Latin for "My soul rather chooseth hanging." Job 7:15 (Douay-Rheims).

My dear Henry,

Ah! I acknowledge it, that really is too much. But suffer, even if you should be surprised by it, that Léon Bloy congratulates you.

It is incontestable, is it not? that your arrival in A. is what determined this catastrophe. If you had not made the trip, a perfectly inadmissible supposition, given each person's destiny is irrevocable, it is quite evident that nobody could have *drowned.*

For billions of centuries, the circumstances of this accident were bound, by chains a thousand times harder than bronze or diamond, to the divine *circumstance of your arrival in that place, and both circumstances were absolutely impossible to predict or to avoid.*

So, once again, suffer that I should congratulate you. A man around whom catastrophes can be unleashed, is one of the elect. Woe unto him whose presence displaces only atoms.

You know me well enough, my dear friend, to know that I am not laughing, and you have a lofty enough soul to sense that I am telling you something great.

Recall some of our conversations. We did not bump into each other, random-ly, like two cows in a pasture. We were cast, one on top of the other, by the hand of an infallible Discobolus, since the beginning of time, to a point deter-mined by the duration, – so that a mysterious thing, infinitely agreeable and necessary, might be accomplished on our planet. It is what the eaters of excrement call "Chance."

I have told you, how many times! what I know about my destiny and, conse-quently, about yours, because the two are inseparable. You do not know who I am, *and you do not know who you are. Reread my portrait of Hello. But I tell you, for the hundredth time perhaps, and with what authority! that even if we were in our last agony, each of us; even if we were exhaling our last death rattle, thrown naked onto the most horrible of dungheaps, in the darkest shadows of the most frightening night, abandoned by the entire world and on the point of being disdained by dogs or pigs, – as long as we have the tiniest breath, we will be vanquishers.*

We shall be the vanquishers of God; – do you understand what I am saying, my dear Hello, who cannot die? – the

*victorious of God, who made us ex-
pressly so that in the end we would triumph by Him, and who asks for nothing more than to remain a captive.*

*Listen to that "Voice from Below";
that Voice so distant, which speaks to
us from the bottom of the "terrifying
Pit," and which so easily drowns out
the vain clamor of men; that Voice of
the Consoler in exile, who gives us his
word that we have the right to apothe-
oses.*

*I just received your letter, and I want-
ed, although very pressed for time, to
respond to it without delay...*

Your,

LÉON BLOY.

19. – "We live our life nourished by the bosom of
God," my very dear wife said to me, "like a child
nourished by its mother's breast. We are suspended
from that bosom, avidly, with eyes closed, without
even knowing that only a few centimeters above us, a
Face regards us. And it is a totally eye-opening experience to discover it!"

Jeanne is easily visited by marvelous
thoughts. It is not joy that we seek, it is the *glory* of
God that solicits us, and we feel, more and more, with
each passing moment, the vicinity of an infinite Pres-

ence.

Modern science. Instead of *Fiat Lux!* read this: *Let the Electricity flow!*

21. – God is alone against everyone. Evidently there is a mystery there. It is certain that a man, were he a wicked one, against whom all the world aligns and who is *alone against everyone*, has in himself something DIVINE which makes him amiable.

23. – Rosny's mind resembles a smoking lamp in a water closet that is too narrow.

25. – To Forain:

> *My dear Forain,*
>
> *I presented myself, yesterday, at your place, in your absence, armed with a copy of my recent booklet:* Léon Bloy devant les cochons. *It seemed to me that this serious persiflage could amuse, for a few instants, a Sagittarius, and I learned that the runt Lepelletier had attempted to bite you. An imprudence that surprised me.*
>
> *I owe it to that stinkbug for having been deprived of my daily bread, an account that will be settled to the very last sou, one day, believe me. While*

waiting, I do what I can, and here it is, quite simply, the rather noble proposition that I brought to share with you, yesterday, together with my sympathetic face.

Do you not think it would be honorable, *as much for you as for me, to show support for an artist whom everyone abandons in order to punish him for having appeared to belong to a superior order, and for having refused, for ten years and counting, any association with the imbecilic pimps who have an iron grip on publicity?*

A set of drawings accompanying the text, illustrating my poor Swine, *would assure the booklet a very great success. At the same time, you would be helping an oppressed writer, whom you have declared yourself, recently, an admirer of, and you would help to break the famous conspiracy of silence, the unique resource used against me by a pile of riffraff whose ignominy is known to you.*

That is it, my dear Forain, all that I had to say. On your soul, which I know so little, depends the favorable or unfavorable acceptance of this proposition which would ardently seduce me, I swear, if I were in your place and you were in mine.

Cordially,

– LÉON BLOY.[76]

Reread *Morgane*, one of the first dramas by Villiers. More than in any other of his works, I note this appeal, this violent predilection for the tenebræ and the empire of the tenebræ, which Hello pointed out as the characteristic of Shakespeare himself.

26. – No more shirt, no more shoes, no more hat, no more clothes. Our distress increases with each passing day and no expedient presents itself.

Why does God not show his Hand to those who love him? His Hand of bounty, his Hand of glory?

---

[76]Original footnote: this letter, accompanied by the booklet, both sent by *certified* mail, never received a response. Forain must have feared losing Scholl's esteem and the voluptuous embrace of the catamites at the *Américain*.

I was informed, in addition, not long after this so-pointless letter, that Forain, possessing a deliberative voice among I do not know what group of cyclists or bookmakers, of whom he is, incontrovertibly, the decoration, shot down, one certain day, a *charitable* motion, with a simple and generous cry: THE DOWN AND OUT! S'NO MORE NEED FOR 'EM!!!

To fully appreciate the eloquence of those words, one must needs be familiar with the impoverished past of the horrible dog who suddenly bellowed them.

"Lovely country"! What a delight it is to lie down in the stable and eat in the kitchen, when the domestics take the place of their masters!

27. – Why is Gold so precious? Because it is worth a lot of money. The word *precious* is inseparable from the idea of *money*.

30. – Received a letter by certified mail yesterday, at the office on the avenue d'Italie. The sender, who signs himself P.D., supposing that I find myself in a "difficult situation," sends me 25 fr. This letter is of an extreme simplicity. The money order is in the name of Dupont, obviously a pseudonym.[77]

  Mercure de France. Very amicable article by Julien Leclercq, about *Swine.* One cannot defend me with more generosity. This will likely be the only one.

31. – To Julien Leclercq:

> *My dear Monsieur,*
>
> *You are the* first, *and only, until now, and I honor myself by soliciting your friendship. I do not know if I am the equal of my books, but it is not above the strength of man to shake my hand without disgust, despite legends and clichés, please believe it.*
>
> *People have written a great deal about*

---

[77]Original footnote: After three years, I urge this mysterious friend to make himself known.

*me, as you know. The famous conspir-
ation of silence went, many times, un-
observed, alas! and the most savorous
absurdities were not always written by
those who hated me. You are one of
the rare few who have applauded me
without exasperating me.*

*"Long live Bloy!" you say. Rest as-
sured, Bloy will live, no matter what
all the sons of bitches do. He will live,
just as he has lived, for his enemies
and his friends. They may have made
him starve to death for many years,
but what of it? He has endured
famines and mournings, been flouted
by meteors, and gnawed on by the
filthiest of worms, without once man-
aging to* sober up *about his God. He
is, and will always be, "He who did
not wish to know anything," the black
soldier, autobiographied in* Sueur de
Sang, *who could not be demolished
and whom a Prussian officer had to
besiege by cannonfire, like a citadel.*

*What shall I complain about? Could I
have written* The Desperate Man, *or*
Salvation Through the Jews, *etc., if I
had not benefited from this demonic
existence which was divine to me?*

*First of all, all that happens in life is
adorable. Secondly, perfect accord between divine freedom and human free-*

dom. Throughout eternity, God knows
*that on such a day, such an individual
will* freely *accomplish a* necessary *act;
and finally, all that which is not strictly, exclusively, desperately Catholic,
must be thrown into the latrines.*

*In consequence of these three points, I
pronounce that any individual who
does not think exactly as I do, is, sooner or later, in the absolute necessity of
admitting to himself that he is a rascal, hypocrite, or imbecile; and I declare that the first of all duties, for a
man who has not renounced the use of
his reason, is to afflict, as much as
possible and by all imaginable means,
that same individual.* Qui no est
mecum, contra me est.[78]

*That's all I've got. I expose everything
to you. Impossible to draw anything
else from me,* in æternum. *When I do
not say it in proper terms, I say it in
allegories, as you will see in the* Histoires désobligeantes, *which will soon
be published. But have you not admirably understood that already?*

*Once again, dear Monsieur, I offer
you my friendship. It is not a virgin,
but I swear to you that it has almost
never served. Here then are my two*

---

[78]*Qui non est mecum...*: Latin for "He that is not with me, is
against me." Matthew 12:30 (Douay-Rheims).

hands, and all my heart.

– *LÉON BLOY.*

August

1st. – "One is always what one believes himself to be, but in reverse, *in the mirror*." I wrote these words just as they came to me, in a dream.

The Incarnation is the consummate Creation. This world being a system of "invisible things manifested visibly," Creation is renewed, one could say, every time our eye perceives a sensible reality. Genesis begins with the *Fiat Lux*.

3. – With an eye to an article for the *Mercure*, I undertake a reading of *Lourdes*. The pedanticism and sottishness of the author overwhelm me. All the basest commonplaces of the journalism of the countryside and the table d'hôte of traveling salesmen are there, on display in this abject book, like luminous truths. Not a single one is overlooked.

And with what style! – that of the gendarme, the factory worker, the sentimental level-crossing guard and swine! Ah! The task will be easy for me.

What a brute! I was saying to a friend this evening that Zola, having a gift like that of "The Tisane," the first of my tales in *Histoires désobligeantes* (170 lines), he would need at least 500 pages to unwind the tenia of that fiction.

Correction of the proofs of the new book. To the habitual mention of works that have preceded it, I add this:

The Desperate Man being, to this day,
the most well-known of my books, I
feel it is my duty to inform good folk
who do me the honor of reading it that
the Tresse and Stock edition, pub-
lished last year and antedated by six
years, *is apocryphal, defective, and*
absolutely disavowed by me, – having
been put before the public in a clan-
destine manner, to my prejudice and
without my knowledge. I do not recog-
nize as my own any other text than the
Soirat edition, actually published in
1887 and having become, today, al-
most rare.

– *LÉON BLOY.*

This notice, already given on the cover of
Swines, will be, I want to hope, *disobliging* to the
cunning publishers, while I wait for the time when I
am in a position to trip them up by throwing a lawyer
into the mix.

4. – Still reading *Lourdes*. Such a large number of
hours given to sottishness and filth have produced a
profound melancholy in me. I would like not to dispense more than two or three lines on this dirty and
vilifying idiot. I begin my article: "The Cretin of the
Pyrenees."

8. – Events are not successive, but *contemporaneous*,

in an absolute way; contemporaneous and simultaneous, and it is for this reason that prophets are even possible. Events unfurl before our eyes, like an immense canvas. Our vision alone is successive.

10. – Finished my "Cretin."

13. – Everything, in this world, is inexplicable without the intervention of the Demon. Those who habitually remember this Enemy can glimpse, with as much admiration as fright, the underbelly of things.

The priest, so goes a very miserable commonplace, is the doctor of the soul, as if the priest should not heal, simultaneously, *the soul and the body*. Is this not the spirit of the Church and the letter even of the Gospel? Why do priests receive the power to chase out demons if it is not to heal ALL ills? Why the liturgical benediction of bread, water, salt, fire, the prayers of Extreme Unction, etc.?

Rigorous consequence. Doctors are priests of the Demon. They confess those sick in body, console them, absolve them in their manner, give them, finally, *the communion of the tenebræ*.

Pharmacies resemble the sacristies of hell: those men who speak in whispers, those jars labeled in Latin, that odor of poisons, those little mysterious packets!...

Everyone seems to abandon us. God doubtless enjoins us to take up generously our share of the solitude wherever and whenever He wills it. Who on earth feels and thinks like we do?

15. – After a night of physical suffering: The ill in body are more tormented at night than during the day, so that the word of David might be accomplished in them: *"In die mandavit Dominus misericordiam suam, et* nocte CANTICUM *ejus."*[79]

To a very young man:

My dear friend,

I am perfectly happy to have given you the pleasure that you so enthusiastically thank me for, and I would have responded to your letter at once if I had not been entirely submerged by the last turd of Zola's, which I had promised to render a faithful account of to the Mercure. *Try to read that article, towards the end of the month.*

In addition to that task of a sewer cleaner, I needed to watch over the typographic execution of the Histoires dé sobligeantes, *which will appear in print next month and one of which is dedicated to you.*

I greatly despise, it is true, the contemporary youth whom the universities

---

[79]*In die mandavit...*: Latin for "In the daytime the Lord hath commanded his mercy; and a canticle to him at night." Psalm 41:9 (Douay-Rheims).

and slaves of every sort confection for us, but I know that not everything falls into their nets and that it is not in their power to kill France entirely.

That is not in anyone's power, believe me. France is not like other nations. It is the only one that God has need of, *de Maistre said, who was sometimes a prophet. There will always be in her, no matter what anyone does, a sovereign principle of life that nothing will be able to destroy.*

Your letter, postmarked from Lescar, surprised me. I thought you were a captive in one of those young pig farms that one calls the Paris lycées, and I was hoping to see you soon. I renounce that thought with displeasure. You have pleased me, and I could have told you profitable things, for I assure you that Marchenoir is anything but a litterateur. You are right to understood that The Desperate Man *is an autobiography, but you cannot possibly know just how much of an autobiography it is! Chapters 39, 64, 65, and 68, for example, should have warned you that the author has not yet delivered himself of all his thoughts.*

In reality, I have received much, having terrifyingly endured, and much remains in me to give to my sad contem-

*poraries. I am, then, unshakably per-
suaded that God will not allow me to
perish before I have fulfilled my task.*

*One has done what one could to kill
me, however. My stupidest enemies,
divining, instinctively, a force that
menaces them, have tried everything
in their power to reduce me truly to
despair.* Circumdederunt me canes
multi; concilium malignantium obsedit
me.[80] *They have reduced me to being
unable to live by the quill, and to having to search for my subsistence every
day, God knows at what price!*

*They have primarily obtained this re-
sult by making the work infinitely difficult for me, of delaying, like demons,
and as much as God has permitted
them, the accomplishment of my work.
And the same diabolical instinct has
distanced from me those who had the
duty to succor me, to restore me, to ex-
alt me.*

*The most fervent, most implacable,
most perfidious hatreds have come to
me from my very dear Catholic
brethren, whom I have shouted down,
on every occasion, the inexpressible
cowardice of. No one from among*

---

[80]*Circumcederunt me canes multi...*: Latin for "Many dogs have
encompassed me: the council of the malignant hath besieged
me." Psalm 21:17 (Douay-Rheims).

these Pharisees, from among those even who declared themselves my admirers, has come forward, hands outstretched, nor has sought to know whether I was on the verge of succumbing to grief, cold, or hunger...

Being a few years younger, I was surprised by the marvelous shamelessness of certain individuals, basking in every possession of this world, who could so easily have assisted, out of their superfluousness, the one writer who has something to say for the glory of their abominably-outraged Lord God.

I came to the understanding that this God wanted me in his Hand, uniquely in his adorable Hand, and now you understand how my daily existence is a sort of miracle.

Therefore, once again, I will go the full distance, have no doubt about it, and the indigent Marchenoir will give some bread perhaps to those even who did not have any pity for his suffering.

May the Holy Mother, whom the Church today pays tribute to in her glory, bless you yourself, dear child, as you bless me.

Your friend,

— LÉON BLOY.

18. – A collector just acquired, from a merchant of autographs, an old letter, of which here is the exact content:

> *Paris, 26 April 1889.*
>
> *Monsieur Edmond Lepelletier,*
>
> *I have read, with satisfaction, your ig-noble article, on my return from the cemetery immediately after Barbey d'Aurevilly's burial. You were obviously specially selected for that task, and something would have been lacking in the glory of the great Writer if the most notable scoundrel of the profession had not dropped that filth on his casket.*
>
> *– LÉON BLOY.*

19. – Epistle of the day: "*Si spiritu ducimini, non estis sub lege.*"[81] What is that then but obedience? – It is the *accomplishment* of the Law, in the same sense as the "*non veni solvere, sed adimplere,*"[82] in the Gospel. He who obeys *exceeds* the Law, because he accomplishes it.

---

[81]*Si spiritu ducimini...*: Latin for "But if you are led by the spirit, you are not under the law." Galatians 5:18 (Douay-Rheims).

[82]*Non veni solvere...*: Latin for "I am not come to destroy, but to fulfil." Matthew 5:17 (Douay-Rheims).

As for those who "crucify their *flesh*," according to the precept of the same Saint Paul, do they not recommence, in an ineffably holy manner, the *salutary* [act of the] executioners of Jesus crucifying the Word made FLESH, for the Redemption of the world?

I can easily kindle a poor man by telling him that a perfectly true thought expressed in extremely fine terms can satisfy reason, without giving an impression of the Beautiful; but that, then, most likely, there is something false in the account. *It is indispensable that Truth be dressed in Glory*. The splendor of style is not a luxury, but a necessity.

20. – The cemetery is the earthly Paradise... "There is a lamp, therefore, lit for us which does not burn for others," murmurs Jeanne.

21. – "God said: You shall honor your [business] affairs, and you shall satisfy your clients."

– Response from a *blind* usurer, to whom I was childish enough to plead God.

23. – The priests almost never make use of their power as exorcists, because they lack faith and fundamentally they are afraid of disobliging the Devil.

We want to habituate our children to living in the thought of death, to loving the vicinity of the dead. People like us are necessary to counter the im-

pious prejudice that wants death and images of death
to be desolating.

24. – Every writer must carry his books in his face.

26. – With respect to Suffering, we are struck by this.
The Immaculate Conception, that is to say, Mary, –
alone, – could not suffer except *by miracle*; in the
same way as the martyrs given to the flames could not
be saved from suffering except miraculously. And yet
Mary could not suffer, it seems, *except in her soul*.
Not having, like Jesus, assumed Sin, suffering *in the
body, although miraculous*, is absolutely inconceivable. Nor could she die, because death is the consequence of sin. Also, the Church employs for her, ex-
ceptionally, the word *Dormition*.

I dedicate the last of my *Histoires désobligeantes* to the FRIEND WHO COMES WITHOUT BEING
EXPECTED. Who knows whether that will not make
him come, that stranger, who certainly exists, who is
perhaps two steps away, and who would be so glad to
deliver me?

I point out to Jeanne that the only profitable
way of reading the Psalms, or the book of Job, for example, is to put oneself *in the shoes of the person
speaking*, because He who speaks is always, necessarily, the Christ, of whom we are the "members." But
this way of reading presupposes a very exceptional
disposition, which God alone can produce.

28. – To de Groux:

My dear Henry,...

You came to me because you are an artist, like a fish throwing itself at a red scrap, supposing, by a marvelous error, that I was, myself, an artist. But the hook has transpierced your mouth, and you have become my prey, – the prey of a voracious fisherman, whom you absolutely do not know, for whom art is nothing but a vulgar bait, good for capturing eel or whiting, who let themselves be taken through the eyes.

When you have embraced indispensable practices, *which you do not yet feel the need for, and whose profound beauty remains unknown to you; when you have removed the* obstacle, *– for I sense an obstacle in you, – then, the* real *magnificence which you are starving for, and which you sought so vainly for among some scraps, will jump out at you. At that moment, I will be able to open the door for you, the small door hidden behind my sumptuous and derisory tapestry of a writer.*

But what am I saying? You feel the need for these practices; only, you do not recognize the need, and you drink vitriol instead of pure water.

When you have formed the habit of confession, and frequent communion, you will recognize me for myself, because I incarnate that need that consumes you, that pushed you towards me, that led you into my hand, – without your having understood anything of your supernatural evolution, absolutely nothing.

Obedience *walks in front of us, in a column of clouds; we have no other guide in the desert, and we must follow it.*

You have often told me, today even, that your confidence in me is perfect. You are persuaded that "a vain remark or one of mediocre importance" cannot come from me. So be it. How does it happen, then, that after your Confirmation, after that enormous event, which has established between us a bond of SUBSTANTIAL kinship, *which nothing can break; how, I say, could it be that you have not come, I do not say very often, but not even once, crying to me: "Instruct me, help me, show me the way, carry me if I cannot walk"? What prodigious blindness!*

You have disarmed me thus, and you have disarmed yourself. You have deprived yourself of the Joy that I could give you, and you have deprived me of the Bread that had been entrusted to you in order to satisfy my hunger.

Both of us, for your fault, are short of MONEY. Recall, reread chapter IX of Salvation Through the Jews.

Henry, I say it to you vehemently, authoritatively, on the part of God, – of that adorable Moloch whom I receive every day and who burns [inside] me, – it depends on you to deliver us both. This power has been given to you, and if you do not make use of it, you force me to accuse you. You will become, in reality, the author of my sufferings and the most merciless of my enemies.

How many times have I heard you speak about the important steps that you needed to take immediately and that brooked no delay! Everything depended on it, etc. How could you have believed me if I had simply told you to go and kneel before any priest whatsoever, with the certitude of acting more usefully in this way? In doing so, you would have spared yourself, and you would have spared me, many months of atrocious misery, all the anguishes, snubs or humiliations that ensue from it.

I wrote about it to you, in my last let-

*ter, which caused you so much fright
and from which I cannot find a single
line to be struck; there is something
redoubtable about you that can instantly turn into something very fortunate, if you are* obedient, *if you do
what you have been given the power to
do. Until then, you are [merely] frightening.*

*For you do not know who I am, you do
not know who you are, and you ignore, with infinite ignorance, your admirable share [of the bounty].*

I embrace you,

– LÉON BLOY.

Saint Paul is a universal type. In the life of every human being, there arrives an hour, a unique moment, when one receives the divine astonishment,
when Jesus distinctly speaks. It is a matter, then, of
saying: "*Domine, quid me vis facere?*"[83] Everything is
there, and the rest is nothing. If one were an assassin,
an ignoble traitor, an empoisoner of multitudes, an
enchained slave of the most fetid *populo*, a
journalist!... everything resides in this precious moment which can confer the Resurrection and the
Light. But one must respond like Saint Paul.

29. – Beheading of Saint John the Baptist. Anti-

---

[83]*Domine, quid...*: Latin for "Lord, what wilt thou have me to do?"
Acts 9:6 (Douay-Rheims).

phonies of the day: "*Domine, mi rex, da mihi in disco caput Joannis Baptistæ. – Nihil aliud petas, nisi caput Joannis.*"[84] That, then, is what must be asked for, and NOTHING ELSE. The Head of John *in disco*, in a disk. (?)

This disk makes one think of an aureole, a piece of money bearing the effigy of a prince, the circular movement of worlds...

In disco. Anne-Catherine Emmerich, – compared to whom golden poets seem like fly speck, – says she saw the Beheading of John, by means of an instrument both singular and terrible, rather like certain wolf traps, the two branches of which, *demi-circular*, and internally garnished with sharpened blades, had cut off the Head while containing it.

Would that not happen to be what is meant by the mysterious *discus*? Nothing in the text of Saint Mark, nor in that of Saint Matthew, opposes this interpretation, despite the universal tradition of a *platter*, on which the Head of the Precursor would have been deposed.

Montparnasse Cemetery. Jewish quarter, in the neighborhood of d'Aurevilly's tomb. Received two strong impressions. The first, at the sight of a gigantic tomb of black marble, which I want to painstakingly describe, one of these days. The aspect of that monument is diabolic, and it oppresses the heart, like a nightmare of damnation. The second is

---

[84]*Domine, mi rex...*: Latin for "Lord, mine king, give me John the Baptist's head on a plate. – *Nothing else* do you ask for, but John's head." from a chant for Office and Mass.

procured by the discovery of a Jewish custom, which consists in setting down stones on certain tombs, in consequence of, I suppose, the *text* of the Law (Leviticus 24:16), which condemns blasphemers to being stoned. Each visitor, according to my conjecture, puts a stone on the tomb of his enemy.[85] It is in this way that one finds a very large number of those sepultures, on which may be noticed a more or less considerable mass of stones. Sometimes the pile is enormous. I think of my own sepulture, I think of the Himalayas.

The absence of the Cross horrifies me, it is true. Nothing anymore of the refreshing peace that I feel amidst Christian tombs. Of course, I do not wish for my little daughter to come and play in this accursed place, where the visitor stirs up the enormous rats and I do not know what other ghastly beasts!...

30. – Come tomorrow, a benefactor tells me. Only tomorrow will I do what you ask of me. Assuredly, I do not have the right to complain, given that I am a solicitor, a beggar, and because my interlocutor is so sure of not *owing* me the thing I solicit. However, how is it that he is really so very little put out by making me

---

[85]Original footnote: Someone assures me that I am mistaken, and that it is exactly the opposite. So much the worse! My idea was awfully more beautiful.

But no! I am not mistaken. It is still Leviticus, actually. Only, the Jews, who have forgotten their Law, have come to the point of believing that they honor their dead by applying to them an altered rite of lapidation and anathema. *Lapidibus opprimet eum omnis multitudo*, etc. Equivocation both terrible and supernatural!

come from so far away, knowing that I am poor and in a state of anguish. When, then, will I habituate myself to not counting on any man?

It would have been, I think, quite easy for him to do today what he wants to put off until tomorrow, and he surely would not have condemned me to return if I were a wicked person or an imbecile millionaire. But I am a poor artist. Lord! Give us John's Head, *in disco*.

Execution, in Laval, of the abbot Bruneau, robber priest and libertine, condemned for murder, after an enormous scandal. To the very end, he said he was innocent of the assassination for which he was guillotined, – which is possible, after all. I think about what I could write, if I had a journal. Abomination of an atheistic law striking a priest whom the Church alone has the right to judge and punish!

31. – Illumination through the Psalms. At first, several rare and feeble points of light in the immensity, then a great number, an inconceivable multitude, – the brightness of a single flame passing to a thousand others, – finally the conflagration, the universal conflagration!

September

2. – Saint Lazarus (Paris Diocese). *"Jesus diligebat Martham, et sororem ejus Mariam, et Lazarum,"*[86] that is, Faith, Love, and Hope. But Hope is dead, for four days now, and Jesus *weeps*, because Hope is in the tomb, because she is already starting *to stink*. For her to revive, *the* ROCK *must be lifted*.

Lacrymare, O Jesu, et magna voce clama:[87] Lazare, veni foras.[88]

Apparently, in New York, one can see a mechanical gentleman who walks through the streets, with all the appearances of a real man. He greets, climbs onto the omnibus, pays for his seat, articulates some words and acts in this same way, in an irreproachable manner, for a certain number of hours.

The journalist who informs me of this finds it very *amusing*, and he does not understand anything of the dark horror that his tale fills me with. I imagine a large city peopled with like phantoms!...

3. – Jeanne tells me: "When one quits the world, one is never alone. One is only alone when one has been

---

[86]*Jesus diligebat Martham...*: Latin for "Now Jesus loved Martha, and her sister Mary, and Lazarus." John 11:5 (Douay-Rheims).

[87]*Lacrymare, O Jesu...*: Latin for "Weep, O Jesus, and in a loud voice call out."

[88]*Lazare, veni foras:* Latin for "Lazarus, come forth." John 11:43 (Douay-Rheims).

quit by the world."

4. – Small success of my *Cretin of the Pyrenees*. Some serious journals reprove me. It appears that I hit the mark.

5. – People speak about the lack of money that prevents certain souls from withdrawing from the world. Response by my wife: "There are no obstacles, neither on the side of the poor, nor on the side of the rich. The truth is that, rich or poor, *everyone has a horror of solitude*."

6. – To a village curate (Dordogne):

> *Monsieur the Curate,*
>
> *My memory is faithful and I have not forgotten your name, despite your silence for twenty-two years. I have never forgotten that in 1872 I had the fortune of saving you from dissipation and being the instrument chosen by God, so that you might become a Christian and, much later, one of its priests. You have, apparently, completely forgotten this memory, given that for a third of a man's life the destiny of your* Ananias *was unable to interest you for a single day, and you do not notice his existence until the mo-*

ment you think you have need of him.

It is regrettable, monsieur the Curate, that you were not better informed. You suppose me, quite wrongly, to possess an influence, some sort of power.

The truth is that having, to this hour, employed all my strength and all my courage serving God by my quill, I have not received any other wage than perfect poverty and universal hatred, which I am far from complaining about, moreover.

Unbelievers detest me because I scorn their sophisms, and believers abhor me because I shout down their cowardice. To whom then could I turn to be really useful to you?

If you were still the little milner, of simple heart and candid spirit, whom I knew in 1872, I would calmly tell you: Do as I do myself. When I have need of something, I ask for it from God and from the friends of God who are his saints. I ask for it, with great faith, from the suffering souls of the dead, to whom God often gives the strength to assist us, and it happens then, almost always, that I am fulfilled in some marvelous fashion. Pray then with all your strength, monsieur the Curate, and do not count on men.

*(Here, several roborant texts, appro-
priate to a parenthesis.)*

*Do you not think, monsieur the Cu-
rate, that it is more surefire to be
faithful to those divine precepts than
to beg as you do for publicity from
those agencies of prostitution and
blasphemy that go by the name of
journals, or to implore the succor of
worldly men, condemned by Our Lord
in so terrible a fashion:* Non pro mundo rogo?[89]

*Please accept, monsieur the Curate,
the assurance of my respect,*

– Léon Bloy.

8. – Inspired by the XVIIIth Psalm: In the morning,
one opens one's eyes for consolation, compassion.
One closes them in the evening *for knowledge.*[90]

9. – High mass. Enormous sacrilege in the substitu-
tion of *Salvam fac rempublicam* for *Salvum fac
regem,*[91] in the Holy Text. Nothing is more like Peter's Denial than the Concordat.

---

[89]*Non pro mundo rogo:* Latin for "I pray not for the world." John
17:9 (Douay-Rheims).

[90]*In the morning...:* Perhaps in reference to "Day to day uttereth
speech, and night to night sheweth knowledge." Psalm 18.3
(Douay-Rheims).

"*Omnes dii gentium dæmonia*,"[92] says the XCV[th] Psalm. This *republic*, sung in our churches, was it not predicted by the Psalmist? I am terrified to think so.

Abraham, Isaac, Jacob, Patriarchs, Kings and Prophets! It is a shame for Occidental Christians never to invoke such saints.

To someone who piously abandons us: "You have left us for those who live only with Jesus and who, consequently, possess *Money*. We remain with the Holy Spirit and Misery."

10. – Modern men, almost all slaves of the Devil, have a sure instinct for what is excellent and energetically push it away. They detest sanctity, just as they detest Beatitude.

The Jewish race is so debased that it is impossible to imagine a *noble Jew*. How to think about Abraham, other than with the traits of a Christian?

The Parables of Moses. What a sublime work of exegesis! Each of the articles of the Law interpreted as an evangelic parable.

> *"He dreamed of having such an aura*
> *of mysterious fascination that every*
> *woman, instantaneously, could be*

---

[91] *Salvam fac rempublicam...*: Latin for "Save the republic" and "Save the king."

[92] *Omnes dii gentium...*: Latin for "For all the gods of the Gentiles are devils." Psalm 95:5 (Douay-Rheims).

dominated. And all his life, which was long, he suffered for not having that aura. At the hour of death, he apperceived that he possessed it..."

– Epitaph on an abandoned tomb, in an unknown cemetery.

11. – *"Anchoram animæ tutam ac firmam, et incedentem usque ad interiora velaminis."*[93] Saint Paul, addressing himself to the Hebrews, thus symbolizes Hope.

"The anchor," Jeanne told me, "is the Cross thrown into the abysses of below, and the Cross is the anchor thrown into the abysses of on high."

"We cannot perish," adds the same voice. *"We walk on water,* like Saint Peter; we are with Jesus then. Faith must suffice us."

12. – To a Lyonnais scribbler who is a millionaire, the unnameable author of a *Life of Ernest Hello*, who had sent to me, in the month of May, a TWENTY-*franc* coin, that I might wrap him in glory:

Monsieur,

I am happy to learn that you have read my poor Swine. *It is the response of a hideously calumniated writer, who is*

---

[93]*Anchoram animæ tutam*...: Latin for "[Which we have as an] anchor of the soul, sure and firm, and which entereth in even within the veil." Hebrews 6:19 (Douay-Rheims).

alone, absolutely alone, against an army of riffraff. Unicus et pauper, sed non erubescens.[94]

You have seen in it the war on "pornographers," on the "men of below." There is perhaps something more, something like a living word, a word of the Absolute uttered before impure phantoms, a manner of exorcism thrown in the face of a society long since polluted in the tenebræ and which agonizes. The Sword of the Lord, have no doubt about it, laments in spirit as in truth. After Hello, I appear to be the only one, from now on, who hears that great mysterious Voice which I have a mission to repercuss.

You speak to me again about that great man and about your book. I believe that I have written to you about it: a small number of lines on a like subject do not suit me. I have much to say and I want an important article, if only to address some inexactitudes.

That work would have already been done if I had been able to collect myself enough for so great an effort. It is less easy to speak about Hello than about M. Zola, for example, or about any other buffoon relentlessly at the

---

[94]*Unicus et pauper...*: Latin for "Alone and poor, but not ashamed."

work of demons. But I am literally dying of poverty, my dear monsieur, and I would see myself as the vilest of all Christians if I felt the ignoble need to hide this resemblance to Our Lord Jesus Christ.

Do you know what my life is like? I get up, each morning, with this thought: What will I do today to feed my family? I strongly doubt that you could imagine the frightening anguish of that awakening... I am errant, the entire day almost, searching for the God of pity in his inattentive creatures. Quare me repulisti, et quare tristis incedo?[95]

Ah! I have no intention, believe me, of acting like a mendicant with you, – even if the King David, speaking in the Name of the future Christ, called himself a mendicant. I was told that millions stirred or lay quietly, – I don't remember very well anymore, – in your immediate vicinity, and I feel sorry for you with all my soul, if you are one of those about whom it is said: Quam difficile, qui pecunias habent, in regnum Dei intrabunt![96] *But I owe you*

---

[95]*Quare me repulisti...*: Latin for "why dost thou cast me off? and why do I go sorrowful." Psalm 43:2 (Douay-Rheims).

[96]*Quam difficile, qui pecunias...*: Latin for "How hardly shall they that have riches enter into the kingdom of God" Luke 18:24

the truth, because you write to me, because you are asking me yourself for something...

What a misfortune if you were exposed to the injustice of accusing me of negligence! As soon as Providence allows, I will write what I must write about your book and, especially, about my great friend, Ernest Hello. I have spent my life doing for others what nobody wanted to do for me. Thus will I always do, for the love of God's Kingdom and his Justice, in the hope that what remains, moreover, will be given to me. Thus will I do, without bitterness, I hope, and with no concern for happy consequences or unhappy ones.

You know, undoubtedly, that the surest way to harm a writer, – the way that was efficaciously employed against Hello, for twenty years, – is silence. *Why did you need to use it against me, – becoming, unbeknownst to yourself, the ally of my enemies?*

All imaginable names are cited in your book, – except mine. Humbly, you will object, of course, that it is an omission that incurious posterity will have no reason to profit from to my detriment. But your intentions as a historian pre-

---

(Douay-Rheims).

vented you from ignoring that nobody in the world, – not even Hello's wife, – could have known better than myself the intellectuality of that unfortunate man of genius and suffering, who did me the honor sometimes of consulting me, going so far as to write to me that he saw in me a sort of prophet and the greatest mind of his time. It was, in any case, extremely difficult for you not to have read the Brelan d'Excommuniés, *wherein I had taken the trouble to write what I think of your hero.*

Ah! monsieur, what an occasion you lost, to raise your standing by manifesting yourself as my witness, my only witness in the Catholic world, and how indignant my poor great Hello would have been for this sin of omission, *with respect to him, if he were still alive and able to suffer the astonishing misery of soul of the [current] worshipers of Jesus Christ!*

Please accept, etc.,

– Léon Bloy.

Montparnasse Cemetery. The story of Barbey d'Aurevilly's tomb has exasperated in me the need to see, to touch, the Cross on tombs. I can barely stand the thought that d'Aurevilly was deprived of this Sign for nearly three years. Having so passionately adored women, all his life, he needed that chastisement of being condemned, by a woman, to the sepulture of reprobates.

The Church tells us that the Spirit of God rests on the bones of the Saints, and I know that the Cross is the sign of the Spirit of God. What to think of a poor deceased who is deprived of it? And what to think of the woman who took it upon herself to inflict a like opprobrium on the great writer?

I pointed out to Jeanne that the tombs without crosses, the tombs of atheists, always end up by sinking, more or less, into the ground. Some even *disappear* completely. I would be curious to verify this in various cemeteries.

13. – Words of an inventor: "You cannot imagine the DIABOLIC *simplicity* of my apparatus!"

14. – "Must not the Sacraments," Jeanne says to me, "realize, *in Glory*, all the physical needs of man?"

Baptism would correspond to the need to wash oneself;

Penitence, the need *purgandi ventrem*,[97] or the need to *sleep*.

Confirmation, the need to grow;

The Eucharist, the need to eat;

Extreme Unction, the need to heal;

---

[97] *Purgandi ventrem*: Latin for "to purge the stomach."

The Order, the need to be *clothed*;

Marriage, the need for love.

15. – A bourgeois person to our Lord Jesus Christ dying of hunger:

"My friend, I am charmed to be chosen to hear
your supplications. This proof of confidence honors
me, and I wish to strive to make myself worthy of it. I
will apply myself, therefore, to assuming charitable
habits, and I do not doubt that, after ten or fifteen
years, I will be in a position to make a SPONTANEOUS
act of almsgiving of a beautiful two-sou piece to you.
Rejoice."

16. – XVIIIth Sunday after Pentecost. – *Cum* VIDISSET
Jesus cogitationes eorum.[98] Jesus sees [our] thoughts.
Quid est FACILIUS?[99] etc. This comparative is surprising. One of the two things proposed is *easier* than the
other. In the end, the crowd glorifies God for having
given such power to *men*, while Jesus just said that it
is the Son of Man who has this power.

17. – Feast Day of the Stigmata of Saint Francis of
Assisi.

---

[98]*Cum vidisset*...: Latin for "Jesus seeing their thoughts." See
Matthew 9:4 (Douay-Rheims).

[99]*Quid est facilius:* Latin for "Whether is easier." Matthew 9:5
(Douay-Rheims). The full verse is this: "Whether is easier: Thy
sins are forgiven thee: or to say, Arise, and walk?"

The infallible Liturgy mentions the words of Saint Paul to the Galatians: "*Ego enim stigmata Domini Jesu* IN CORPORE MEO PORTO."[100] Saint Paul, then, also had the stigmata, as did Saint Francis!

18. – Feast Day of Joseph of Cupertino, one of the most extraordinary men that ever lived. He resuscitated *animals* and made manifest, in his person, the truth that the Glory for bodies consists in *no longer having any weight.*

20. – *Membrum virile symbolice Crucis effigies ab antiquitate videtur. Christus moriens in patibulo, emisit Spiritum. Vir Coïtans et hoc modo cruciatus in muliere anhelans, emittit semen.*[101]

There are no worse executioners than those who make it a law never to act spontaneously. I have a publisher who is like that.

22. – Pilate is the only individual of the Passion mentioned in the *Credo*. Then come the Offertory, the Oblation of the Host, and the Oblation of the Chalice: *sacrificium præparatum.* Then, the priest WASHES HIS

---

[100]*Ego enim stigmata*...: Latin for "For I bear the marks of the Lord Jesus in my body." Galatians 6:17 (Douay-Rheims).

[101]*Membrum virile symbolice*...: Latin for "The virile member is symbolically seen [as] an image of the Cross from antiquity. Christ, dying on the gibbet, released his Spirit. A man during coitus, and in a kind of crucifixion, releases semen into his heavily breathing wife."

HANDS *among the innocents*, in fulfillment of the Law
(Deut. 21:6). Here, I distinctly see Pilate himself... It
would be marvelous to develop that and to discover,
by means of such insight, the external, sensible life of
all the liturgical phases of the Mass.

Ironic letter from my historian of Hello, displeased with the allusion to his wealth, and he throws
into my face a church, schools, a vicarage, and I do
not know what other pious foundations which have
cleaned him out. Response to that perfect Catholic
from Lyon:

> *Monsieur,*
>
> *I do not believe a word of what you
> write to me. I inform you, however,
> that each of my autographs can sell
> for twenty francs in Paris, at Sapin's,
> rue Bonaparte, or at Sagot's, rue de
> Châteaudun.*
>
> *I would be happy to contribute in this
> way to the prosperity of your
> "church", your "schools," and your
> "vicarage," "not to mention the rest
> of it."* Decimas do omnium quæ pos-
> sideo, dicebat Pharisæus.[102]
>
> *The absolute omission of my name
> was, you said, a mere oversight, a dis-
> traction. My God! I consent, with all
> my heart, if that might be profitable to
> you. But* literary *minds, if any should*

---

[102]*Decimas do omnium...*: Latin for "I give tithes of all that I
possess, [said the Pharisee]." Luke 18:12 (Douay-Rheims).

> *exist among your readers, will un-*
> *doubtedly deplore that in your book*
> *you did not, "by pure distraction,"*
> *forget to mention Ernest Hello him-*
> *self! On this point, as well as on sever-*
> *al others, the* entire *truth will out,*
> *soon, and before a numerous public.*
> *Rest assured.*
>
> *Please accept, etc.*
>
> *– LÉON BLOY.*

The *Figaro* begins the serialization of a story by Bourget, which the *New York Herald* will simultaneously publish an English translation of, because we are at the height [of literary excellence]. It is called *Outre-Mer* [Overseas]. Impressions of Paul's trip to America.

From the outset, the most abundant foolishness bursts out. The "peon's child" is no longer recognizable, being in the land of money.

23. – Gospel reading of the day, 19th Sunday after Pentecost. The guest "not dressed in nuptial clothing," who says nothing in response, might he not be taken for the silent Joseph, whom I see everywhere where "bonds," "tenebræ", and "silence" are spoken of, and who is excluded from everywhere, while waiting for his Word to arrive, *donec veniret verbum ejus.*[103]

---

[103]*Donec veniret verbum ejus*: Latin for "Until his word came." Psalm 104:19 (Douay-Rheims).

Jesus, who is the Word, said: VADO AD PATREM. When this mysterious journey will have ended, Joseph will finally be in possession of his Word. There will no longer be bonds, nor tenebræ, nor silence, and he will dominate "all the land of Egypt."

To M. de M., former magistrate, very honorable landowner, in a small canton of the Meuse:

Monsieur,

I feel compelled to write to you, on the occasion of the fifteen anniversary of the death of your brother. He forever holds an immense place in my memory. I see, I will always see, his face of an apostle, at the point of departure of my intellectual and supernatural life which has been, I want to believe, hardly ordinary. It was because of him that the internal meaning of the Scriptures was made manifest to me.

I was twenty-three years old then. God had wanted me to be absolutely nothing, before my having encountered that man, and that I should experience enormous suffering when I lost him soon thereafter. I still have, however, the consolation of having given him, if only for a few days, the recomfort of a great hope.

You know that your brother, very cruelly afflicted and sad to death because of it, because of the terrible mediocrity of the Catholic world, had believed that he discerned in me the writer, long awaited for, whom he needed to breathe life into, to nourish with his words, and whose assiduous collaboration would have finally permitted him to glorify Our Lady of Salette and the Holy Sepulcher, in an astonishing and magnificent way, the only way that could satisfy his heart. We were supposed to live together from then on and journey, while praying and working, from pilgrimage to pilgrimage. "No longer suffer for your life," he used to tell me.

But being one of those about whom it is written that the "world is not worthy," your brother had to go away, before having seen the realization of that too beautiful dream of his. Overwhelmed with sadness, invested with a mourning much greater than the death of my father according to the flesh, I deeply felt the duty to guard, like a treasure, the marvelous instructions that I had received. It was demonstrated to me that I had a mission to accomplish the will of that deceased, sooner or later, and in whatever manner possible.

I undertook to write a book of exegesis on La Salette and I wrote, God knows at what price! a rather large number of pages. Halfway through it, I had to stop. I was too feebly equipped for that gigantic enterprise, and my perfect denouement condemned me to powerlessness. How to undertake the absolutely necessary research or journeys? The abbot T. de M., your brother, understood extremely well that a work of that exceptional *character could not be accomplished except by dint of meditation, and in perfect security.*

I had thought, then, that I might be able to count on you, just as the deceased, doubtless, counted on you in his agony, and my disappointment was enormous.

"... Your familiarity," Father B. wrote to me, "with the Missionaries of La Salette, who cared for him until his last moments, had given him hope. The two last days of his intellectual *life, he spoke much to me about you and about the work that you two had undertaken together. He had no doubt about succeeding. I dare believe that he awaits on high... In one interval of delirium, he made this remark: 'If I had my wits about me better, it would behoove me to write a scrap of a testament.' 'Do you really think then that you are ill?' I said to him. A small*

time later, he wanted to get up, took a quill in hand, and wrote these final and indecipherable *words."*

The letter, from which I extract these lines, is dated 10 October 1879. Ten years later, on my formal request for certain enlightenments, the same father responded to me:

... My very demanding affairs prevented me from making long explanations to M. de M., but I believe to have done better. I communicated to him your two letters, by softly dropping into his ear that, for the genius who brings forth and who suffers, a *Maecenas* is needed. If he wants to be him (and he can), he must have already apprised you of it, or he will not delay in doing so... He is an excellent man... But, perhaps, She whom you have undertaken to praise wants you to purchase your success through suffering and privations.

Presentiment that has become too true. Always forced to adjourn my book, so as not to die of hunger, I entered into the literary tourbillon where I finished by conquering a sort of celebrity, at the price of sufferings that have been almost immeasurable.

In fact, I brought into that frivolous milieu the same need for independence and absolute rectitude that had formerly pushed me toward your brother, and which infallibly had to excite, around me, universal defiance. Despite my effort, judged considerable, I could not live by my quill alone except with infinite suffering.

Today, at forty-eight years of age, I find myself in this hardly banal situation of passing for a writer of lofty value and being, nonetheless, each day, extremely put out for my subsistence.

It is, then, rather natural that I should sometimes remember your brother's promises. You must have known that his intention was to accomplish them, dead or alive, *and you certainly have easily divined what could be his will, when he wrote his* INDECIPHERABLE TESTAMENT.

If Father B. had had a more ardent soul, he would have spoken to you more forcibly and would have counseled you, – quite vainly moreover, – to be my Maecenas, whenas it had uniquely *to do with exhorting you to* JUSTICE. *He would have made it a duty for you to execute the last will of the deceased, a will so well known to him and to you, and all the more respectable that he did not have the time to write it.*

In the month of September, 1880, you sent to me, for a journey to La Salette, one hundred francs(!), *on the pleading of a certain someone who vigorously pressed you – and that was all, absolutely all.*

Result: fifteen years of black misery and the impossibility of achieving a necessary work, which I have not stopped thinking about, which I am, more than ever, disposed to pick up again energetically, in the plenitude of my intellectual strength, if leisure is accorded me, and which the realization of, perhaps, is indispensable to the eternal repose of your brother's soul.

The anniversary of his death, I repeat, has irresistibly compelled me to ask you in his name, for the first and probably last time, if it is your intention to appear, in turn, before the court of God, without having tried to repair that frightening injustice.

Please accept, etc.

– Léon Bloy.[104]

24. – Our Lady of Mercy. Reading the Psalm *Exspectans*, I suddenly imagine the Apparition of La Salette, – that central preoccupation of my life! – the mysterious Lady seated, in tears, on the rock, and reciting to Herself this psalm which one could believe concerned her, for three thousand years:

> *Exspectans exspectavi... exaudivit... eduxit [me] de lacu miseriæ... statuit super petram... Et immisit in os meum canticum novum... Ecce venio... Annuntiavi justitiam... Labia mea non prohibebo...*[105]
What a vision! What drama!

In the psalm *Nisi Dominus*, I notice also: *Merces fructus ventris*. The "Mercy" is the fruit of the womb. One needs to have God in one's heart in order continually to be visited by such thoughts!

I compare the Book of David to a vast plain that one cannot believe is of such hopeless uniformity. One walks for a long time, without seeing anything other than the flat ground and heather, like the area surrounding the sublime chateau of Crozant in Berry. That famous fortress is invisible and, yet, the guide assures us that one has arrived, that one is practically standing on top of the ruins. Just the plain, nothing but. One step more and a gaping hole ap-

---

[104]Original footnote: No response, naturally. I have already remarked that the addressee was one of the most honorable Christians.

[105]*Exspectans exspectavi...*: See Psalm 39:2-10 (Douay-Rheims).

pears. The formidable donjon, because it is itself halfway down the road to the abyss. Brusque vision of an
unforgettable magnificence.

So with the Psalms. One comes to contemplate them; no more than a drop of light is needed, a
single drop, and one will be bathing in the splendor
and dazzlement.

Clearly, one can say the same thing about
each of the holy Books. But the psaltery is so very
much the umbilicus of the Scriptures, and Jesus is so
often called the Son of David!

25. – A day of torture.

Read in the *Figaro* an interminable story
about the death of the Count of Paris, by Mgr.
d'Hulst. That valet, an imbecile moreover, surprised
by his prince's grandeur of soul, does not hesitate to
compare him to the greatest saints and sacrilegiously
asserts that the Countess, on her admirable spouse's
death bed, resembled the Virgin at the foot of the
Cross!

The inexpressible platitude of that story has
given the wings of the condor to my general contempt
for modern Catholics.

27. – Day before yesterday, a person who had had the
imprudence of recommending Henry de Groux *was
struck by lightning*, immediately thereafter. They just
buried him today.

See my letter from July 17.

The same de Groux informs me that the extra-ordinary physician who had succeeded in putting him back on his feet *poisoned himself by* imprudence, and that his death had something diabolical about it.

Whether he likes it or not, whether he realizes it or ignores it, each man is forced, at every moment in his life, to declare the death of Jesus Christ. *He who buys a loaf of bread, announces the death of Jesus Christ.*

"I cannot give the drop of Blood whereby I am saved, but here is a piece of money that is its representative sign, and it is because Jesus Christ is dead that this piece of money has the power to pay for the morsel of bread that will nourish me." Everything is like this.

29. – The Holy Text is not obscure, but mysterious. The Mystery is luminous and impenetrable. The obscurity is essentially penetrable, as a man can be engulfed in it.

30. – By dint of suffering, I have something like a black veil over my eyes...

Jesus can do nothing for those who suffer with him. Before his Glory comes, he cannot, – and this is a divine irony that instills fear, – he cannot succor anyone except those who have no need of his succor, that is to say, the fortunate in the world. By this title, he is, in a redoubtable and profoundly hidden sense, the *friend* of the bourgeoisie, who hold the Holy Spirit in horror.

Now, the unfortunate are the lamentable flock of the Paraclete, to whom no one is so close as Jesus himself, because he is the *Man of Sorrows*. The poor and the desolate cannot, then, have any hope, in the present, no succor from those two frightening Captives, *nailed* one to the other.

All that remains is the Father...

October

1ˢᵗ. – Sorrow suffocates me... So many accumulated menaces; so many deceptions for so many years; the diabolical stubbornness of my ill fortune; that climacteric last September, which I had so much hope for, from the very first day, and which disappointed me; these joys even from Prayer which have been given to me in abundance and which resemble a sterile voluptuousness; all that fills my soul with horror...

2. – *Sancti Angeli qui videtis Faciem Patris...*[106]

3. – In the Catholic Epistle of Saint Jude, the Archangel Michael and the Devil struggle over the body of Moses, that is to say, *the body of the Law*, that is to say, Mary: LEX DOMINI IMMACULATA. This, I see it very clearly. Lucifer had need of that Body, of that Tabernacle. Clearly, in order to incarnate it. And he always has that need, to be sure.

When someone receives money, – which hardly ever happens to me, – would it not be that he has betrayed and sold Jesus, like Judas, in some manner?

7. – XXIᵗʰ Sunday after Pentecost. Admirable mystery of the Liturgy. In the Epistle, Saint Paul gives the *ar-*

---

[106] *Sancti Angeli qui...*: Latin for "Holy Angels, who see the face of the Father." See Matthew 18:10.

mature of God in order to resist the snares of the devil. In the Gospel, the rich man hands the miserable debtor over to the executioners, and finally, in the Offertory, Job suddenly appears, handed by God over to Satan.

He who would see the hidden connection among all these things would be a bit greater than an angel. He would know everything, and he could do anything. I say, on this topic, that he must possess, on every occasion of peril, a divine word of certain effect, whose magical formulas can only be a sacrilegious forgery, and it is the amorous intuition of the saints that reveals this word.

13. – Usury is the foundation of commerce, just as avarice is the foundation of wisdom.

"The *breath* of street entertainers, that small breath, short and light, when they want to make vanish an object that they conjure away, is an act likely derived from dark places. It is the trace of some forgotten ancient rite."

This was said to me by my wife, apropos of the fire that a breath can extinguish, but which is not at all abolished, which mysteriously *disappears* without being annihilated.

17. – Thinking all that I can about our abominable situation, that does not mean "sinning by my lips," by uttering words of rebellion. In such hours, so fre-

quent, alas! after so many years, my sad heart must resemble that sponge saturated with bile and vinegar which the Jews imagined they could quench the dying Savior with.

19. – *In quamcumque domum intraveritis, primum dicite: Pax huic domui.*[107] It is Jesus' recommendation to his disciples, when he sends them out into the world. Each of us is really a disciple, and the word *quamcumque* leaves no doubt as to the absolute meaning of that precept. One must, then, obey, and not enter into any house without uttering that phrase. Who knows whether these three words are not a *second key* to enter with? It is added that others' *peace* and our own depends on this act.

Bagneux, the poor people's cemetery. The proud crosses of stone or marble are a vestige from paganism. The cross of Christians must be made of *wood*, like that of Jesus. But the wooden cross, *always scorned*, remains the portion of the poor, and this PRIVILEGE stands out particularly in cemeteries.

21. – I pray like a robber asking for alms, at the door to a farm that he wants to set fire to.

25. – What will Tomorrow bring us? What a life! We drag ourselves along in this way, reeling, drunk with

---

[107]*In quamcumque domum...*: Latin for "Into whatsoever house you enter, first say: Peace be to this house." Luke 10:5 (Douay-Rheims).

desire and mad with anguish, from one day to the next, from one week to the next, from one season to the next, from an appalling year to a homicidal one, waiting for the Lord and his *new Canticle*...

Our misery is unrelenting, but our souls, each day, become stronger for enduring it. Our immortal hope resuscitates, each moment, under the knife, and we feel so valid a blessing in our two children who are so beautiful, so strong, so clearly turned toward the Light!

26. – Visit by a young buck millionaire smitten with literature, come to make off with my last copy of *Salvation Through the Jews*, with the declared intention of being useful to me by purchasing it from me directly. Lovely procedure. After this benefactor's departure, I notice the disappearance of a rare book, which I had not yet had the courage to sell, and whose very particular format seemed to attract the pocket of every book lover with agile hands.[108]

27. – There need to be mendicants at the gate of cemeteries! Mendicants dressed in fire!

29. – In execution of my promise from September 22, I most assuredly will write a copious article on Ernest Hello, apropos of the miserable book by his so-called

---

[108]Original footnote: I would willingly write the name of that young hero, known on the new literary couches. Unfortunately, I do not have any *proof* of the larceny. July 1897.

historian. I want to show, above all, the Hello whom one does not speak about, and who is so little known: the oppressed and poor great man, belittled, ridiculed by his wife.

This latter person, a dreadful bluestocking, once published, under the pseudonym of *Jean Lander*, many stories, regrettably edifying, some of which, – fifteen years ago, – appeared to me to be stamped with a certain beauty. I will call out that remarkable transposition of the wife, passing her own foolishness and bourgeois narrow-mindedness onto a husband whose greatness she siphoned.

Fortunately, I possess a few important letters from Hello... On rereading them, I find the trace of old impressions that made an impact on my life. 1880! It was the dawn of dreadful tribulations.

30. – To the [Minister] General of the Carthusians, at the Grande Chartreuse.

> *Very Reverent Father General,*
>
> *One of my friends, M. Alcide Guérin, who must have seemed an intriguer to you, thought he could take it upon himself to write to you in order to apprise you of my more than difficult situation, which profoundly afflicts him. I could not blame him for his zeal, but I fear, naturally, lest his actions might appear too equivocal, and I would like to remove any uncertainty, by writing*

to you in turn.

I know that M. Guérin has spoken to you about my past relations with your predecessor, the R. F. General An-selme-Marie, who was my protector and my friend, at the start of my liter-ary life; but he could not have told you to what point that venerable and holy religious, from whom I piously possess a rather large number of letters filled with the most vivid tenderness of feel-ing, deigned to honor me with his friendship.

He encouraged me in the difficult path that I settled on, preserved me, some-times, from the sufferings of poverty, sustained me, from my first steps, with a perfect charity and a marvelous sweetness.

Much later, I had the honor of cele-brating the Grand Chartreuse in that one book of mine that has garnered the greatest attention, and joy was ac-corded me to influence, even among enemies of the Church, a respectful curiosity that God will want, without a doubt, compassionately to use for their souls.

M. Guérin must have sought to make you understand that R. F. Anselme-Marie, knowing me to be menaced to-

day, would have hastened to succor me, and that is certainly not in doubt. M. Guérin could have been carried too far in the expression of that thought. You are the sole judge. But, to be sure, he told the truth.

It is quite true that I am in danger. It is also true that, more than once, I have spoken to him, melancholically, about the illustrious House of Saint Bruno which I have sung into the face of an incredulous world, by which I would have been, in the past, so promptly delivered of my anguish, but which, since then, no longer remembers me.

Please deign to accept, etc.

– LÉON BLOY.

31. – The work on Hello takes shape in my head. What a gorgeous subject! and what an occasion to exact justice!

For the first time, today, it seems to me, I am struck by this thought that, living in abundance and knowing me to be deprived of everything, Hello never offered me the hospitality of his vast house in the countryside, at the edge of the sea. His wife alone, I think, must be accused of that cruel and inconceivable omission. He cherished me, however, in his manner, until the day when Mme Hello's jealousy suggested to him that he abandon me; but what a prodigious obliviousness!

Extract from a rough copy of a letter to Hello, with the date of August 18, 1880:

> ... *As for the way in which the Holy Spirit must manifest itself, it is the secret of the "glory of the Just" which Isaiah speaks about:* Secretum meum mihi, secretum meum mihi, *a divinely guarded secret, and which no human or angelic creature – with the exception,* perhaps, *of Mary, – could possibly know about.*

> *People have mocked, with more or less agreement, that same Lucifer who was* ignorant, *they say, of the Divinity of Jesus Christ and who had him crucified to his own detriment. I do not know to what extent that great Intelligence was bound at the time. But, to be sure, the Perverse One knew the Scriptures and penetrated the esoteric meaning of them much better than all our doctors [of divinity] combined. It was impossible for him not to see that something infinite was being accomplished on Calvary, but he was seeking the Secret that I am telling you now, and he had to see very clearly that* THIS WAS NOT IT!

> *In this sense, he was not deceived, for*

God does not deceive anyone, not even the devil. This secret, he sought it out desperately, for five thousand years; it is this secret which is his hell, and it is because of this secret that he "trembles," as the apostle Saint James says.

... I have strong reasons to believe that the Discourse of La Salette, which I called the Verbum novissimum *of the Holy Spirit, contains, under an extremely symbolic and hidden form, the Secret that Lucifer despairs of. It is the first* public *and* universal *Word that Mary has pronounced since the Wedding at Cana, just as I have pointed out to you. The eighteen centuries separating the two epochs are the mysterious and terrible abyss of her Silence...*

November

2. – The only true devotion is the pity for Jesus, that is, the Compassion of Mary.

I learn that Remy de Gourmont and one of his female friends who was curious to meet me, in '92, after *Salvation Through the Jews* came out, are furious with me, I do not know why. It is instinctual, undoubtedly, these people having their "conversation *in inferis*."[109] The friend would be mixed up, I am led to believe, in the practices of *inverted* masses, and would have suggested to Huysmans some of the most dreadful pages in *Là-Bas*.

Montparnasse Cemetery. The crowd, fortunately, is not too compact. But this annual trip of Parisians to visit their deceased is so banal that I pick up, in the ambient air, the following idea: Why wouldn't an agency of publicity exploit the tombs, as one exploits the walls of urinals or the ceilings of omnibuses? One could read, in this way, the announcement of a new chocolate or of an American toothpaste on the tumular slabs, and the available walls of burial vaults would display the eighty thousand recent cures obtained through the employment of such and such pharmaceutical preparation whose praises no longer need to be sung, etc., etc.

One thing, however, that is not ridiculous is the illumination of little chapels. Never having visited a cemetery on the Day of the Dead, I am ignorant of this custom. If they did not close the gates, what a

[109] *In inferis*: Latin for "In the lower world."

walk, while praying, through the solitary and illuminated *streets* of that city of souls who suffer, souls who cannot speak, and who are in this way the souls of *children!*

Exited from there and sitting in a café, we are surrounded by so-called human beings, also come from the cemeteries, and who appear to us less living than the *dormientes* who so moved us earlier. Frightful mannequins, beneath the rags that lend them an appearance of humanity.

3. – The emperor of Russia just died, on the first day of this month of the dead. Happy prince!

Recollection of one of my oldest ideas. The Tsar is the spiritual head and father of one hundred fifty million men. Horrifying responsibility which is merely *apparent*. Perhaps he does not really have under his charge, before God, any more than two or three human beings, and, if the poor people of his empire are oppressed during his reign, if immense catastrophes must result from that reign, who knows whether the domestic charged with waxing his boots is not the real, the only, responsible person? In the mysterious arrangements of the Depths, who is the Tsar, then, who then is the king, and who could flatter himself for not being a domestic?

4. – Visit by Marius Tournadre, escapee from a hospital. In vain do I try to make him acknowledge the stupidity, ignorance, and inexpressible ignominy of mili-

tant anarchists.

5. – The General of the Carthusians sends me two hundred francs. It was time. But I would need about ten times this amount.

To Marius Tournadre:

My dear Tournadre,

I think that you cannot doubt my affection for you. When I found out you were ill, I was with you with all my heart, with the disappointment of being unable to do for you all the good that I would have wished. I believe also that, on your side, you have desired to be helpful to me, and I want us, as much as you yourself do, to remain friends.

But you refused to make the Sign of the Cross in my house, at my table, and you will not be surprised, doubtless, to learn that I consider that refusal to be a danger for me and my family.

I will not refuse to see you and shake your hand in the street or in some café, especially if I can be useful to you in some way. But I cannot let you into my home anymore.

Your friend,

– *Léon Bloy.*

8. – Letter from Tournadre who claims that I am trying to get rid of him, under any pretext. Immediate response:

> *My dear Tournadre,*
>
> *I do not relish causing pain to those
> whom I receive at home and whom I
> call my friends. I have proven, as
> much as I could, that I was yours, and
> I am still. I would like, with all my
> heart, to be able to be useful to you
> and the occasion will present itself
> perhaps.*
>
> *But, once again, I cannot allow to en-
> ter into my home a man who, – were it
> my father even, – judges ridiculous the
> things for which I would immolate my-
> self. I have spent my life in order to
> write that, and, if you had read me, my
> letter could not have surprised you.
> You would have understood that I did
> not pick a "German quarrel" with
> you, and that that affair of the Sign of
> the Cross was not a pretext at all, but
> a vital, essential, and absolute matter
> for me. The effort that I took immedi-
> ately to remove my daughter [from the
> room] should have made that clear to
> you.*

I am not one of those people who "respect all opinions," as the bourgeois say, of whom you are one. Ah! no. I am for perfect intolerance, and I estimate that whoever is not with me is against me. *It may be that, replete with the need to serve me, even to devote yourself to me, you are, in reality, an enemy.*

Your refusal on Sunday caught me off guard, stunned me. I should have expected it, you will say. I am persuaded that you can succeed in your endeavor that we had planned to work on together, and that your success would have been for me a deliverance, as you know. I have sacrificed that, however. It seems to me that this sacrifice must demonstrate to you to what degree certain sentiments are profound in me. I do not consider life as a collection of fumisteries.

How can it be, my poor Tournadre, that you have so poorly understood my character?

Your friend, forever,

— Léon Bloy.

11. – End of my work on Hello: *Ici on assassine les grands hommes.*

12. – Not only is this work joyously accepted, by the *Mercure de France*, by our amiable Vallette, but they decide on the offprint of a small book at two hundred fifty copies. The title will shine in gold letters on a black cover, because it has to do with a deceased and because I have primarily a tumular imagination.

13. – Christian necessity to be disinterested in diamonds, – *quorum fulgur, oriens de locis tenebrarum, proecto carnis concupiscentiæ flammas* excitat, *in despectu et desperatione pauperum.*[110]

The Wind, which symbolizes the Holy Spirit, is particularly menacing for navigators, who cannot, however, do without it. The Navigator *par excellence* is Peter in the Barque of the Church. What will become of Peter and what will become of his boat, if the Wind is unleashed and if Jesus, alone capable of appeasing it, is absent?

Now watch as the Master seems to distance himself... *Expedit vobis ut ego vadam: si enim non abiero, Paraclitus non veniet ad vos.*[111]

14. – Jeanne tells me, after having read it in Anne-

---

[110]*Quorum fulgur...*: Latin for "Whose splendor, rising from places of darkness, actually excites the flames of carnal concupiscence in contempt of, and disregard for, the poor."

[111]*Expedit vobis...*: Latin for "It is expedient for you that I go: for if I go not, the Paraclete will not come unto you." John 16:7 (Douay-Rheims).

Catherine Emmerich, that the unique explanation of the perpetuity of the Church is the communion of the priest, – not of the faithful, but of the priest. This was, I believe, always taught, but divine truths are such that the more one knows, the more one discovers.

Office of Mary and Matins of the Dead. Immense Joy traversed by lightning, as if some storm of light was about to break forth.

Gospel of Saint Matthew. Temptation of Jesus. – *Diabolus tentat* Christum *esurientem, SEMEL in nomine David;* TER *Christus refutat illum in nomine Moysi.*[112] A gleam of light in the abyss.

15. – Moses, "the man of God," the greatest of men; he whom Noah *saved from the waters* was but the figure of; Moses, in his cradle, had already *fulfilled* Noah.

Pax hominibus bonæ *voluntatis.*[113] To men of goodwill, a God of goodwill is needed.

Several marriages have just been blessed, in the parish: marriages of rich people, marriages of poor people. At the gate, an opulent vehicle encumbered with flowers was waiting. A poor woman, newly united with a young man of lamentable aspect, and leaning on his arm while walking, found herself, all

---

[112]*Diabolus tentat*...: Latin for "The Devil tempts the hungry Christ, once in the name of David. Thrice, Christ rejects him in the name of Moses."

[113]*Pax hominibus*...: Latin for "Peace to men of goodwill." Luke 2:14 (Douay-Rheims).

of a sudden, in the presence of that vehicle which she was obliged to turn away from, like an obstacle, to pass through the crowd. Naturally, the crowd, composed primarily of poor people like her, insulted her.

Occasion to admire, for the thousandth time, the servile boorishness of a Godless people and the spontaneous abnegation of its idolatry before all signs of wealth. One deplores, at such moments, not being at least the caliph of Bagdad, in order to put things instantly in their place.

16. – Horrible situation of landlords, condemned, by their status, to persecute the poor from whom they receive money, without wishing to know the privations, the sometimes atrocious sufferings, or even the *mournings* that that money represents... – "I demand," said Moloch, "that children die."

The nothingness of everything that is not divine. I think of music, of the most beautiful music in the world that could not be for God. This music, in the palaces of Justice and Light, would it not amount to silence? And all the other noise of the world, all the vain words uttered by doormen or famous orators, would they not appear below the silence, infinitely below perfect Silence?

17. – Visit to the Catacombs. Descent amidst a hateful crowd. Some swine born malign try to sing canticles or derisively chant a few phrases of the plainsong for the Dead, punctuated by bursts of boisterous

laughter by several hussies who accompany them. These beasts are excited, doubtless, by the light of lit candles that the rules demand of visitors.

The immense ossuary, where the bones of eight million dead are piled up in an orderly fashion, transfuses us with joy, fills us with peace and sorrow. They must contain, to be sure, the relics of unknown saints, on which the silent Spirit reposes...

We think of a church whose walls would be covered within with this debris, the sublime ex-voto of a house of prayer that would be dedicated to Our Lady of Death. This church would need to be subterranean and, on feast days, those who are called the living would hear the carillons rise from the bowels of the earth.

18. – When someone claims to be a Catholic, I said to a very young man, I demand that he be just as I am myself, that is, in absolute obedience, – and in absolute contempt of the practical jokes of occultism or magic, which disgust me.

19. – Death of Francis Magnard, the powerful flake. The Macedonian phalanx of the *Figaro* was in his grip, and he died without having done ANYTHING for Justice. He glorified in being the greatest skeptic of his century.

Nice bit of journalistic nonsense: "To the last, he persisted in fulfilling his duties... as editor in chief."

The very brief account of Moses conceals from us the *duration*, in the opening chapters of Genesis. One is accustomed to the idea that the Fall was followed immediately by the creation of Woman. However, our first parents, before their disobedience, were exempt from death. The nine hundred thirty years of the First Man would need, then, to be counted from the time of the Expulsion, *as Time could not have begun without Sin*. Adam's stay in the earthly Paradise would belong, consequently, to Eternity and would be inexpressible in human numbers. That could take several thousands of centuries, according to our reckoning.

21. – We had spoken again about the surprising multitude of friends who have abandoned us; about one of them in particular, whose memory presented itself to Jeanne, and whose behavior is horrible. – "Nothing is simpler," I responded, "*I am the enemy,* everyone's enemy, *cujus manus contra omnes, et manus omnium contra eum: et e regione universorum fratrum suorum figet tabernacula.*[114] My friends themselves sense it. One must be very much with me to be my friend!

Immense difficulty in truly serving God. God wants everything, he demands everything, and one cannot escape him. "We are sold to God," my wife tells me, "we have been caught in his net, and we

---

[114]*Cujus manus contra...*: Latin for "Whose hand [is] against everyone, and everyone's hand [is] against him; and he will pitch his tent opposite all his brothers."

know that that net cannot be broken. Terrible joy
which begins with a cry of distress!"

24. – So atrocious a week that I renounce writing
whatsoever it might be.

29. – A kind of occultist, thirsty for my esteem, believed he needed to inform me of his pious practices.
Thus do I learn that he assiduously recites the *rosary*.
The ignorance of this individual is so compact that I
suspect that he does not know the meaning of this
word. He must have thought it the synonym of *chap-
let*, a vocable judged, probably, too little noble.

"Demons," Jeanne tells me, "must *recite the
rosary*. They draw their strength, in effect, from the
sacrilegious defiguration of practices through which
we receive Life, and they must be of a redoubtable
exactitude."

30. – To Périvier, who had made me hope for my
more or less imminent reintegration at the *Figaro*:

> *My dear monsieur Périvier,*
>
> *I thank you for having responded to
> me* yourself, *benevolently. I am sel-
> dom accustomed to such a show of re-
> spect, as you can imagine. "It is not
> impossible," you say. So be it. Re-
> member, then, that the day you need*

*someone to settle an account with re-
spect to that terrible fellow (Zola), I
am all yours. Having obtained that
hide, I can be calm.*[115]

Your devoted [servant],

– LÉON BLOY.

My very dear friend, Alphonse Soirat, the one
and only publisher of *The Desperate Man*, tells me
that, after the cruel death of one of his boys, having
arrived at Le Pré Saint-Gervais, last April 16, he

---

[115]Original footnote: At the very moment that I am correcting the
proofs of this part of my Journal, Emile Zola has just been
sentenced to arrest by the court of assizes, to one year of prison,
and a fine of three thousand francs. Such is the result of the
huge trial brought against that scoundrel by several heroes, for
the stirring up and *universal* stench of a society in putrefaction.

One year of prison will be easy on him, doubtless, and three
thousand francs will not make him starve. "I WANT TO BE TREATED
LIKE A ROBBER AND AN ASSASSIN!!!" he shouted at the first
audience. Would to God that the judges had heard and
understood that clamor of his conscience! There is no other
writer that has so vilified the French language, there is no other
sophist who has squatted on French thought in lower places, and
I cannot imagine a semblance of a man who better deserved the
ultimate punishment.

The author of *Rougon-Macquart* and of *Three Cities* had only one
means to exceed his frightening infatuation, and that was to act,
out of the blue, as the defender or avenger of oppressed
innocence, to appear thus, suddenly, unimaginably, as the last
pilaster of national generosity!!!!!

I do not know whether Captain Dreyfus could, one day, be
rehabilitated from his supposed treason; but, supposing such a
victory, how could he ever be rehabilitated and scraped clean of
the chivalry of M. Zola? (February 24, 1898).

went, naturally, to find the curate of his parish and begged that ecclesiastic to take into consideration his extreme poverty by giving him the equivalent of an alm, the humblest of all religious services.

"Have him buried civilly!!!"

Such was the response by M. the abbot Lavalle, curate in charge of Saint-Gervais, whom I draw attention to for the admiration of his superiors and confreres.

He is still at the same post, where he waits, with the serenity of a blissful ignorance, the tempests of smacks and the typhoons of kicks promised to such a clergy.

"The sacred clergy makes the people virtuous," said a great philosopher; "the virtuous clergy makes the people honest; the honest clergy makes the people impious."[116] I ask Monseigneur the Cardinal-Archbishop of Paris: M. the Curate Lavalle, would he not happen to be a precious cutting of the clergy to come, the *impious clergy*?

---

[116]The sacred clergy...: Attributed, by Bloy, to Antoine Blanc de Saint-Bonnet. See Chapter 16 of *She Who Weeps* (published by Sunny Lou Publishing, 2021).

December

1st. – A poor man who makes it a regular practice to share banal ideas, regales me with the hackneyed argument of the watch and the watchmaker, not to establish the existence of a Worker, but to say that that worker created a *definitive* object, with no other motive than to create it as such, and that this proves nothing. I am ashamed to write about such things of emptiness.

But here is my response:

That watch is so scantly definitive that, in a few years perhaps, the watchmakers will sell others with an infinitely simpler mechanism and which will cost barely a sou, which watches will mark the Hour of God.

It seems to us that death is the ultimate despoilment, because our body is a visible thing. If one only knew, that despoilment would probably appear as insignificant as the sweeping of a thin layer of dust off a precious piece of furniture. How many more layers will our soul have yet to remove?

3. – To Henry de Groux:

I want to try to "say something " to you, my very dear friend. I would be quite unworthy of your friendship if I did not make an effort to console you. You are mistaken when you tell me that your letter is pitiable, I find it quite beautiful, I do, and I have even inscribed it in my journal, the arrival of that letter being something of an event. It would be difficult for me to tell you how much I love you. Your appearance in my terrible life has been one of the rare and complete joys that divine pity has accorded me. I would like you to be convinced of it.

When your letter was delivered to me, I had just finished re-reading, in the Mercure, *my article on Hello, and I was struck to see that that article, read by you also probably at the same moment, was like an anticipated response. You must have felt it, on the first page even, that it had been written* for *you.*

Is it not admirable how God has shared such an affinity of thoughts and feelings between us? Everything that afflicts you has been so painfully endured by me, for so many years! You believe yourself to be "deprived of superior intuition," when you are precisely overflowing with that gift, when you are completely shaking and sobbing in the proximity of Splendor!

My beloved Henry, without knowing it, you touch on the profoundest mystery when you speak to me about "poor beasts"; and the "chagrin" that you complain about, believe me, is merely an aspect of divine Joy which lurks around you, in order to devour you. Our souls redeemed by the Blood of Jesus Christ are not "cursed," but condemned to give birth to God in suffering. When God is born, torrents of joy will rain down on us and we will hear the songs of angels.

I find in you, with what emotion! the same sensibilities as that extraordinary man whom I encountered at La Salette, in '80, and whom I call "The Friend of Beasts," in my Histoires désobligeantes, *a copy of which will be sent to you. He was a sublime being. I had astonishing proofs of it, and I do not believe that I have made him any greater than he was. From him, I understood how one must be the friend of God, to that degree, in order to love the animals, whom man abuses and who suffer for his fault.*

For his fault, – *and therein lies the mystery. Before the Fall, man had to nourish himself exclusively on herbs and fruits. And the animals themselves, no matter what wisemen might say, had no need for other aliments. The text of Genesis is definite on these two points. The Fall came and dislo-*

*cated that order, and we are still in
the period of dislocation. Nothing is in
its proper place.*

In punishment for that first crime, the
plenitude *of which is another absolutely impenetrable mystery, man was
condemned to devouring the animals;
and those among the animals that
most resembled the guilty Leader who
led them into his disgrace, those which
are called, for that reason,* beasts of
prey, *were condemned, by the same
stroke, to eating other beasts, to eating
man himself. Such is the* human order
*substituted for the divine Order, in
other words, the frightening disorder
that makes you suffer and that can
only be glimpsed by individuals such
as yourself, rare species, take it from
me.*

*No one else but God could reestablish
all that, and it is in this sense that
King David, directly inspired, wrote:
"Your judgments are a great abyss,
Lord, you will save men and* beasts.*"
You who speak affectionately of the
humble creatures who warm the infant
Jesus, know that this same Jesus, the
Son of God, was born expressly to die
for them, as well as for us, and that it
is the Holy Spirit who said that. But do
not forget that the* poor *Jesus could*

*only save creation "in expectation,"
as Saint Paul asserts;[117] that his Sacrifice is not consummated; that he is
still nailed to his Cross; that he continues, after nineteen centuries, to suffer with those who suffer; and that his
Redemption cannot be* fulfilled *except
by the coming of the Third Person
through whom all must be
"restituted."*

*However obscure these thoughts might
seem to you, you are prepared for
them, no doubt. Many of our conversations and, especially, the reading of*
Salvation Through the Jews, *have habituated you to believe, at the very
least, that something truly great could
be involved here.*

*Jesus says in the Gospel: "I am the
Truth," and the truth, my dear Henry,
is that one must suffer, because he
who calls himself the Truth, he who
declares his* Family Name *in that way,
is precisely the Leader of sufferers and
of the tormented. One must suffer just
as he suffers, for others and in others,
men or beasts, by telling oneself that
the words of God are not empty, and
that it is completely certain that the
most humble among the oppressed will
be avenged in the end and consoled in*

---

[117]In expectation: See Philippians 1:20.

*the end, when the hour of infallible re-
tributions come. We are in a state of
torture merely to confess the Glory.*

*Do you know that in order to be a true
Christian, that is, a* Saint, *one must
have a tender heart inside a bronze
carapace? Saint Luke recounts how, in
the midst of the most inexpressible
pain, Christ had pity for the brutes
who were crucifying him, and that he
supplicated his Father to pardon them.
"They do not know what they do," he
cried to Him. Think, now, how butchers or filthy pork butchers, who, not
content with massacring poor beings,
disfigure them ignobly, ridiculously,
after their death, – how they continue,
in a way, in the most unfathomable
tenebræ, the immolation of the Lord,
and how they are enveloped in His
Prayer. They have all the more need
for it as they are more abject, more
unconscious, more insulated in a terrifying ignorance of what they do.*

*Jesus is at the center of everything, he
takes everything on himself, he bears
everything, he suffers everything. It is
impossible to strike another being
without striking Him, to humiliate
someone without humiliating Him, to
curse or kill whomever it might be,
without cursing or killing Him. The*

vilest of all louts is forced to assume the Face of Christ to receive a slap, from whatever hand. Otherwise, the clout could never reach him and would remain suspended between the interval of planets, for centuries upon centuries, world without end, until it would have finally met the Face that pardons...

The grief and indignation, perfectly noble, which return to your heart at the sight of the disgusting vulgarities that you have spoken to me about, would become an equilibrium to you if, being habitually reminded of profound realities, you thought on the immensity of that Pardon. The people who kill or who make suffer, those who degrade or who dishonor the divine work, in whatever way, and who, consequently, cannot possibly know what they do, are themselves in so horrible a misery that it was necessary for Jesus dying to insert them into the testament of his Passion, that they might obtain compassion.

Lift up your soul, then, in the contemplation of things that are not seen. *Be a man of prayer and you will be a man of peace. Tell yourself, I implore you, that everything is merely an appearance, that everything is merely a* sym-

bol, even the most wrenching sorrow. We are sleepers who cry out in their sleep. We can never know if the thing that so greatly afflicts us is not the principal secret of our ulterior joy. We currently see, said Saint Paul, per speculum in ænigmate,[118] *literally: "in enigma by means of a mirror," and we cannot see otherwise, before the coming of Him who is completely ablaze and who must teach us all things. Until then, we have merely obedience, amorous obedience, which gives back to us,* on earth, *the paradise lost by disobedience.*

You see, my very dear Henry, I am trying to tell you "something," as you have asked of me, without knowing too well whether I succeed. But I do what I can, to be honest, all that I can, because I am a suffering and poor man myself. I consider myself honored, *– take it for what it is worth, – I consider myself honored and strongly favored beyond my merits, to have been chosen to operate some good in a soul such as your own. There is nothing greater than a soul. In this sense, I am your servant before being your friend, and the gift that you make me of your affection is an alm whose value you*

---

[118] *Per speculum*...: Latin for "through a glass in a dark manner." 1 Corinthians 13:12 (Douay-Rheims).

are unaware of.

Well did I know what paternity would be for you. Before being a father myself, I poorly understood the Lord's Prayer. Pater noster... *When my little girl speaks to me, it seems to me that* my kingdom comes... *You will feel that.*

Our life is always dolorous, impossible even, and it resembles an on-going miracle. We understand nothing about it, and nobody understands anything about it. We needed to pass through infinite anguish. But we are held in the hand of God, in the crux of His Palm, and he watches over us.

– LÉON BLOY.

P.S. No news from Tailhade. What does this phantom matter? It may be useful to you to know that de Gourmont and the old person that you know have made the greatest effort with respect to Vallette that he should no longer publish anything by me. I do not remember, however, having offended them. As [apparently] they feel the need to avenge themselves on the Tongue of God!

4. – Finally, *Histoires désobligeantes* comes out. It has been six months or so since I handed over the

manuscript. This new ray of my glory shines on a man without a sou.

Borrowed thirty francs from a Capuchin father who speaks to me about Zola and his ignoble book on Lourdes. Nobody lays a finger on Mary without impunity. There are examples of profaners of the Body of Christ who later became saints. Jesus suffers everything, pardons everything. He who pierced his Heart is now on altars. But he will not suffer anyone to touch Mary, nor his Cross, nor his Vicar, nor the Relics of his Saints, and Zola's situation is certainly frightening.[119]

Executed at Dentu's that famous corvée of the "press service" which consists, for me, in having my books sent to my creditors so as to economize my own copies. I have no end, moreover, of writing dedications. Surprising banality.

6. – Tacitus and Nero. The role of this latter seems exceptional. There exists a sibylline prophecy mentioned by Lactantius: *Matricidam profugum a finibus*

---

[119]Original footnote: See above [November 30]. When this book appears, Emile Zola will he still be alive? Something more than audacity will be needed to presume it. The pontiff of Naturalism, immolated, shredded, and dragged through excrement, *under any pretext*, by the beautiful youth that he engendered, -- is this not the most plausible and consoling dream?

The utter defeat of the abominable boor will have been, at least, the occasion to verify, once again, the marvelous abjection of the entire press, completely prostrate only yesterday before the novelist's print run of one hundred fifty thousand copies, and today hurling torrents of filth into the face of the condemned man (February 24, 1898).

esse venturum,[120] etc., which was applied to Nero, whose burial place is unknown. Among the Christians of that period, it was believed that that individual had been hidden, kept in reserve, so as to reappear in the end, before being the precursor of the Antichrist. The babblings of the fat Ernest [Renan] on this matter are enough to disgust you with nothingness.

It is strange, after all, that the plenary abomination of the persecutors should have been placed under this one head, when one thinks of the so many other executioners of the nascent Church who were no less atrocious. It is true that Nero had the Saints Peter and Paul put to death and that, in a sense, the punishment of those two apostles continues today.

7. – *Redit angor, redeunt cruciatus.*[121]

8. – I do not know why Nero recomforts me. I wonder what a writer of genius could do with the following banal idea: The throne was a refuge for criminals of exception who, having weaponized all the laws against them, rushed towards the purple with an intent of escaping them.

---

[120]*Matricidam profugum*...: Latin for "The fugitive matricide is about to come from the ends [of the earth]." From *De Mortibus Persecutorum*.

[121]*Redit angor*...: Latin for "The anguish returns, the tortures come back."

9. – To Henry de Groux:

My dear Henry,...

Your letter lacked simplicity. You were looking at yourself *with a great deal of attention; you were practicing, – O de Groux, – you were practicing* psychology, *and consequently it was bad, to say the very least.*

For the love of God, dear friend, leave analyses to the stinking swine whose profession it is, and get down on your knees, simply, to hear the song of your heart. You are so good in that posture!

What got into you [to want] to contradict me? I wrote, published, once again, that Henry de Groux is a great artist, "the greatest" perhaps. Eh! well, and then? If it pleases me, myself, to speak in this way about you, will you contest me the right? And if I do not see the means to speak in any other way, must I renounce the use of words or writing?

Ah! so that's it, is it: your stay in the countryside deteriorates you to the point of believing that one becomes *a great artist, and that this title of artist can only be legitimately awarded to individuals who have produced works of a certain comfort or expected dimensions?*

He who is not the greatest artist in the world before having drawn a single line will never become one. One does not become anything, not even an imbecile, not even a pig. One is born *a great artist just as one is born a saint, just as one is born whatsoever it might be, and education is merely a* discernment. *Nothing more. Caesar is not permitted to suckle like other men.*

But I hope that you have already gotten over that attack of commonplaces and that you will believe me from now on.

I am happy about the good effect on you that my new book has, which will probably be stifled like the others, better than the others, if they judge it to be superior, let's not kid ourselves. It has gotten to the point now for me, moreover, of no longer even suffering for this injustice. I find it quite simple that Bourget, for example, should be adorned in glory and covered in gold, – while I am considered a scoundrel.

Doesn't Remy de Gourmont's example prove that no one, among those who write, must espouse me? But who better than that fellow knew just how false my legend is? Who better than him can know how true it is that I am an artist, and with what marvelous in-

iquity I was always deprived of my wages, oppressed by the multitude of cowards or imbeciles, to the point of dying?

Nobly, he has swelled the ranks of these latter fellows by one. But he should take care. I say what I want, when I want, at the precise moment determined by me, and it is a game in which I pass for having outplayed my contemporaries. It would be human to remind him of it.

And I end my letter here. We are extremely unfortunate. Yesterday, I could not have written to you, for lack of three sous. Our distress is infernal and begins anew every single day. We are dying slowly of misery, waiting for the hour when we will no longer be able to die even, because that would be yet another manner of being.

All that is merely the human point of view, which we despise. The other is to wait and believe, whatever happens, even if we were agonizing. We do what we can. But each instant must be snatched from despair.

Your LÉON BLOY.

Necessity and Freedom are identical – in God. The Necessity of God is his Glory.

10. – Hello's historian has asked the *Mercure* for three copies of my booklet *Ici on assassine les grands hommes*, and paid for them in advance, "even though," he says, pathetically, "I have already paid very dearly, being Léon Bloy's victim." It would be amusing if these copies were destined for the journalists of Lyon who would have undertaken my carnage.

Law. When all that remains in a household is twenty sous, it almost always includes a coin for the Pope. Occasion, for poor devils, to curse the Vicar of Jesus Christ.

11. – This morning, at mass, I had the idea, for one instant, of offering my coin for the Pope to the chair attendant, to see if he would refuse it. The fear of upsetting some devout rich woman, whom he would have promptly handed it to, held me back.

"There is nothing doing with you," a lady told me, "you walk in the Absolute."

"*In what*, then, do you wish me to walk?" I responded.

12. – Woke up, in the middle of the night, to the carillon of the Basilicas of Heaven...

14. – One seeks how not to die.

15. – Saint Matthew, chap. VIII, v. 16 and 17. Jesus was healing all the maladies. In what way? *By taking them on Himself*, mysteriously and invisibly; so as to become, in truth, the *leper* announced by Isaiah, the absolute cripple, *in quo omnia constant*.[122]

Physical illness being merely the consequence of sin, Jesus always begins by remitting the sins of the ill person who is presented to him, and he takes that burden on himself. The ill person, then, is suddenly healed. But his illness is merely displaced. It is now on the Person of the Christ, with the sins that He just assumed.

It is terrifying to tell oneself that it has always been like this and that the Gospel continues...

I imagine transforming into prayers, according to my usage, the evangelical story of a few miracles:

Saint Matthew, chap. IX.

Domine, tange oculos meos, et secundum fidem meam fiat mihi, et aperiantur oculi mei.[123]

Saint Mark, chap. VII.

---

[122]*In quo omnia constant*: Latin for "in whom all things consist." See Colossians 1:17.

[123]*Domine, tange oculos meos*...: Latin for "Lord, touch my eyes, and according to my faith, heal me, and let my eyes be opened." See Matthew 9:28-29.

> *Domine, apprehende me de turba se-*
> *orsum: mitte digitos tuos in auriculas*
> *meas; et exspuens, tange linguam*
> *meam; et suspiciens in cœlum, et inge-*
> *mens, dic mihi: Ephpheta, quod est,*
> *adaperire. Et statim aperiantur aures*
> *meœ, et solvatur vinculum linguœ, et*
> *solvatur vinculum linguœ meœ, et*
> *recte loquar.*[124]

Saint Luke, chap. V.

> *Domine, ego sum jacens paralyticus.*
> *Dimitte pecca mea, ut surgens et am-*
> *bulans coram omnibus, et tollens gra-*
> *batumm meum, vadam in domum*
> *meam, magnificans Deum.*[125]

Saint John, chap. XI.

---

[124]*Domine, apprehende me*...: Latin for "Lord, remove me from
the multitude: put your fingers in my ears; and expectorating,
touch my tongue; and looking up at heaven and sighing, say to
me: *Ephpheta*, i.e., be opened. And straightway let my ears be
opened, and let the fetters of my tongue be loosened, and let me
speak correctly." See Mark 7:33-35.

[125]*Domine, ego sum jacens*...: Latin for "Lord, I am lying
paralyzed. Forgive me my sin, so that rising and walking before
everyone, and taking my bed with me, I might go home, glorifying
God." See Luke 5:23-25.

*Domine Jesu, ego sum amicus tuus, et
dormio de dormitione mortis. O Jesu,
Resurrectio et Vita, mortuus sum et
fœteo. Bone Jesu, veni ad monu-
mentum meum, et vide, et infreme
spiritu, et turba teipsum, et lacrymare.
Nonne poteras tu, qui aperuisti oculos
cœci nati, facere ut amicus tuus non
moreretur? Dic ut tollant lapidem, et
voce magna clamans, jube me venire
foras.*[126]

18. – The Gospel! How delicious this reading is to
me, even in the grip of the most poignant anguish!
How many times have I not felt and expressed that
the hardest part of my penitence was to be unable to
give my entire days to this study! God knows what he
does and he is the only one who knows it!

The earthly Paradise was necessarily the entire
earth. Otherwise, the earth could not have been
cursed, because by supposing the Garden of Voluptuousness a determinate place, *everything*, beyond the
limits of that place, would have been what we see,
and by consequence, would not have had any need for
malediction.

---

[126]*Domine Jesu, ego sum amicus*...: Latin for "Lord Jesus, I am
your friend, and I sleep the sleep of death. O Jesus, the
Resurrection and Life, I am dead and putrid. Good Jesus, come
to my tomb, and see, and groan in spirit, and be troubled, and
weep. Will you be unable, you who have opened the eyes of
those born blind, to keep your friend from dying? Speak, that the
stone might be removed, and calling with a loud voice, command
me to come out." See John 11.

Adam, before his fall, was in an unimaginable state, analogous, it seems, to that of Our Lord in his glorious Humanity, after the Resurrection: luminosity, agility, subtlety, ubiquity, etc., matter being unable to be an obstacle to him.

Adam, before his fall, was like a piece of coal in a state of incandescence. Brusquely snuffed out, he lost his light and he grew cold and dark.

25. – At my marriage, we had ten absolutely *sure* friends around our table. All of them have appallingly abandoned us, except one who is on the verge of disappearing. And how many others besides, who were not at that wedding banquet! Who even thinks of coming to see an unfortunate man? I have always been, moreover, someone whom nobody concerns himself with. Those even who claim they love me, and who demonstrate it to a certain point, have they ever tried to put themselves out?

29. – It is something to notice: the shadow of the Hand of God.

31. – Melancholic end to this year which was so important for us, so laden with suffering, so filled with divine suggestions and marked, for us, by such great progress.

1895

... Terram tenebrosam et opertam mortis caligine:
Terram miseriæ et tenebrarum, ubi umbra mortis,
et nullus ordo, sed sempiternus horror inhabitat.[127]
– Job X, 21-22.

---

[127]*Terram tenebrosam...*: Latin for "A land that is dark and covered with the mist of death: A land of misery and darkness, where the shadow of death, and no order, but everlasting horror dwelleth." Job 10:21-22 (Douay-Rheims).

January

1st. – My books with their numerous dedications, such as *Sueur de Sang* and *Histoires désobligeantes*, could almost be consulted for a list of the names of my abandoners.

On a copy of *Léon Bloy devant les cochons*: "The most delicate of those swine, would it not happen to be Laurent Tailhade himself, for whom I sacrificed six thousand francs of rent, when the entire press was drowning him in insults and who resolutely stopped seeing me, soon after the publication of this brochure?"

We were speaking about the Jews. "There are only two people loved by God," I said, "the Jewish people and the Gaulic people, the Lion and the Cock. *The Jew, the Lion of Judah, will become pastor again and will weep when the Cock has crowed.*"

5. – To be sure, I will be happy, I will even be *blessed*, the day when I have definitively, resolutely, exchanged every *pleasure* for JOY.

6. – This morning, Three Kings's Day, at 11:30 a.m., *one sou* remains in the house. Terrible cold. Impossibility of warming ourselves.

7. – Sedative study of Solomon's *Proverbs*. All these

Sentences or Parables, which a transcendent exegesis would realize the Unity of, appear to me like an *uninterrupted* poem, like the seamless Robe.

What a miracle to be able to enjoy the Holy Word in this way, amidst the threats that surround us, more than sufficient, one might believe, to cause despair!

8. – In general, I am particularly prone to being put off by my own efforts, so sure am I that God himself does everything within me. This remark applies above all to my hermeneutical studies.

My insuccess, for some time now, is a bit confounding. Everything I attempt fails.

This morning, at church, a singular idea came to me, I do not know whence: "You are looking for money, poor man. Nothing is simpler. Go find such and such a rich person and speak with authority: 'I need this,' you will say, and it will be given to you. It is no longer a question of imploring: demand [it]. Is not everything yours?"

9. – The *Proverbs!* Certain verses pass before my eyes like lightning flashes.

15. – I pay a visit to Dentu. I ask him why he publishes my books if he is doing nothing to sell them. Not a single line of advertising mentions the *Histoires dé-*

sobligeantes, which my habitual readers are not aware exists and which cannot be found on the shelves of any bookstore.

16. – To Louis Montchal, to whom I dedicated *The Desperate Man*:

> *My dear Louis,*
>
> *I am taking advantage, in complete haste, of several* sous *that have come my way to return to you your manuscript, which I could do nothing with, and which I have kept for much too long a time, I admit.*
>
> *It is completely incontestable that I* appear *to have forgotten you. What does that prove, if not that I am very badly off and that suffering makes me silent? After ten years, the dedicatee of* The Desperate Man *must know his Léon Bloy.*
>
> *Your letters and those of Mme X. have sufficiently informed me, have sufficiently shown me your hell. It is all the more mysterious that you do not appear to believe it, either one of you, – the persistence and duration of our ill fortune. Since '85, we exchange only lamentations or sad confidences; except when, tired of reciprocally afflicting each other, we keep a glum si-*

lence.

*Nothing that we have tried, to sur-
mount the misery, has succeeded for
either of us. It is, on the contrary,
worse now, alas!*

*Would to God, however, dear friends,
that you were as little beaten down as
I am! The more I suffer, the less I despair. No snub knocks me to the
ground, no reef makes me founder, no
hammer crushes me. I am indestruc-
tible.*

*How many times have I not written to
you that I was full of hope, ready for
anything, even if it were from the bottom of a pit, from the lowest and most
horrible pit! I would have written that
to you more often if I had always had
the 25 centimes for a postage stamp,
for I have, in all honesty, nothing else
to say.*

*My very profound and very unshake-
able conviction is that I am* reserved *to
be God's witness, the very sure friend
of the God of the poor and the oppressed, when the hour comes and
when nothing will prevail against that
call. I have the incomparable and
miraculous honor of being necessary
to Him who has no need of anyone,
and I have been* salted *with grief and*

sorrow for a long voyage.

Literature, which I do not aim for and which is not my object, appears to me, for a long time now, like a kind of instrument of my punishment, while waiting for my time to come. But the special form, the desired aspect, the essential species of my tribulation, it is Misery.

You do not know, Louis, and you cannot divine how perfect that misery has been. How could I make you understand it, given you have never known how to penetrate into the Absolute, which is my abode? Of all men, you assuredly are him whom I have loved the most. I did not see any other to whom to dedicate the terrifying poem of desolation and love that is called The Desperate Man. *But by what necessity was it that I could never draw your soul into my light, and that such chasms should exist between us?*

It is terrifying, my dear Louis, to think that we have nothing to say to one another. "You are always right," you wrote to me, not even several days ago. Under one form or another, here it is ten years now that you approve of me with the same energy, without having, one single time, tried to inquire about my principle and my God. Is it not incomprehensible and desolating?

I had some bread for you but you did not want to partake of it. You did not even seem to notice. I was so clearly called to draw you into the immense orbit of Contemplation, of superior Joy! Who knows if the dreadful torments that have come to us from men and things might not have been made impossible even? For I know, with a certain knowledge, that everything that one truly asks for is eventually obtained and that peace is the patrimony of men of goodwill.

To be frank, you should have been a Catholic with me many years ago. Having met me, having found the man of certitude and equilibrium whom, so many times, you declared to be "the one," all you ever had to do was follow him, by modeling yourself after him. You had a huge need to renounce your prejudices of love and hate, to keep nothing for yourself, to give with all your heart, to make yourself like a child and to become my disciple. We would have suffered infinitely less, each of us, and I would have set a precise goal to your marvelous activity which has none, which has never had one, you recognize it yourself.

In one of your earlier letters, you

spoke to me about your plan to write a book on Geneva. I did not have the courage to respond to that letter which profoundly afflicted me. The book on Geneva must not be and cannot be written by anyone but me, *and you are not unaware that it is one of the projects closest to my heart. That project would have already been executed, if I was not an indigent.*

Recall what I have written to you so many times... As well researched as I can be, I would like this book to be the most terrible book in the world. But I would approach the thing from an infinitely lofty vantage point, as is only fitting.

Geneva is different for me than for you. It is not a city where someone has personally offended me. Nor is it a city where hypocrites exclusively abound, who pullulate elsewhere no less, in England, for example, or in Germany, to say nothing of France. Those are your points of view.

For me, Geneva is the basest city in the world, the most infamous among infamous. Dico vobis, quia Sodomis in die illa remissius erit, quam illi civitati.[128] *It is the hearth and home of the*

---

[128]*Dico vobis,...*: Latin for "I say to you, that it shall be more tolerable at that day for Sodom, than for that city." Luke 10:12

filthy hypocrisy and egoism of the modern world, for three hundred years, and that is what I wish to show.

Such is the Church's point of view. One must be a Catholic for such a task, one must be so absolutely. But it is indispensable that it be done in a de-finitive manner. For that, my quill is necessary and not yours, and it would be criminal of you to deflower me of a like subject.

There you have it, my dear Louis, what I had to say to you on this head. You would have stopped being the "brother of election" if these remarks or reprimands revolted you.

Will you believe me, my friend, when I say to you that I would willingly suffer that you might partake of my faith and my hope? that you might pray with me? My hope, alas! I am without means, not to make you espouse it, but to make you understand it, for I would be forced then to speak a supernatural language to a man who does not have or does not want to have any views but what are simply human.

It is sublime, nevertheless, my dear hope is, and its greatest beauty is be-ing invincible. To the grace of God

---

(Douay-Rheims).

then, my very dear Louis.

– *Léon Bloy.*

17. – I prevent a miserable wretch from killing himself this evening. I interest him in life, by offering him the spectacle of my moving out, which will take place tomorrow.

18. – A dark moving out, and our moving in at the end of the Cœur de Vey cul-de-sac, in Montrouge, in the sinister, dreadful pavilion. The miserable wretch of yesterday came to assist us. What a presence that self-condemned man is, already vacillating, but so feebly, on the side of life and light!

26. – Woke up, at about 4 a.m, to Jeanne's terrible cries, and I rush to witness the last exhalation of our son André. Terrifying moment. New episode in my frightening life!...[129]

---

[129]Original footnote: The incidents preceding that death and the horrible circumstances that accompanied it and followed it, have been told in *La Femme pauvre*. One does not recommence a like effort. Once is enough and too much. Silence, then.

I only wish to mention by name the doctor of the dead, – who remained anonymous in that veridical novel – warty cretin and molester, whose unparalleled loutishness so diabolically aggravated our grief. That doctor, practically begging to be slapped, is named Lecoq and continues, it appears, his farces in Montrouge, without anything being able to explain the miraculous patience of an entire population who have not yet battered him to death and dragged him through the dirt.

27. – "...Never a mother and child, never two spouses, came together with an ecstasy of love comparable
to that of the body and soul of the Just reuniting." Father Faber, *Aspects de la mort*.

28. – Interment... *Me autem propter innocentiam sus-
cepisti: Et confirmasti me in conspectu tuo incæter-
num...*[130] *Fac nos, Domine, in Paradiso cum beatis
parvulis perenniter sociari.*[131]

"All that I had of the most precious, I have offered it for you," I said to the desperate man who
wanted to kill himself several days before. Here it is,
my God, this little, deplorable body. I offer it to you
so that this miserable man might know you. I offer it
to you with a broken heart, and I can do no more, in
all honesty!

30. – Horrible stink in our house. We have to ask ourselves whether this tabernacle of grief and misery,
which appears to have killed one of our two children
already, is not maleficent, in every way, because of
the presence of some terrible *relic*...

---

[130]*Me autem propter...*: Latin for "But thou hast upheld me by
reason of my innocence: and hast established me in thy sight for
ever." Psalm 40:13 (Douay-Rheims).

[131]*Fac nos, Domine...*: Latin for "Unite us, O Lord, in Paradise
with the blessed little ones, forever." From the *Ordo sepeliendi
parvulos*, Rite for the Burial of Children.

February

3 . – *Exégèse des Lieux Communs*. – "The occasion makes the thief." The Thief is called Dismas, and the Occasion, it is the dying Jesus. *A solis ortu usque ad OCCASUM.*[132] "Life interest," is yet another commonplace. What is it? It is the Presence of Jesus. *Interest vita.* In the Gospel of Saint John, Jesus declares that it is he himself who is the Life.

4. – With disgust, scanned the morning journals, relating the triumph of Rochefort, who has just reentered Paris, with the acclamations of the vile multitude. Paul Adam himself applauds the victory of the old bed soiler. Shame of shames and presentiment of the end of ends.

To the Prince Alexandre Ourousof, in Moscow:

Dear friend,

Here is my new address... I had to move out, last month, from a comfortable apartment to install myself in a tiny, frozen and insalubrious pavilion, habitable only in summer. This move cost the life of my youngest of two children, marked for death from the first day. The terrifying humidity of the place immediately gripped that poor

---

[132]*A solis ortu*...: Latin for "From the rising of the sun unto the going down of the same." Psalm 112:3 (Douay-Rheims).

being who was already suffering, and whom we could not warm up again as he clearly needed; one week later, on January 26, he expired in our arms, at 4 o'clock in the morning. I think, my friend, that the simple announcement of this event must exempt me from phrases and commentaries.

It is another dark chapter in my dark life, and the grief of a man such as myself must be modest. I was able to find money for the funeral. What could I complain about?

The "Swine," being unable to exterminate me, have succeeded at least in killing my little boy. Great joy for them, if they learn about it. But they do not know who I am, nor what I am, the filthy demons! nor that accounts will be settled exactly, on a certain day.

Your,

Léon Bloy.

6. – In the street. A few louts amuse themselves by torching rats in an iron cage suspended above a door. This spectacle makes Jeanne despair, urging me to intervene. Not understanding at first, then hypnotized, I finally rush forward into the middle of that ignoble group which I dissipate in the blink of an eye. This vi-

sion has filled us with the most painful horror. The world is frightening...

Ecclesiastes. Struck by the expression *sub sole*, particular to that book, and which one meets mysteriously twenty-nine times, I realize that I should interpret it by *sub imagine* SOLIS, and that gives me a sort of key to penetrate into the vestibule of the closed house of the King of Glory.

10. – The man I saved from suicide last month, – condemned by God this time, – collapses in our home, agonizing and destitute, in order to look death in the face there. The installation of this moribund completes the demoniacal appearance of our place. Larvae teem and the shadows seem as if they are about to howl. Terrible cold, as always.

13. – Continuation of that hospitality. We obtained from the moribund, an ignorant and heavy man, fifty years old, banal ideas that he confessed yesterday. This evening, he spoke again about suicide. Crushed by fatigue and forced to leave him alone, I tell myself that perhaps I will find him dead in his bed in the morning, only two paces away.

15. – Our guest has disappeared. One of his relatives came looking for him. He will not die in our midst then. But immediately this nightmare is replaced by another, a more terrible one. Our beloved little girl,

o u r Véronique is in turn in danger, in this house
where the inhabitants of graveyards walk around,
whom we haven't the means to escape.

17. – While watching over the little sick person, tried
to read O'Meara, adapting the perfect anguish of my
own heart to the account of the hateful persecutions
that Napoleon was the victim of.

Napoleon's surprising intellectual mediocrity.
That great man is the father of all 19th-century commonplaces; the more abject they are, the more their
extraction makes sense.

18. – Our suicide passed away yesterday evening, in
the arms of a concierge. His last words: "Thank you,
monsieur, this time, this is it!"

This man, the memory of whom will be more
than somber, and who was not even our friend, has
entered into the Past as if a chasm had swallowed him
up. I could be made to believe he died twenty centuries ago, such is the duration of an illusion.

Our house is not only freezing, dark, and foul-
smelling, we also get impression that it is *haunted*.
"Anything can happen," my wife tells me. As for myself, I'm losing my mind, and my soul is clenched
when night falls.

No assistance to hope for. Our doctor refuses
to attest to the obvious insalubrity of the place; the
municipal administration does not wish to intervene;

an attorney, whom we consulted, discourages me, and the filthy proprietor pats his belly. *Torrentem pertransivit anima nostra: forsitan pertransisset anima nostra aquam intolerabilem.*[133]

23. – The most ruinous of follies, to be sure, is not to be a pimp or an imbecile.

24. – Always the same horrible stink, that carrion cheese. It reminds me of the torments of my hebdomadary visits to the *Gil Blas*.

We are ineffably alone. Will I ever find the unknown Friend whom I have so often sought?

---

[133]*Torrentem pertransivit...*: Latin for "Our soul hath passed through a torrent: perhaps our soul had passed through a water insupportable." Psalm 123:5 (Douay-Rheims).

March

1st. – A cleaning woman, admirably a bitch, has me called before the XIVth arrondissement's justice of the peace, an old Republican imbecile, like the majority of justices of the peace.

So far as I can tell, the entire function of these magistrates can be summed up under the extremely stupid and cowardly rubric of *conciliation*. A thieving domestic demands what is not her due, and the mechanical judge, without any concern to look more deeply into whatever it might be, without any regard for the most legitimate moral presumptions, invariably seeks to strike a balance, a sort of middle ground between the unjust request and the indignant refusal... The wisdom of Solomon would be rather difficult in such employments.

Certain inutility of resistance and, moreover, filled with disgust, I let myself be fleeced by this upstanding judge.

9. – Appearance of the captain Bigand-Kaire, until now a stranger to me. This sailor has read me, it appears, on the oceans. Then he learned or guessed that I was dying of poverty, and he visits me. Plan of a lottery. An indeterminate number of artists, friends, or victims whom this seaman knows, would give paintings or drawings, and the investment, highly hypothetical to be honest, of three or four hundred tickets, would provide me a viaticum for the completion of

La Femme pauvre.

14. – "Understand, monsieur Léon Bloy, that I am an atheist and a materialist." "Very good, dear monsieur, you see me charmed to know that I am in the presence of an imbecile."

The pestilence redoubles and the misery does not diminish.

15. – To a benefactor:

My dear M.S.,

I did not think I had the right to refuse the twenty francs that I received from you this morning, this money being sent to me by Someone whom you do not know and whom you are merely the messager of, – benevolent for me at the present hour, I want to believe. But as I always was and always wish to be a man of irreproachable uprightness, I do not think that it would be permitted to me to hide to M. Bigand the enormous accusations that you charge him with. He will read your letter then. I have a horror of raising a quarrel, especially between two men who have shown me their friendship, but it would be ignoble in my own eyes if I allowed one of them to take advan-

tage of my silence in order to condemn the other. It is necessary then that M. Bigand know at least what he is being accused of.

I saw him the day before yesterday. He came to bring to me a list of the names of artists and works of art collected for me with great fatigue. His behavior, evidently upright and without any shadow of equivocalness, had the primary object of giving me hope in an imminent and happy outcome. His good faith was as bright as the day... If I could conceive of the least suspicion, the verification would be too simple. What could I do, if not admire the devotion of a man who is no longer young, who may have lost the foolish illusions of adolescence, who has, doubtless, a right to repose, and who benevolently takes upon himself a like concern for me?

Take care not to believe, however, that these reflections were the result of some conversation or another that I could have had with M. Bigand. I have no need for any external suggestion to think in this way. It is enough for me to interrogate my conscience. You must not accuse a man – whether he be my friend or not, – *of shameful acts and which pass for dishonorable, even among riffraff, without immediately providing the proof. I could not, at this point, approve such behavior without contradicting myself, given that you say that I am, and I quote, "loyalty itself."*

I see too well that this letter will change the dispositions of your heart. Experience tells me that I have everything to fear in this regard, and you can be sure that the sudden and inexplicable loss of a friendship that I must believe providential will be among the most bizarre catastrophes of my life. Whatever the case, I reject, until now, with all the energy of my soul, your proposition of succoring me "in whatever way possible." That, you will have to agree, is absolutely unacceptable, even if I were more unfortunate than I currently am.

I am quite willing to acknowledge that, since February 25, I have lived only on what you have given or procured. But do you not think that the very numerous dedications that you extract from me, and the confidential letters that my confidence in you dictated to me, and which you will make a scant noble use of perhaps, are more than sufficient compensation, – not to mention the honor that you did your-

> *self even, by introducing yourself to*
> *me,* against my initial will, *you under-*
> *stand, thus abusing my poverty which*
> *forced me to endure everything? I*
> *have sometimes received assistance*
> *from* anonymous *admirers who know*
> *me to be poor but do not wish to be*
> paid *for their benefaction. Evidently*
> *you are not of that school.*[134]

16. – The unhappy de Groux writes to us from Brussels, where he suffers in body and soul, abandoned to misery, ill and gnawed on by cares. He exposed a painting there that he hopes to sell. If he does not succeed, he will bring it to Amsterdam. His situation oppresses us. Why so many sufferings for so noble a creature? and why such sufferings in the tenebræ? For well do we know, despite his protestations, that he is attached to the world by some bond that he himself ignores, and that it is the obstacle he is dying of. He speaks to us about prayer, he affirms that he often prays. But this vast confidence in God which we subsist on, we others, and which would deliver him from so many pointless endeavors, we know only too well that he does not possess it. We ask ourselves what could humanly save him, and the feeling of our powerlessness overwhelms us.

On our way to consult, once more, the afore-

---

[134]Original footnote: Such was the end of a most dangerous liaison. In response to this letter, I received several epistolary pieces of filth, with insulting suggestions on the envelope, and the "Ungrateful Beggar" was delivered of this benefactor.

mentioned discouraging lawyer, against my landlord, I suddenly feel very miserable, very disarmed, absolutely incapable of interesting so important a person in my cause, and I renounce it in order to confess myself, forming a plan to write. But write what exactly? Must not that confession suffice, must it not be preferred to everything else, and must I not count on God exclusively? My landlord is a ghost, my lawyer a ghost, I am myself a ghost, but God will not wish the oppressed to be confounded.

Excellent effect of conscience. I breathe God, as others breathe the breeze from the sky through the open window.

17. – That poor Bigand who is thirsting for peace, was ill inspired, really, when he undertook to act on my behalf.

18. – In the XVIIIth century, an old woman bequeathed, by testament, her fortune to her cat. That testament, naturally, was annulled by humans. But God did not annul it. The act remained *irrevocable*, as all human acts, and that villainous old woman's cat will ask her for its inheritance until the end of time.

22. – To de Groux:

> ... *I accept. I will give talks in Belgium. In principle, I hate them, you are not unaware of this. I am too much*

of the Absolute for the role of a Tail-hade to suit me. A single *bomb, however, would be entirely insufficient for my apotheosis or extermination. I deserve better, don't you think? and my person invokes more "beautiful gestures."*

No matter, I accept. I will speak to your Belgians and I will be insolent, as it is always proper to be, when one is a good Christian.

Ah! I have no right to be fussy!

You encourage me to violence, Demolder too. What childishness!... Have a bit more faith in me then. Well! What the devil do you want me to do? Yes, for the love of God! what do you want me to do, in the presence of any public whatsoever, *if I do not vociferate disagreeably.*

Henry, my heart is riddled like a target, I am saturated with horror, and the world is infinitely, indescribably hateful to me. If your dogs want insults, they will have them, for their money, for their filthy money, which they would never have the velleity to purify, by offering it gratuitously to an artist, were he even the greatest in the world!

Do you know what convinced me to

accept? It is knowing that you will be there with me, you, the valiant friend, the only perhaps among those who will come to see me suffer...

Your,

– LÉON BLOY.

23. – Began reading *En Route*, the recent book by Huysmans, whose painful art exhausts me, and whose documented ignorance turns my stomach.

24. – Continued *En Route*. The real title of this book would be *Broken Down*. Huysmans keeps churning out the same foolishness and filth, without having advanced one bit. However, he discovers Catholicism and is profoundly astonished by what he finds. Enormous boredom.

The indigence of imagination of that discoverer and the hollowness of his brain give me vertigo. He has only eyes and ears, – in the most carnal sense, of course, – and still. A few pages, it is true, relative to his confessions or communions, can touch, but it is a foreign effort to him, and one sees so clearly the trace of certain readings! In sum, identical compilation to previous compilations, but infinitely more annoying. Nothing more exasperating than to see this man examine his conscience, in four hundred fifty pages, using a microscope purchased the day before, and which he does not even know how to operate.

Simple trait, profoundly characteristic. In *En Route*, children, hated and despised, as in all his earlier books, are invariably called *brats*. What to think of this: the defense of Catholicism undertaken by a writer whose instinct has always been to vilify?

25. – Finished *En Route*. Why am I not Huysmans' friend anymore! I would give him a precious piece of advice.

After *Là-Bas* and *En Route*, why would he not entitle his next tome: EN HAUT! EVERYONE DESCENDS?

27. Exhaustion and languor. To be sure, my youth is quite defunct, – the poor youth that was mine, but which appears to me now to have belonged to another and which I was never able to enjoy, even while offending God.

30. – Someone speaks to me about the universal hatred of which I am the object. How many times have I heard that! This hatred seems to form part of the duty of citizens. It is unjustifiable and mysterious, in this sense: that it is espoused by people who do not know me, whom I have never heard speak of, and to whom I was unable to do any harm. I must be quite an astonishing person!

31. – Passion Sunday and the last day of March very pale, neutral like Belgium.

Letter by one William Picard, writing on behalf of the anonymous society *"l'Art,"* of Brussels. In fulfillment of dazzling promises, they offer me one hundred fifty francs for a single talk, *travel expenses included.* If my talk attracted five hundred attendees at forty sous a head, it would be the same price, evidently. Good business for anonymous people.

Response:

Messieurs the Anonymous,

I consider your offer of one hundred fifty francs! travel expenses included!! to a writer whom one supposes vanquished by misery to be insulting for that writer and dishonorable for Belgium.

– LÉON BLOY.

Here is the exordium, happily preserved, of that talk, which would have been one beautiful attempt at a literary unmuzzlement:

Mesdames, Messieurs,

I begin, naturally, by soliciting your malevolence. It is too evident that the height of injustice and ridicule would be to cover in applause or suffocate under flowers, a writer, supposedly great, whom the journalists have loathed.

You know full well that it would be monstrous of you to deprive me thus of the wages for my efforts, and that you could not inflict on me the affront of a welcome without outrageously violating the sacred laws of most elementary hospitality.

I add that that would be a betrayal and an unmentionable cowardice.

And yet! For fifteen years, I would have worked night and day to render myself insupportable to all my contemporaries; I would have died of misery during the three most beautiful lustra of my very bitch of a life; I would have endured hunger, thirst, nakedness, excessive cold, extreme heat, cantankerous demands by countless landlords whom I became the terror of.

And what does that entail? Just heaven! I would have heard sobbing, I would have seen cherished beings, wrapped in my destiny, perish; I would have ripped out my heart with claws or pincers, so that one day, O almighty God! so that one certain day Belgian citizens might lure me into the trap of their courtesy! so that being in their midst I might notice, around me, their sympathetic faces, their outstretched hands, their open hearts!...

How is it possible that you could have abused my trust to such an extent! What a fall, then! and what would become of that beautiful dream of my life to become the spittoon of the universe's maledictions? to be arrayed, as with a luminous coat, in the infinitely agreeable contempt of honest folk? never to receive but vile insults and riffrafferous defiances? to appear, finally, as the vilest scrap of the literary shoe-scraper and to squat gloriously in the dejections of the most muck-laden swine of journalism?

O desirable, voluptuous, and refreshing ignominy! Fountain of delights which every proud artist must yearn for! do not deprive me of it, messieurs, I beg of you. Throw some excrements at me, some good excrements, from the heart. Fortify yourselves in the thought that I have the ambition to displease you and leave me the hope of succeeding.

I formulated the plan of entertaining you with a lamentable individual whose misfortunes will disgust you, I am sure of it.

His name is Caïn Marchenoir. We have but one heart, and one soul, and I am, after God, his only friend. He is a writer among the most obscure. He is unknown to the ladies and cannot be read fruitfully except by a small number of arsonists.

When I say that he is obscure, it is by an indigence of vocables. He is at the heart of obscurity, at the deepest recess of a black cave. Rare beings endowed with night vision who have visited that solitary could not approach him without groping their way, and they went away disappointed. I myself who have tried it many times, I confess to knowing him poorly; however, our commerce having been among the most assiduous, most intimate, I dare flatter myself for having offered a few first-hand references as to this enigmatic individual.

Ah! it is a most difficult enterprise, I admit, and of an execution all the more difficult that I have strictly forbidden myself from counting on the intelligence or longanimity of my audience.

It is true that I am not here to amuse myself. Judge for yourselves!

On the one hand, I am forced to lack respect, – oh! but absolutely – for an entire lot of notorious louts, generally honored in all the countries of the world. Let's see, you do not expect, I suppose, especially given the topic of my talk, that I might speak to you in an affectionate manner about the swine of the quill whom you, doubtless, are delighted by, and whom the grossest among you, – indubitably, – are accustomed to regarding as peerless writers: the Daudets, the Bourgets, the Zolas, the Maupassants, and the nauseating rabble of imitators and thurifers. It is abundantly clear that any expression of my feelings toward these adored masturbators can only disoblige an audience from which capitalists or merchants will not have been carefully extirpated.

On the other hand, I am unfortunately suffering from an infirmity, a sort of vile goiter: I believe in God, *like Marchenoir, and I am Catholic to the tip of my hair, like him also. You see me ensconced, no less than him, in an absolute intolerance. In a word, the two of us figure that the Inquisition was parsimonious in its punishments, and that true apostolic charity is, above everything else, in the abundance and quality of its massacres.*

That having been made abundantly and insolently clear, I come now to my character... Etc., etc.

April

3. – Gave to Bigand a copy of *Sueur de Sang*. Dedication: "To Edmond Bigand-Kaire, who was sent to me, in his Agony, by the Adorable One who sweated his blood for everyone"; and one of my most rare copies of *Swine*, on Holland paper: "*Cupiebat implere ventrem suum de siliquis quas porci mauducabant: et nemo illi dabat.*[135] Léon Bloy according to Saint Luke."

8. – "Léon Bloy?... Don't know 'im." Fine response by Alphonse Daudet when my name came up among millionaires.

12. – Good Friday. *Domine, memento mei, cum veneris in regnum tuum.*[136] These words by the Thief, are they not the excellent archetype of a dolorous and spontaneously answered prayer?

13. – A poor devil of a Protestant said to me a few days ago, after how many others, that people saw much hatred in me. The words of this man, otherwise benevolent, came back to me this morning, I do not

---

[135]*Cupiebat implere ventrem*...: Latin for "And he would fain have filled his belly with the husks that the swine did eat: and no man gave unto him." Luke 15:16 (Douay-Rheims).

[136]*Memento mei*...: Latin for "Lord, remember me, when thou shalt come into thy kingdom." Luke 23:42 (Douay-Rheims).

know why. Yes, it is true, I am full of hatred since my childhood, and no one loved other men more naïvely than I did. I have hated the World to no end, and the experiences of my life have served merely to exasperate that passion. Who then, among Christians even, could understand that?

Waited for consoling letters that do not arrive. Jeanne asked me whether, among the prophetic and figurative sufferings spoken of in Scripture, I had not noticed the Silence, – that terrible and torturing silence of friends, which I have greatly suffered from. It is odd that I have never thought to investigate this.

14. – Easter. I am cold to the core of my soul, and I am also as close as possible to despair. Such is, on me, the effect of this great feast. Easter Sunday is ordinarily painful for me, sometimes terrible. Impossible to hide my distress, which is expressed nearly like this: I do not arrive at feeling the joy of the Resurrection because the Resurrection, for me, never arrives. I always see Jesus in agony, Jesus on the cross, and I cannot see him in any other way.

Then, this morning, I was too much reminded of the past, already so distant (1879-1882) and, all the same, so very much alive still when I saw the *veritable* Véronique, in tears and shredded by the tigers of compassion, in front of the image of Jesus being handed over to his tormentors...[137] How to climb out of that chasm again?... That perpetual recommencement of the ecclesiastical Year, ever the same, with-

_____
[137] *Veritable Véronique*...: See Chapter 65 of *The Desperate Man*.

out the Lord ever breaking out, from behind the clouds, and shining!...

Non venit regnum Dei cum observatione.[138] Well do I know it. But because this Reign must not be accompanied by any sign, does that mean that I must wait forever?

15. – Words by my dear Jeanne: "One voluntarily asserts that Godless people suffer more than others. This must be a commonplace. It seems to me, on the contrary, that deep suffering cannot be known except by the friends of God."

16. – Having been unable to pay my rent, at the exact minute due, the landlord, a sordid second-hand dealer of old pants, issues me a command. Noticed, in the garden, the abject face of that funny old man. O God! what a face of a base profiteer, what a dirty churl's frontside *with rosy cheeks*, like the buttocks of a swine! He remains there, in our sight, perorating, for one or two hours, with his workers, and I would be unable to say just how much his vicinity makes me suffer. To be what I am and to feel myself oppressed by this miserable man among ignoble men, who triumphs over my distress, after having procured the death of my child!...

---

[138]*Non venit regnum...*: Latin for "The kingdom of God cometh not with observation." Luke 17:20 (Douay-Rheims).

20. – The sending of one of my *Swine* to old Mar-cellin Desboutin: "*Dœmones rogabant eum dicentes: Mitte nos in gregem porcorum. Et ait illis: Ite.* S. Matth. VIIII."[139]

25. – Feast of Saint Mark. I put a lot of hope in this evangelist who said that Jesus "was with the beasts." I said to my Véronique: "Today is the Feast of Saint Mark, and it is little papa who is the lion of Saint Mark!" The dear child listens to this with her bright, beautiful smile.

27. – To a friend from Brussels:

> *Dear Monsieur,*
>
> *Once more, I take recourse in your obligingness. The* Argus de la Presse *informs me, by summary communiqué, that Durendal(!), a sort of Catholic review published in Brussels, has just offered to its public a long article entitled "Léon Bloy, the miserable," by Pol Demade.*
>
> *It is certainly unlikely that this poor Demade, who has taken so much trouble to raise himself to the intellectual level of a Charles Buet, has enriched, by some happy find, my famous* cliché

---

[139]*Dæmones autem....:* Latin for "And the devils besought him, saying: If thou cast us out hence, send us into the herd of swine. And he said unto them: Go." Matthew 8:31-32 (Douay-Rheims).

on this occasion.

He most assuredly must have re-hashed, like so many others, the tired imbecilities that make up, after fifteen years, the Bloyian legend.

I would not waste any more time on it, then, and I definitely would not have written to you about it, – life being too short, after all, – if I did not suppose, unwarrantedly perhaps, that this good Demade, incapable of disobliging a fly, must have been, in this instance, the scribe for a certain lady whom I suspect of having abused his inno-cence.

I would like to verify it myself, then, and I beg you to send to me a copy of Durendal(?!?) *as soon as possible.*

Your,

– LÉON BLOY.

30. – Jeanne's idea. – The Priest is hidden in the man, just as Jesus is hidden in the poor.

May

2. – Reading of the *Life* of Saint Anthony of Padua, by Father de Chérancé. One really has to love the saints to consume such mediocre books! "It seems," I said to Jeanne, "that superior ecclesiastics and the Heads of orders should implore, on bended knee, that artist-writers write and popularize the life of saints in the world..."

On further reflection, this complaint is not worthy of me, the author of "Fou," in *Brelan d'Ex-communiés*. For here is the mystery: Jesus vanquished the world merely "by hope," and he is the Poor. The magnificence of Art is not appropriate to him. The verminous literature of books of devotion, which he is forced to be content with until the advent of the Vagabond is, consequently, a sort of miserable and ignominious language, divinely appropriate to his condition; what am I saying? a *reserved*, occult language accessible only to a limited number of people, insupportable to the proud world of people who cannot be purified except in the furnaces of the Consoler.

"This language," adds Jeanne, "is perfect poverty. As soon as one exits this language, one necessarily falls into the dark or bright abysses of the Paraclete, and one belongs to it like a prey."

3. – The drawing of a tombola, organized, to my profit, by the terrific captain Bigand.

I have sent packing the strangest individual I

have ever met, a chaser of inheritances and heiresses, who persecutes me, for several days now, that I might use my eloquence to bring back to him a certain recalcitrant fiancée, *two or three HUNDRED times a millionaire*. It is enough to cause vertigo to think that he should address himself to *me* for a like negotiation! It is inconceivable that our door was able to be open, for one single hour, to that adventurer who brought the abomination of the World into our home.

...Terram tenebrosam et opertam mortis caligine: terram miseriæ et tenebrarum, ubi umbra mortis, et nullus ordo, sed sempiternus horror inhabitat.[140]

Here is the Absolute; and here is the Kingdom of the Prince of this World, who is also the Prince of Darkness. *Per signum Crucis, libera nos, Domine.*[141]

4. – The most beautiful of lotteries is the one that David prophesied: *Super vestem meam miserunt sortem.*[142]

Mine is less redemptive. Our most pressing debts paid, we have little or nothing left, and we can-

---

[140] *Terram tenebrosam...*: Latin for "...[to a] land that is dark and covered with the mist of death: A land of misery and darkness, where the shadow of death, and no order, but everlasting horror dwelleth." Job 10:21-22 (Douay-Rheims).

[141] *Per signum...*: Latin for "By the sign of the cross, deliver us, Lord."

[142] *Super vestem meam...*: Latin for "upon my vesture they cast lots." Psalm 21:19 (Douay-Rheims).

not even escape from our dreadful abode.

The most important pieces were won by strangers or the indifferent. An old atheistic million-aire, who had disbursed merely twenty-five francs, bagged two remarkable drawings, one of which, by Charles Maurin, is worth about twenty times that. Virtue recompensed. It is the law of supposed games of *hazard*, whose prince abides in the realm of Dark-ness and whose results are always disenchanting.

6. – Entirely unbeknownst to me, Bigand had taken it upon himself, several days earlier, to write to Tail-hade, inviting him to take part in the tombola. The naïve mariner believed this step to be totally simple and more than appropriate, supposing, candidly, that the individual would be only too happy on this occa-sion to make his villainy be forgotten.

Here is the response, which he communicates to me under the title of a "historical literary docu-ment":

Neuilly-sur-Seine, May 3, '93.

Your two letters, monsieur, arrived to-day by the same courier, in the nurs-ing home where I am being cared for since the beginning of winter. Al-though I am not at all accustomed to receiving solicitations presented in the rather uncivil and, so to speak, com-minatory, format that you use, rather inappropriately, so it seems to me, I very sincerely feel for the unfortunate Léon Bloy, my being unable to come to his aid on account of my feeble strength.

You will find, enclosed, a money order for twenty francs, in exchange for which I kindly ask you not to send me any tombola ticket in return.

As for the legend that you make an allusion to of Léon Bloy losing his job for having come to my assistance, – at the same time, moreover, as Octave Mirbeau, Georges Vanor, Jean Carrère, and many others whom I currently forget; for I was at that time a brilliant "subject of an article" – for all I know that could be the favored legend in Cancale;[143] *but here, we all know that Léon Bloy was forced to leave the* Gil Blas *for having refused to a vituperated confrere a reparation by arms. In your friend's selfsame interest, I do not believe that it is too smart to insist on that upsetting adventure, nor to violently play, as you do, the gratitude card. However contemptible today's gazetteers might be, at least they kept in tact the prejudice of the épée. Also, monsieur, and although you seem the most unlikely person in*

---

[143]Original footnote: Captain Bigand was, at that time, usually residing in Cancale. I think it is pointless to insist on the exquisite subtlety of that geographic allusion.

the world to be involved in revendica-
tions of honor, suffer me to advise you
some restraint in the story that you
make of the quarrel between Léon
Bloy and Lepelletier. By too much em-
phasis, you will harm a writer whom I
love and whom you appear curious to
serve efficaciously. I have, monsieur,
the honor of saluting you, – LAURENT
TAILHADE.

The recipient of that overwrought epistle informs me that he immediately sent back the money
order, it having arrived too late for the tombola, and
that he wrote, at the same time, a *compassionate* letter. Tailhade is fortunate to be a hospital patient!

8. – Money order certificate for twenty francs, with
these words: "Laurent Tailhade's best compliments
come too late for the tombola."

Response by the ungrateful beggar:

The twenty francs received from you,
Tailhade, will go to noble things that I
will not waste my time explaining to
you. I renounce my original idea of
sending the money back to you, proud
step that would clearly be misunder-
stood. Your insolent and lying *letter to*
the captain Bigand-Kaire, moved to
pity for you and who gave it to me like
a "historical document," does not sur-
prise me.

It was natural that I should be denied by you. I know that one must not expect intrepidity of anyone, particularly not of a morphine patient. However, you could have, when, because of you, the most vile and loutish letters insulted me, – you could have murmured a few syllables into the ear of the interviewer. You knew admirably well what went down, and, as a result of some riffraffish schemes, a poor writer, who had stood up for you, had been deprived of his daily bread. Those few syllables which you considered compromising to you, would have been extremely useful to him, at that time. He was hoping for nothing more, having done the thing freely and spontaneously, without a second thought. But it appears that even that was too much [for you], and the extremely belated letter that now decorates the frontispiece of Léon Bloy devant les cochons, *it required Henry de Groux to wrest it from you. Later, still fearing to appear my friend, you so perfectly hid yourself that an entire year passed without my having received two lines from you, without my having encountered you again.*

In the end, you write an abominable letter to the only man who undertook to heal the frightful wound that I was suffering from because of you, abusing your situation of a valetudinarian which prevents this man from punishing you.

That exceeds all measure of rakish tomfooleries, *monsieur the tolero. Be restored then to the esteem of "gazetteers who have kept in tact the prejudice of the épée" and accept the assurance of my absolute disgust.*

– *LÉON BLOY.*

10. – Received a copy of the Belgian review Durendal with "*Léon Bloy le misérable*," by Pol Demade, in it. Rare stupidity. Rather long tirade. It is exactly what I had expected. But I was wrong to speak about *a* woman who could have left her imprint on the mastic of that brain. There is more than one, it seems. I have even recognized the oafish paw of the big Buet, whose intelligence is glabrous and sex intermittent, as everyone knows. This Demade, I am told, is one of the candles of Belgian Catholicism. He has made for himself, in that funny milieu, a sort of reputation by using the ideas or butt ends of phrases of countless French writers, among whom Barbey d'Aurevilly, Ernest Hello, Villiers de l'Isle-Adam, and myself. It is disarming.

The entire effect of this imbecilic labor has been to bring me to reread the brochure: *Ici on assassine les grands hommes*, which is imputed to me as a black crime. Would to God that I had always written such noble pages!¹⁴⁴

12. – Read an article by d'Esparbès on Joan of Arc
(!), of the most exact infamy. The poor devil who declared to me, in '92, that he did not to want to have
his son baptized, seems to me, today, struck by cre-

---

[144]Original footnote: Letter, completely unexpected, from the so-
called Pol Demade who solicits the "cruel" documents that he
supposes me the possessor of. Solicited himself by the most
pressing need to shine, at my expense, he provisorily forgets that
I am "a miserable wretch, a brigand of letters, an exceptional
lout," and grovels even to proclaim me: "hungry for justice."
Come on, Pol, a little self-respect, my boy! – May 29, 1897.

To finish up with that *Durendal*.

To Henry Carton de Wiart, member of the editorial committee:

August 19, 1897.

Monsieur,

I came across, in the imbecilic review Durendal, *the
"Introduction" to* Belluaires et Porchers, *the handwritten
manuscript of which I had given to you, nine years ago,
when I thought you were a friend.*

*You took it upon yourself to give that to the public,
without my authorization, in a clandestine manner and
in an absolute disinterestedness of prejudice, which
could result for me in an anticipated and defective
publication, – villainously abusing the insufficiency of
the law which feebly protects literary property.*

*Your conduct in my regard was so odious and so
marvelously loutish that I ought not to be surprised. But
this vile, very Belgian hand [laid] on the goods of the
poor, borders on FRAUD, in the sense that I find myself
deprived, thereby, of an unpublished manuscript that,*

tinism and rage. It is enough to believe that he has been ambushed by some Masonic lodge whence he receives abject instructions.

Pol Demade again. Article on *En Route*. This new stupidity, which is sent to me from Belgium, I don't know by whom, does not even amuse me. It is really too stupid.

On this occasion, I think back again on the sad book by Huysmans which makes some noise, after two months. I recall that in one place the unexpected doctor considers the ritual of marriage mediocre, not knowing, doubtless, that marriage is a Sacrament, and even "a great sacrament" according to Saint Paul. What's more, he has the equity to condemn King David, and in what language! without suspecting for one minute the colossal majesty of an individual whom the Holy Spirit constantly names the Father of Our Lord Jesus Christ... It is true that one must not ask for, from the author of the *Sœurs Vatard*, any sort of intelligence or even an approximate notion of the Holy Bible. In general, that apostle seems to believe that Religion is an aesthetic. What a brain!

The pages of *En Route* that attempt to be lyri-

---

one day or another, might be profitable to me, – and I did not know that you were at precisely the same point as the little brigands of the Patriot.

Do not cry out too much against it then if, from now on, I avidly jump on every occasion that presents itself to express to you, publicly, the perfect contempt that I offer you here the investiture of.

– LÉON BLOY.

cal give rise to thoughts of *artificial* flowers offered to Mary in a chamber pot.[145]

18. Conversation with Jeanne. We make fun of science, art, honor, dishonor, laws or proprieties of all sorts. Everything that is not strictly the Love of God appears to us on a level with filth.

20. – To a pharmacist of Montrouge:

> *Dear Monsieur,*
>
> *You urge me to fix a date for the settling of your account. I fix, then, the 15th of the following month and it is, in truth, the best I can do.* – Si contuderis me in pila, quasi ptisanas, feriente desuper pilo, non auferres a me amplius.[146]
>
> *That said, not without deploring that you are, at this point, a victim of the demon of impatience, I instantly urge you no longer to send your employees to [harass] me.*

---

[145]Original footnote: Everyone knows that the two "vessels" of the present hour, the two apostles of contemporary gentility, are J.-K. Huysmans and François Coppée. – 1898.

[146]*Si contunderis me*...: Latin for "Though you shouldst bray me in the mortar, as when a pestle striketh upon sodden barley, you will not get any more out of me." A variation on Proverb 27:22 (Douay-Rheims).

*It would afflict me to have to sadden
the least woodlouse, being – as every
literary rascal knows –* mitissimus vir
super omnes prophetas, et monstra pla-
cans in verbis.[147]

*But I will not suffer anyone to insult
my wife, especially in my absence, nor
that a domestic, emboldened by the
appearance of our poverty, should excite his loutishness to the degree of* os-
tensibly doubting *what was said to
him by way of response.*

*I urge you to consider, monsieur, that
I could find myself at home one day, at
the precise moment that that caballero
presented himself, and that it is satan-
ic to tempt poor humans.*

*Alas! My reputation is filled with tales
of overburdening apothecaries with
work, by damaging contemporary car-
casses, and the nickname of Caïn has
stuck with me.*

*I entreat you, then, quite simply to
count on me, and, once again, don't
send your flunkies my way again.*

*Accept, dear monsieur, the assurance
of my rage, my goodwill, and my perfect consideration.*

---

[147]*Mitissimus vir...*: Latin for "a man exceeding meek above all the
prophets, and placating prodigies with [his] words." A variation on
Numbers 12:3 and Ecclesiasticus 45:2 (Douay-Rheims).

– LÉON BLOY.

21. – Why is it so difficult to escape serious thoughts, or, at least, – if one is a brute, – a kind of oppression, in the proximity of a decedent? The fact is that this decedent, even if he were the most banal person alive, has just fallen under the domination of Someone who is absolutely unknown and whose Presence one *senses*... This presence is particularly perceptible in the phenomenon, so little explained, that is commonly called *the cold of death*. Jeanne's idea, with respect to our son André whom we were talking about this evening.

Similarly:

That one should have money or not have any, it is the same thing, in the sense that one is always in God's Hands. In the first case, money is held by someone who is visible, and, therefore, it is *visible*. In the second case, it is held by someone invisible, and, therefore, it is *invisible*.

22. – To one of my abandoners who wants to see me again:

You were simply dreadful. You were nowhere to be found, like so many others, when misfortune struck us. I will never forget that end of winter, in a homicidal house. We were shivering with misery, between a small dead boy and a little dying girl, and nobody presented themselves. Nobody, among former admirers or guests, asked themselves, at that time, if I had the need of any assistance and did not give me so much as the alm of a visit.

It is God alone who knows what was going on in your heart, but how could I count on your friendship? *"Faithful, despite appearances," you say. Do you not feel, then, the appalling irony of that formula? As a Christian, however, I do not have the right to absolutely reject you and I do not refuse to shake your hand, when I might see you again. But you are not welcome in my home.*

– *LÉON BLOY.*

23. – Ascension. – Ascension is, for me, a strange celebration, and I have a great need for the supernatural in order to support what Saint Luke said about the Apostles returning to Jerusalem, *cum gaudio magno.*[148] How to rejoice for Jesus' departure? I have always seen it as an occasion of infinite mourning.

24. – I have thought long and hard about that thing of my distant past: the obstinate prayer I said every day,

---

[148]*Cum gaudio magno*: Latin for "with great joy." Luke 24:52 (Douay-Rheims).

for hours and months, more than twenty years ago, offering to my friends, J.B. d'A., Georges L., and Victor L., – the only ones I had then, and who *have all three abandoned me*, – whatever I might have of the most precious. For the love of their souls, I asked to suffer inordinately, to be suffocated by sorrow, trod on by demons, earmarked for injustice, ignominy, ridicule, and misunderstood by those even for whom I sacrificed myself. Admirably answered prayer.

On exiting church, an old man proposed that I become affiliated with the brotherhood of the Holy Sacrament, counseling me, already, to go and see the president whom he sought to qualify by declaring him a *landlord*... My response: "Ah! he is a landlord, your president! In that case, nothing doing. You will speak to me again about your brotherhood when you are presided over by a *beggar*."

26. – Syllogism. – Who asks to be eaten? It is Jesus (Saint John, VI). But the perfect form of idolatry, it is Anthropophagy. Therefore Jesus is God and man, all in one.

But God alone wants to be eaten. God alone *can* be eaten. That there is a pretty abyss [to fathom]. Besides, what does it mean to eat? What does anything mean? Given that we are always ignorant of the limit between the natural and supernatural, the visible and the invisible.

27. – Oh! the infamy, the diabolical laughter of the

bourgeois who are amused by the drunkenness of a small child!

30. – I try to enter the church. Impossible. Barrier on all sides. It is the always odious solemnity, in Paris, of the first communion, and the poor cannot enter. God himself would be forced to pay twenty centimes. The Poor are explused from *his* house, and rich women exhibit their toilettes there. Simony and prostitution.

Véronique. Will I ever forget the consolations that this child gives me? When I came home this evening, she was in bed. I sat down beside her bed and I said to her: "Little papa is sad." The dear creature then held me in her arms and covered me in kisses, *while moaning with feeling*. What sweet tears I shed, my God!

31. – Horrible misery. I was really hoping that I had not made that immense trip in vain. But I need to return on foot, just as I came, without a centime, and my heart filled with sobs. Frequent disappointment. Sometimes it seems that an idea is brought to me by an angel, but soon afterwards I think I hear the laughter of a demon. *Hi sunt qui venerunt de tribulatione magna.*[149] I have endured this torment for twenty years, having *asked* for it, so that my cowardly friends who were bound to abandon me might become God's friends.

---

[149]*Hi sunt qui...*: Latin for "These are they who are come out of great tribulation." Revelations, 7:14 (Douay-Rheims).

Not long ago, Véronique, seeing me extremely sad, comes to me, takes me by the neck and, with an extreme tenderness, says to me: "My dear little papa, do not cry, *I will give you something*." And the little child searches among her playthings for something to offer me.

Today, at mass, this memory moves my heart with too much force for it not to correspond with something divine. Is there anything more heartrending than the compassion of someone who has nothing, but who wants to give something? And God, is he not the Poor of the poor?

June

1st – Jeanne tells me she is feeling a sort of enthusiasm at the thought that, tomorrow, the Feast of Pentecost, we will be without any type of resource.

2. – Pentecost. Day of abstinence and fasting. Véronique has what she needs. Everything is excellent in that respect. We hope in vain for this child's godfather. He knows full well that we are suffering and that he could assist us. Two francs alone would do us so much good! On such a feast day! It is hideous! In the past, for three years, he was regaled at our table, every Sunday and holiday. Now, we could die for all he cared.

The day ends, however. The salad too. We have survived, the whole day, on salad. All that in the "external" tenebræ. For here is one of the strangest circumstances: This evening of Pentecost, we are *without light!*...

5. – To evade the most probable of melancholic crises, studied the three first chapters of *Acts*. Immediate relief. I rediscover that divine feeling of feasting on the powerful and *invisible nourishment* that Raphael speaks of, in the book of Tobit.

Jeanne asks whether the twenty-four old men, in white vestment and gold crowns, in the IVth chapter of Revelations, would not simply be the *twenty-four small children.*

An idea of overwhelming beauty, stemming from the notion that old age *must* be envisaged, not like a decadence, but like an embellishment, in the example of youth. *Introibo ad altare Dei,* said a very old priest, before approaching the altar, *introibo ad altare Dei: ad Deum qui lætificat* JUVENTUTEM MEAM.[150]

7. – To the Count Roselly de Lorgues, for whom I gave two years of my life, and *gratuitously* accomplished enormous labors:

> *My dear Count,*
>
> *Yesterday I received through the offices of one of my rare friends, a sum of forty francs, which you had entrusted to him for me. That devoted friend had taken it upon himself to go and see you, even though he knew of my resolution no longer to importune you, even in case of mortal danger. I thank you, not for me who no longer has need of anything, having become or forcing myself to become exclusively a man of prayer, but for my little girl, a frail child of barely four years old, whom this money can prevent from dying.*

---

[150]*Introibo ad altare..*: Latin for "And I will go in to the altar of God: to God who giveth joy to my youth." Psalm 42:4 (Douay-Rheims).

Please accept,

– LÉON BLOY.

8. – To the right of our vile abode, on the side where the sun goes down, a monstrous building is rapidly going up, to which our garden will seem like the bottom of a well. That enormous structure, which we see men working at every day, without exception, appears to us like some positively infernal thing.

To Henry de Groux, in Spa:

My very dear Henry,...

Everything that happens in life is adorable: *I maintain this, with all the authority of my misery, which is perfect because God is perfect, and which is itself adorable, consequently. We may complain all we like, the two of us, but we cannot avoid this law and we will never succeed in giving life to a plausible grief against Providence. If we lack money, it is because money would be disastrous for us, but we will certainly be overwhelmed by it on the day when this metal stops being an occasion of peril for us.*

To believe that, to see that, such is the unique means offered to us not to fall below the level of brutes. If your feet hurt, my poor Henry, locomotion would be harmful to you at this time, and if I myself am immobilized until some future time, with my wife and child, in this diabolical cul-de-sac, it is indubitably because pure air and the perfume of flowers would be less favorable to us than the odor of pits of easement and the stink of rotting car-casses that we breathe here.

I think, my dear godson, that you know me well enough to feel that I am speaking seriously to you. It is a bizarre remark that, when one is, like me, installed, domiciled, in the abso-lute, – you understand me, surely: in the Absolute, – it becomes nearly im-possible to affirm or deny whatsoever it might be, without sounding ironic. Example: the Histoires désobligeantes, *a book forever incomprehensible to the scribes of the banlieue, such as your "cousin" Pol Demade.*

Apropos of which, Demolder sent me the lofty work of that pious boor who does not at all like it that I should hap-pen to be poor: Léon Bloy le misérable, *dictated or inspired by Mme. Hello, Mlle. R., Buet, perhaps also George L., my friend of thirty years, etc., etc., for an entire people was consulted. That's just great.*

To return to my argument, note, and I

entreat you, how much right I have to invite you in the adoration of God's gestures. Imagine that we almost never possess one centime, for fifteen days nearly, that the threats press on us from all sides, that we observed a very strict fast on Holy Saturday, the Sunday of Pentecost itself, and that the day before yesterday Véronique fell ill again, giving us to fear the same fever that failed to kill her in February, in that terrible February when all humanity appeared to have abandoned us. I hasten to add that it was a false alarm and that the dear little one is already doing much better. I do not mention a few other torments whose telling would fill about twenty-four pages of cramped text.

Eh, well! And then? Do we not know that at the very moment when we suffer a painful shock, that it is Jesus, covered with wounds, who falls on the mud carpet of our souls, supplicating us, at least, not to bristle too much against him, and that in this way we are overwhelmed with the most unimaginable honor?

You know how Job speaks about the earth: Terram tenebrosam, *etc. What about it? But it is the dwelling place of fallen man, the tabernacle of the dis-*

obedient, what one is used to calling the ball of the world, and we are sufficiently warned by these unequivocal Words that it would be goiters or malice to suppose that what the Church calls a "vale of tears" is, on the contrary, a luminous and comfortable place. Happy are the poor, happy the meek, happy those who weep and those who are avid for justice; happy still are those who have pity, those whose heart is pure and those who are peaceful. Happy finally are those who suffer persecution. Well! Doubtless. Do you not see that all these elect, of whom we ourselves, *more or less, although very unworthy, are admirably situated to decipher the text of Job, and that it is always a beginning of Paradise to glimpse, even if barely, a lineament of the Word of God,.*

All that to say this to you, my dear Henry, that we must not afflict each other. I find it excessive and terribly unjust that you should feel such great distress for having put me in an awkward situation, as if you wanted to cause me the unbearable ridicule of making me appear your creditor. My reprimands, as you have seen, bore on another point. I immediately understood that I had had the most celestial, most mysterious, and most pressing need to swallow that bitter pill, and that it was necessary for you to offer it to me yourself so that we should experience this suffering together, *for it is a characteristic of Providence to economize catastrophes.*

So let's not get on each other's nerves, my very dear friend, but let us adore [each other]. It is the only proper thing for us to do. Why should we perish? Are we not extremely precious, and the superfine quality of our tribulations, do they not prove the exceptional solicitude of Him who has been working on us, like works of art, for so long a time? I tell you that we will not perish. I am even perfectly sure that we would have already been delivered if you had had more confidence in God than in yourself. Reread my letters.

I embrace you,

– Léon Bloy.

P.S. The Osterwald Bible is a Protestant Bible and, by consequence, garbage. *It is, Henry, I who will give you a Bible.*

9. – To Jeanne, apropos of a curate's demands and rapacity:

*Priests of this sort have this in com-
mon with the Jews: the inconceivable
blindness that hurtles them toward the
catastrophe that everything ought to
warn them against. They both know a
thousand times over that the cynicism
of their avarice upsets the ocean of the
poor. One might say that this certitude
serves only to exasperate their imprudence, and it is something supernatural to see them gallop toward their
destiny. Judas sold the Son of God for
thirty deniers. These horrible priests
redeemed him from the Synagogue,
with benefice, only to sell him again
with usury to the multitude of Christians.*

11. – In reprisal for my letter of May 8, Tailhade, who
signs himself "Tybalt" in the *Echo de Paris*, and who
imitates me clumsily, publishes, in that issue, a chron-
icle in praise of a book by Léon Daudet, the worthy
son of Alphonse senior, a book in which I am dragged
through the dung.

How distant all this seems to me today, and
how terribly tiring and disgusting all these vanities of
animalcules are! Tailhade accuses me of *poltroon-
ery(!)* and *ingratitude(!!!)*.

14. – Acceptance speech to the Academy [of France],
by the spirited eunuch Paul Bourget. Mucilaginous

secretion which the ladies are forced to be contented with.

Today, I have not only touched the bottom of the abyss, but the Enemy has tried to squash my heart, to crush my brain on the paving stones.

"Lord Jesus, you pray for those who crucify you, and you crucify those who love you!"

15. – Reading of a preface by Huysmans, published in the *Figaro*. Huysmans has decidedly become a pontiff, an oracle in matters of Magic and Satanism. The authoritative tone without appeal by this metropolitan is miraculous.

Astonishing gullibility of the *occultists!* who have a need for rites and grimoires in order to feel the presence of the Demon, but who do not see Satanism, – blindingly obvious, – in their local grocer, for example.

17. – When men of the world lack money, their entire lack and misery is terrifying.

19. – Cemetery of Bagneux. Having decided to live, I return among the dead.

"We cannot have friends except among the invisible," Jeanne tells me, thinking, perhaps, of the improbable multitude of our abandoners. As soon as one becomes our friend, *one is compelled to become in-*

visible.

20. – I learn that Tailhade must have received this:

> *Léon Bloy has always* signed *his at-
> tacks, and he has never praised a book
> or man whom he contemned.*
>
> – HENRY DE GROUX.

On the advice of an individual who believes
himself to be *very well-informed*, I write to the
duchess, alas! of Uzès:

> *Madame,*
>
> *Someone assures me that you will read
> this letter and that even the most de-
> tested writer in the world, the signato-
> ry of these lines, will not be excluded
> from the sweet humor that you refuse
> to no one.*
>
> *I have too greatly excited the rage of
> my contemporaries to resign myself to
> believing that I am totally unknown to
> you. The uproar will have been able to
> carry my name to you. If this confi-
> dence is not the effect of excessive pre-
> sumption, by now you know that I am
> a monster of independence.*
>
> *I write to you, then, madame, because
> I have need of you, and I do not fear
> straightaway to avow it. For what oth-*

er reason would I write to you?

All the gulfs separate us. You live in glory in this world where you are one of the potentates; and I, I stagnate at the bottom of an abyss where the lovers of God have been thrown pell-mell with the friends of Suffering and Light, – for centuries.

If it was just me, I would have nothing to say to you, persuaded that it is better to be unhappy than not to exist at all, and if, for the twenty years that my tribulation has lasted, I am not dead, it is apparently because I am not worthy of so beautiful a decease.

I would not be complaining then. But, not to speak of my wife who feels the same way as I do, do I have the right to expose a little girl of four to frightening suffering?

She is the only child who remains to us, the other having been poisoned, last winter, by the air in the horrible house where the hatred of people of the pen have relegated, in the end, an artist deprived by them of his entire wage, for his crime of being great in the eyes of some...

We need to leave this place as soon as possible, and that is why, Madame, uniquely for that reason, I write to

*you. Give me the means to escape, to
cut the ties that keep us in this place of
pestilence and despair.*

*Tell yourself that this would be for the
honor of God and that you would thus
unchain a writer who must be, all the
same, furiously* someone, *to judge by
the hatred that he is the object of.*

Please accept,...

– LÉON BLOY.[151]

21. – Feast of the Sacred Heart. This feeling of being
in love with God! and this sublime joy that God
gives!...

_____

[151]Pointless, I think, to say that this mendicant epistle obtained no
response and that in this way I was deprived of an occasion to
manifest my ingratitude.

*"...there is no brute as naked as man, and this should be a
commonplace to assert that the rich are bad poor people.*

*"When the chaos of this world in decline has been sorted out,
when the stars find their nourishment, and the most decried filth
alone is admitted to reflect the Splendor; when one knows that
nothing was in its place, and that the reasonable species was
living merely on enigmas and appearances; it could very well be
that the tortures of an unfortunate man divulged the misery of
soul of a millionaire who corresponded spiritually to his rags, on
the mysterious register of repartitions of universal Solidarity...*

*"Ah! really, that would be enough to put one off from immortality,
if there were no surprises, even before what people are used to
calling death, and if the food of the dogs of that* DUCHESS, *vomited
up again by them, was not to be, one day, the only hope of his
eternally famished entrails!"* – La Femme Pauvre, pg. 238.

This joy of love against which nothing prevails, not even crime!

I am guilty of murder, incest, sacrilege, or parricide.

I have murdered little children and I have, like a vampire, drunk the blood of virgins consecrated to God;

I just pierced the Heart of Jesus!

No matter. His Joy burns me, *if He wants it to be thus...*

Universal silence. No letter, not even an insulting one. We are almost at the point of desiring the epistolary duns of our creditors.

22. – To the painter-sculptor Gérôme, who thought of me, with perfect kindness:

> *Master,*
>
> *I had the honor of presenting myself to you, last Monday, but, not finding you at home, I had to leave my card to inform you of my attempt. Not to mention my ambition to be admitted into the home of so celebrated an artist, I would have liked to express to you in person my most personal feelings.*
>
> *I am,* unfortunately, *too much the writer not to recognize the insufficiency, the banality, of letters in certain cases,*

and such is the fear that has kept me from writing to you, at the risk of appearing to justify the thick multitude of noble hearts who are, from morning to evening and evening to midnight, exclusively dedicated to reproaching me for the blackest schemes of ingratitude.

Will you allow me to present myself at your home, once again? And, in that case, would you care to give me notice by a word, nothing but a small word sent to me, twenty-four hours in advance? The request, I believe, is not at all banal. I am, in everyone's eyes, a monster of independence; in the eyes of some artists, a monster of art; and in the opinion of the proud riffraff whom I have fustigated, a monster of turpitude. It is, therefore, highly compromising to receive me, and it would have been entirely inexcusable of me not to apprise you of such danger.

Sincerely,

– LÉON BLOY.

24. – While Jeanne was at mass, Véronique, knowing that today is her mother's feast day, gathered for her, from our frightening garden, some of the sick and sad flowers that are able to grow there, and the poor little girl knew how to make a charming bouquet out of

them, which make our eyes well up with tears.

Reading in the Acts of the Apostles. An imbecile arrives at just the moment when Saint Stephen is looking up at the sky and sees "*Filium hominis stantem a dextris Dei.*"[152] I am, at that moment, several million leagues away from that importunate fellow, and we are forced to tread carefully. We must exhaust our strength to protect the treasure of our peace against the hostile stupidity of the world represented by him, and it is only barely if I succeed at not getting upset.

"I am as religious as you are... I pray in my way, etc." Such are the stupid remarks that one must listen to, with respect to whatever it might be. "My mother was a saint and my sister is an angel." One must swallow that even. "We can do no more." Finally, he leaves rather ill-content, and I hope that he never returns. That [sort of] vanity dies of hunger at our place.

I try to resume my reading, but God has withdrawn.

26. – What must I think of myself?

Thought this up to console myself for the continual mediocrity of my efforts at a holy life; one does not do what one should, one does what one can, in other words, what God gives one to do.

---

[152]*Filium hominis*...: Latin for "The Son of man standing on the right hand of God." Acts 7:55 (Douay-Rheims).

It must definitely be true, otherwise we would be just like Gods and we would have nothing else to do than create the world.

If I did not feel my misery, how could I feel my joy, which is the eldest daughter of my misery and which resembles it so frighteningly?

27. – After painful and vain runnings about, a stranger suddenly approaches me on the street in Montmartre, saying that he is a friend of de Groux and a passionate admirer of me. His name: Whatever. His face: seen here and there *since forever*, – a sort of impersonal face that one would take for an Invisible being, having taken on just enough of the human appearance to deliver his message. Speaking to me as if he were completely up to speed on my distress, he points out one Chausson, a music composer, collector, and very wealthy man, who *must* be one of my readers and on whose generosity I could count, for the obtainment of several pieces of money that were mine from the tombola.

Terrible heat in our hellhole.

28. – I write to this Chausson, so strangely revealed to me, to ask him for an audience.

The heat augments and the vermin pullulates. As if nothing were to be spared us, the masonry work, on the immense and ugly building that is being constructed beside us, had to take place precisely on the hottest days, under a devouring sun. We breathe, we eat, we drink nothing but plaster. No means to escape, to lead Véronique to some less dreadful place, during the thickest hours.

As it turns out, we will need, *by hook or crook*, to move out of here by the 15th of July. God will provide for us, without a doubt.

The poor are rich people without a sou, and the rich are loathsome poor people oozing with money.

My suffering in life is like an old faubourg wall abused for over thirty years, at the foot of which two generations would have... passed away. Famous men who saw me suffering are long since dead and returned to dust. My suffering in life has not changed. How much longer, O Lord?

29. – It is on this day that Saint Peter was freed from his prison by an angel: *Nunc scio vere.*[153]

My dear Jeanne, seeing me agonizing, lulls me with this: "Peter is not free because the door opens. The door opens because Peter is free."

She is persuaded that *I am free* and that *the door will open* – ULTRO.[154]

Rigorous fast. The day ends in silence over all the earth. It is amazing that a writer like me, read,

---

[153]*Nunc scio vere*: Latin for "Now I know truly."

[154]*Ultro*: Latin for "of its own accord."

doubtless, by a few thousand people, a certain number of whom are passionate followers, almost never receives a friendly letter!

30. – Obsession with that totally Christian verse by Juvenal, in his satire on the misery of people of letters:

Servis regna dabunt, captivis Fata triumphos.[155]

Jeanne undertakes the *Mystique* by Görres and then gives up, after having read only a very few number of pages. "It is a book," she tells me, "inspired by the spirit of pride and impurity." For me it is an immense joy and a principle of resurrection almost, to see with what facility my dear wife reads in the Absolute.

We were speaking about the inconceivable mediocrity of the Clergy. What sort of parish priest or religious would find it quite simple that someone called on him in preference to a physician, for a case of hysteria, catalepsy, or epilepsy? Both one and the other would find that ridiculous, or rather they would be afraid of getting caught up in the affairs of men or the Devil.

I think about what I could write, apropos of occultists, on that faithless clergy who is at the point of no longer knowing what power God has given them.

---

[155] *Servis regna dabunt...*: Latin for "They will give kingdoms to servants, Fate will give triumphs to slaves."

One has need of Priests.

July

1st. – Tempestuous heat, stink, plaster dust, and privations of all sorts are killing us.

2. – I am thinking to dedicate a future book as follows:

> *To the very great, intellectual friend, to Madame the Duchess d'Uzès, who has so nobly and so magnanimously helped me in my indigence.*

3. – The other, that Chausson of last week, sends me an apologetic dispatch. Response:

> *Monsieur,*
>
> *The telegram that you honored me with fills me with pride. I was sure that the experiment would succeed. You are rich and I am* notoriously *poor; I knew then, in an absolute manner, that you would be too "occupied" to receive me and that you would "deeply regret" missing the occasion to tell me just how much you are my "admirer."*
>
> *Please accept, Monsieur, the expression of my gratitude.*

– Léon Bloy.

We speak about the horror of living in this world, and about the resemblance with demons that the lack of Christianity positively confers on the vast majority of our contemporaries, rich and poor.

4. – We talk about the Invisible. I say that everything we see, everything that happens, externally, is merely an appearance, – an enigmatic reflection, *per speculum*, – of what happens, substantially, in the Invisible. What is more apparent, more *external*, in my life? It is that having declared war on the world, the world is unleashed against me. The substantial reality of that *sort* is perhaps something to instill fear in the greatest Angel. God alone knows what I unleashed in 1878...

In that epoch, my destiny became clear, my heterogenous destiny which had remained so indecipherable because of the phantoms that made semblance to appear around me.

I was unaware of the literary *gémonies*[156] at that time. I was still unaware even that my contemporaries existed, and I went about weeping for love on the golden carpet of Paradise.

5. – I read the Gospels like a Psalm, in the same way

---

[156]Gémonies: obloquies, superficially; but also places of suffering, punishment, and death. In reference to the *Gemoniae scalae*, or Gemonian Stairs, a flight of stairs in ancient Rome, on the Capitoline (some say Aventine) Hill, where bodies were strangled and thrown down.

that I habitually read the Psalms like a Gospel. M. Chausson could never understand that.

After a very unordinary day, a reading of the Psalm CXVIII. I fall asleep, just like a consoled child, [listening to the sounds played] on the harp of the holy King.

6. – I have spoken with a dead person and he responds to me as best he can, from the bottom of an abyss...

Read, in the *Figaro*, a long article on Naundorff, in whom almost everyone today sees Louis XVII. It would be quite unusual if the son of that Phantom of the Royalty of the Lys became the most likely among the pretenders, and if the end of the century received its historic character from the heir of the darkest Drama ever seen.[157]

7. – Reluctantly, and because someone pushes me very forcefully, I write the following letter:

To Gabriel Hanotaux, minister of Foreign Affairs:

My dear Gabriel,

A friend, a faithful friend, has initiated a conversation with M. Lebon, in view of obtaining a sum of 500 francs,

---

[157]Louis XVII: See *The Son of Louis XVI*, by Sunny Lou Publishing, 2022.

which is absolutely necessary to me,
before the 15th, to keep my wife and lit-
tle daughter from the most banal
catastrophe.

That friend thinks that it would be un-
pardonable of me not to address, con-
fidently, an old comrade who has be-
come powerful.

Your,

– Léon Bloy.

Ah! clearly, it is not very noble of him, Hanotaux having abandoned me in the vilest manner in the
world, on the very day when he seemed to become
someone, and if he complies today I too clearly antic-
ipate that it will be for the unique fear of seeming
manifestly too ignoble, by not doing anything. I knew
him, previously, only too well, this poor Gabriel, having become now – so unfortunately for our prestige, –
a *man of State*, and I do not have any illusions about
the ingenuity of his soul.

But what does it matter, after all? Am I not el-
igible and, consequently, able to participate in secret
funds that a provident Treasury inundates our minis-
ters with?

Besides, why would I repulse an assistance
that is not of men, whatever the hand might be that
brings it?

But above all, by what right would I dismiss,
morally, that lamentable successor to Richelieu, while

depriving, by my refusal, what might justify his ele-
vation?

10. – Hanotaux complied. In the end, his time in the
ministry will have served for something at least. Now,
according to all appearances, he has nothing else to
do than to prepare for an approaching discomfiture.[158]

[158]Original footnote: This prediction soon came to pass, and
Gabriel was restored, for a period of time, "to his dear studies."
But we have become so proud a people that the need for this
excellent minister did not delay making itself felt, once again.

One morning, on September 22, '96, I ran to the quay d'Orsay,
where I tried, without success, to see Hanotaux, forever invisible
to me since '84. Feeling sorry, I have to admit, for having made a
vain trip and no longer knowing to what monster to present
myself, I had to resign myself to leaving a letter in which I
implored him to send me some assistance, immediately,
anything. Several hours later, a lackey of the minister's brought
to me the sum of... TWENTY francs, and made me sign a printed
sheet: "*Received, from M. the Minister of Foreign Affairs, the
sum of twenty francs, by way of assistance.*"

The situation was such that I had to accept that!...

Hanotaux, today, is an Academician, the friend of the sultan, of
the emperor of Germany, of the emperor of Russia, of the queen
of England, and of Paul Bourget. That explains everything. One
asserts even that Abdul Hamid, in recompense for his good
services, has conferred on him the pachalik... This places us at a
rude distance from the "Mignonne" and the breakfasts of rue
Monge. Do you remember them, Gabriel?

Note by the ungrateful beggar, August 1897.

It is frightening to discover in my notes that it was on precisely
this same day, having been implored, my old friends, Fathers of
the Augustians of the Assumption, – publishers of the *Cross*,
organizers of pilgrimages and manipulators of millions, – that I

12. – Noticed this in the Passion according to Luke:
*Herodes autem viso Jesu, gavisus est valde: erat
enim cupiens ex multo tempore videre eum, eo quod
audierat multa de eo, et sperabat signum aliquod
videre ab eo fieri.*[159]

What else could one say about a saint? And
these Words taken from the Bible which must, one
day, damn the world, could they not be believed borrowed from some legendary naïve person among the
Martyrs or Confessors?

13. – We move out finally! Having barely exited that
damned cul-de-sac, Jeanne points out to me that the
Angelus is ringing, the *Angelus* of noon, when our
André was born, as if that child wanted to make us
understand that it is he who is saving us.

Installation in the Great Montrouge. How delicious it is to breathe again! How delicious it is to be
in the vicinity of the cemetery where our Innocent
rests! Threshold of Paradise!

---

received a response that has clearly never been made by any
religious to any poor person since the beginning of the Christian
era, and which seems to have exited from one does not know
what pit of paganism, to chill the bones and confound the stars:

THE RULE OF OUR ORDER FORBIDS US TO GIVE ALMS!!!!

[159]*Herodes autem viso*...: Latin for "And Herod seeing Jesus, was
very glad; for he was desirous of a long time to see him, because
he had heard many things of him; and he hoped to see some
sign wrought by him." Luke 23:8 (Douay-Rheims).

14. – One needs to have suffered like one of the damned to understand what it is like to be delivered from the Tenebræ and black Flames, after only a few days!...

16. – Monsieur the Curate, are you content with your parish? Have you many pious parishioners here?

    – *"Oh! some very small fortunes!..."*

27. – "I find it immoral to ask for credit from the butcher. That would mean a lack of confidence in God who must be our only creditor." – Jeanne.

28. – In the Absolute:

    Idolatry is to prefer visible things to invisible ones.

    Precisely the case with Protestants who accuse Catholics of being idolaters.

    Our superior life begins again at the same time that we begin to suffer again. What a sublime life! To be the anvils of God for joy and for sorrow!

August

5. – Received the *Jeune Belgique*. Article by Arnold Goffin on the *Histoires désobligeantes*. This Goffin who is, it is said, a great man in Brussels, must be, at the same time, a friend of Pol Demade, and entirely deserving to be, for he accuses me of "monstrous co-promania." This critic, surprisingly organized, saw nothing but caca in my *Histoires*. I am, in his eyes, a kind of "Saint Jean-Sewer-Mouth." He likes to express himself like that and appears delighted with his little find.

7. – Vertigo. – When a man has vertigo, the evangelical scene begins anew. *Mitte te deorsum,*[160] said the Devil to Jesus. The second phase of the Temptation of Jesus transported to the pinnacle of the Temple would, then, be – *Vertigo!*

Two sorts of mysteries envelope us on every side, the luminous mysteries and the tenebrous mysteries.

10. – Saint Lawrence. – *Sancte Laurenti, per cremationem carnis tuæ, adjuva me pauperem; per signum crucis, illumina me cæcum... Assatum est jam,*[161] said

---

[160]*Mitte te deorsum*: Latin for "Cast thyself down." Matthew 4:6 (Douay-Rheims).

[161]*Sancte Laurenti*...: Latin for "Saint Lawrence, by the burning of your flesh, help me, a poor man; by the sign of the cross, help

the Martyr to his executioner, *versa et manduca. –
Hilarem datorem diligit Deus,*[162] reads, today, the
Church.

15. – *Assumption.* – We talk about the incomprehensible Gospel of this great day. Mary Magdalene taking
the place of Mary, the Mother of Jesus, which ought
to surprise all Christians and which surprises none of
them. – The Church, here, evidently speaks in a completely *prophetic* manner.

16. – Jeanne says this to me at the cemetery:

"One must dig and go down into the earth,
down to the bed of the dead. Then one will find Joy.

"On caring for the flowers on the tombs, one
cares, in a fashion, for the dead themselves; in this
way they become identified with the dust!"

20. – Saint Bernard. – One reads in the story of this
admirable man that his mother "herself wanted to
breastfeed him, for fear that by entrusting him to another woman he would receive some bad impression."
Idea that we often had ourselves, and which was the
topic of many conversations between us. From the
spiritual point of view primarily, the influence of a

---

me to see. – It is roasted now."

[162] *Versa et manduca*...: Latin for "turn [it] over and eat. God loves
a happy giver."

wet nurse seems to us a danger more to be feared than death itself. Who can tell if one of these creatures, to whom one entrusts the infant, in order that she nourish it with her substance, is not possessed? In an epoch such as our own, the cases of possession must be frequent. *When we speak to someone, we cannot tell whether it is the Devil or not who responds.*

A somewhat rough note to serve for a book on the Late Roman Empire:

Saint Bernard having armed France and Germany, against the East, was urged to put himself at the head of the expedition.

He refused, recalling Peter the Hermit, and he was wrong, frightfully wrong. With that refusal, the Crusade failed, and two hundred thousand men paid with their lives for the ecstatic repose of God's Servant.

He asked the Pope to deliver him from "men's fantasy." Instead, should he not have asked Jesus Christ to honor men with his own fantasy?

Saint Bernard is a saint of Jesus, a saint of the inspirited Word, a saint of the Poor and of the Crucified. In this sense, he was right to refuse, and his place is rightly on the altars of the Man of sorrows.

But a saint of the Holy Spirit should

have acted in a different way.

*Jesus forgives everything, accepts ev-
erything, suffers everything.*

*The glorious Spirit, the Triumphator,
the Burning, the Devouring, and the
Venger forgives absolutely nothing! It
is he whom one cannot insult except* ir-
remediably.

*The saints of Jesus, recompensed by
Jesus for what they have done, will be
judged again by Love on what they did
not do, and the OMISSION will be the
cyclone of flames that will burn all the
tabernacles.*

*A saint of Love will have cried to Je-
sus:*

*"I do not want consolations and sor-
rows awaiting me at Clairvaux. It does
not please me to weep silently, deli-
ciously, at the foot of your Cross. I
want to suffer like someone who would
have lost everything. I want to triumph
in your Name and for your Love, like
the Demons hoping to triumph by de-
testing you. I resist your groanings, I
refuse to listen to your ineffable calls.
I do not wish to hear anything, to
know anything about your Glory, and
if I were to be incinerated by your vol-
canoes, I am dying to decrucify you
before the hour.*

"I will not abandon to the Redemption these poor people, these naked children, these cute little infants, these newborn, who know only how to count on me. I will command them like a general. I will lead them into the deserts, and there will be no means to massacre them without exterminating me myself. For I will always be between them and the infidels, carrying you, Lord Christ, and Lord Savior, in the chalice of my heart. If there are mountains, I will bring them down; if there are rivers, I will dry them up; if there are armies arrayed in battle, I will strike them blind; and if someone lacks bread, I will multiply your Body until the satisfaction of the last churl in this army that will be mine.

"And I will do all these things, even if you would not, because your Glory presses me even more than your adorable Sufferings, and because, having abandoned you to conquer the world for you, you will no longer have anything to refuse me.

"I will eat Constantinople in my passage, and Jerusalem, delivered, will come see me. Then will I speak to the world..."

I spoke in this way in the *Revealer of the*

Globe:[163]

> *I have given to you everything that I*
> *had, when nobody gave to you. Have*
> *pity on a poor man who has glorified*
> *you with all his heart and who is with-*
> *out bread to eat.*[164]

22. – Dreadful day. A cleaning woman, horribly drunk, suddenly shows her insolency, apropos of a thing of little importance. Pretext to exhale her fetid soul, her old soul of a slave, filled with the demon of envy and I do not know what other demons. According to the custom of these bitches, she speaks only about leaving, guessing quite rightly that we have no money to take her at her word and throw her out of

---

[163] *The Revealer of the Globe: Christopher Columbus and His Future Beatification*, published by Sunny Lou Publishing, 2021.

[164] Original footnote: Is there anyone, today, who still knows that this is the title of my first book, published in '84, and unable to be found now? Thus did I designate Christopher Columbus, for whom I implored, – with more than eight hundred bishops, – his *Beatification* by exceptional Way and the freely expressed will of the *only* Sovereign Pontiff.

Six years later, on the eve of the universal masquerade of the Centenary of the Discovery, I renewed, in a more pressing manner, the same pointless wishes, in the brochure: *Christophe Colomb devant les taureaux*.

After that, how to be surprised as to my fate? It is a strange thing, but incontestable, that it is extremely dangerous to busy oneself with love for Christophore [sic], and that the discernment of this colossal *figure* of the Spirit of God, bearing Christ and borne himself "over the waters," is the most efficacious and advanced foretaste of the bitterness of death.

doors, that very instant. Forced to endure that excessive humiliation, we can only give her her one week's notice.

One week! Is that possible? Two hours, covered in slaver and filth, we look at each other, like the indebted souls of the dead, in the piacular Pit. My God: please do not renew this agony often! Finally, I run to my admirable, and always faithful friend, Eugène Grasset, who gives me without hesitation what I need to sack that vile hussy.[165]

23. – Lord, I do not have confidence in You.

No matter how much I know that You love me, that You infinitely cherish me, that You have created worlds for me, and that all that is nothing compared to what You still want to do;

No matter how much I know that "You are with me in my tribulation," that You are slapped, shouted down, flagellated, crowned with thorns, crucified for me, for two thousand years and since forever;

It does not matter, I am a bad Jew, and I do not have confidence in You...

This prayer, which so well expresses my entire soul, came to me by itself, and I wrote it down *as*

---

[165]Original footnote: I need to declare it here and now that Grasset, whose soul is loftier than his very lofty art, was, for many years, one of the two or three people who saved me from dying. May this journal, once published, bear him then the assurance of my eternal *ingratitude*.

if it was dictated to me.

25. – No letter, no visit, no notable incident. It is one of those days, empty in appearance, when God alone acts in silence and in the shadows, in the deepest of the mysterious cisterns of our hearts, – in the middle of the desert. *Projicite Joseph in cisternam hanc, quæ est in solitudine.*[166]

---

[166]*Projicite... in cisternam hanc...*: Latin for "cast him [Joseph] into this pit, that is in the wilderness." Genesis 37:22 (Douay-Rheims).

September

1ˢᵗ. – Dominating Spirit and psychological instinct of the Society of Jesus.[167] It is certainly not to the Poor that the religious of this Order have their hands out-stretched.

It seems to me that Saint Ignatius' *Exercises* correspond, in a way, to Descartes' *Method*. Instead of looking at God, one looks at oneself.

6. – Reading the Gospel of the *Missa pro abbati-bus*,[168] it crosses my mind that I am certainly one of those who will need to travel the world, crying out to men:

"Leave everything, sell everything, and follow us! In recompense, you will be covered in ignominy and you will end up suffering the most frightful torments."

8. – Nativity of Mary. – On taking communion, while my mind is still filled with the Genealogy of Saint Matthew, I think that I am receiving, at the same time as the Body of Christ, the forty-two Patriarchs or Kings who engendered him.

---

[167]Society of Jesus: the Jesuits.

[168]*Missa pro abbitibus*: Latin for "Mass for abbots."

9. – One does what one can. People of genius offer their genius to God, while imbeciles offer their imbecility. All for the best.

18. – To Henry Hornbostel:

> *Dear friend,*
>
> *I am announcing to you, in complete haste, that my dear wife is on the verge of giving me a new child.*
>
> *The first signs of the existence of this child conceived in sorrow appeared at the very moment when my beautiful little boy, killed by the hatred of the swine of letters, died before our very eyes, under awful circumstances.*
>
> *We are expecting this "Benoni" any day now, from one hour to the next. Can you help us to receive him without too much anguish? The smallest sum would be precious to us, for here comes misery, once again. I send a similar letter to each of my very rare friends, who have not abandoned me.*
>
> *Your LÉON BLOY.*

19. – Bagneux Cemetery. What joy again to find, vigorous and flourishing, a small wild rosebush that I had planted myself, several days ago, on my André's

grave, having pulled it out of a random field, and which was almost without roots. I could not have reasonably expected any result. I am moved by it, as if I had obtained a spiritual power, as if my child was speaking to me, encouraging me from the depths of the earth...

Read, in the *Journal*, a column by Coppée, of the most refined cretinism. It has to do with a stinking abbot Victor Charbonnel, and an American, and a crappy *congress of religions* (!!!) which this renegade recommends. Our François, electrified, calls for a universal religion, a decisive and conclusive fraternity of Christians and idolaters. Liquid academician.

21. – A bit of secours has come. Peace and light.

I speak to Jeanne about the mystery of Life, which is Jesus. *Ego sum Vita*. That life should be in men, animals, or plants, it is always Life, and when the moment comes, the elusive point that one calls death, it is always Jesus who withdraws, as readily from a tree as from a human being.

Same thoughts as twenty days ago. Psychology invented by the Jesuits. Method that consists in continually examining oneself, with a view to avoiding sin. It is the contemplation of evil in place of the contemplation of the good. The Devil substituted for God. Is that not the entire genesis of modern Catholicism?

22. – Jeanne said to me: "The Cross of Jesus is his shadow. If a man extends his two arms in broad daylight, before a wall, there will be a Cross behind him. *And when the Sun sets, the Cross covers the earth.*"

24. – Birth of my son Pierre.

May the Lord and his Mother, may his Angels and Saints, may they bless this child of our sorrow, and may he whom we have so terribly lost be thus restored to us!

Today is the feast of Our Lady of Mercy. Will it really bring us the *Mercy* of God?

25. – Baptism. Thinking on the sublime name of Pierre which has been given to this child, I am suddenly visited by this thought, how and whence it came I do not know, but I write it down immediately:

"You complain about being captive, man of little faith! You do not see then that the Angels have removed your chains, long since, that the door to your prison is open, and that Jesus is waiting for you, over there, on the waters, in the sweet luminous night!..."

Everything is there, isn't it? The Angels, Saint Peter, his captivity, his deliverance, and finally baptism signified by the waters, on which Peter alone can walk, in Jesus' footsteps.

Ah! if this child, already beloved to me, had really been sent to succor us, to be the occasion of the deliverance of his father, so cruelly captive for so many years, my God!

26. – Jeanne points out to me the circumstance of this little Pierre being born, with *the cord around his neck*, on the day of Our Lady of Mercy, the liberator of captives, and in the Octave of Our Lady of Seven Sorrows who is represented at La Salette with a chain around her neck.

27. – To Henry de Groux, among several other things:

> ... *Of course, I would be an* ingrate, *a madman, to doubt for one moment the infinitely attentive vigilance of God over us; it would be inexcusable of me to let black Sadness enter the Tower of prodigies where prayer has entrenched us. I know that we live by God's Hand, uniquely, and that we have nothing to fear. But this certainty does not exclude suffering, and we have had our hearts so bruised!...*

> *This morning then, having returned from the first mass of the day, where I had prayed for a deceased who was very dear to me, I felt, with anguish, many ancient wounds reopen, when your letter arrived. Delicious refreshment to learn that you had quite simply and easily done what I had recom-*

mended to you. But you must continue, it is indispensable to establish your-self, to embed yourself in this thought that your godson André has the power to protect you and that it is for that reason that he departed.

You know as well as all the doctors [of divinity] that Christianity means suf-fering, each person for the other. Force yourself then really to under-stand what happened. It is a beautiful story.

Jesus declares, in the Gospel of Saint John, that there is no greater love than giving one's life for those whom one loves. Now, we loved you greatly, and it was fitting, in one way, that the law was fulfilled by us. Be perfectly sure that André Bloy was conceived and given birth to so that you could be his godfather, and he disappeared, soon after, so that you might have a godson who prayed for you, at the feet of Mary, in Splendor. Your soul is worth that.

... You know it, your godson is not dead, he is only sleeping, *as Jesus says. Sleeping a sleep full of clairvoy-ance, in the bosom of the Father of fa-thers, with all the Innocents. That child is a saint, a blessed one full of light, full of knowledge, full of power,*

full of agility, like the Angels...

You must believe me, my dear Henry, for God himself could not tell you anything different, and it is certain that in this way, *we have been crucified for you.*

"I am the Life," says Jesus, at the moment he resurrects Lazarus. "It is not for laughs that I loved you," he says to the blessed Angela da Foligno, speaking to her, one day, from amidst the bleeding bush of his crown. Life is serious, you have understood this...

– LÉON BLOY.

The *Life of Our Savior Jesus Christ*, by Dr. Sepp, is certainly a profitable book to read. By dint of knowledge and also, clearly, true humility, he sometimes encounters beautiful rays of light, but he does not always avoid the reef of moral or sentimental interpretation dear to Protestants. The Absolute of the Scriptures escapes him.

29. – Two things profoundly forgotten by all Christians, without exception nearly:

Primo. We have the duty to ask *everything* of God.

Secundo. God has *nothing* to refuse us.

Dr. Sepp again. This good doctor suffers from

bouts of cretinism. He explains the periodic miracle of the Pool of Bethesda: *"Angelus descendebat, et movebatur aqua,"*[169] as the bubbling of mineral water!!!

30. Fragment of a letter to a young man in Marseille who favors me, sometimes, with his advice:

> *... Analysis! You know that it is a travesty of the Devil, don't you? God help me from speaking disrespectfully about a man whom the Church has put on its altars and whom I firmly believe to be a very great saint. But it is certain that the Society of Jesus has terribly abused Saint Ignatius' Exercises, an infinitely profitable book and method, to be sure, for some souls, but dangerous for so many others! and whence comes the hateful, abominable, depraving contemporary* psychology. *To always be analyzing oneself, anxiously interrogating oneself, looking at one's navel! The Jesuit method, in the final analysis, arrives at substituting the contemplation of oneself for the contemplation of God, and it is in this way that I explain the furious absence of* saints *today which is one of the most undeniable signs of the demise of Christianity. Run from*

---

[169]*Angelus descendebat...*: Latin for "The angel descended, and the water was moved." John 5:4 (Douay-Rheims).

analysis as from the Devil, throw yourself at God like a madman...

You will then have less of a need to oppress with your advice a man who is old enough to be your father...[170]

To a religious of La Salette:

My dear Father,

A deplorable misunderstanding inflicts humiliation on me for being the last person to announce to you, at once, both the birth and the baptism of my son Pierre-Ange-Lazare, come into this villainous and suffering world, last Tuesday, the 24th, feast day of Our Lady of Mercy, in the Octave of the Apparition of La Salette and of the Transfixion of Mary. There is even an arresting particularity that I will share with you. This child of suffering was baptized the day after his birth.

I ask you, dear Father, to pray for him. I ask it of you in the Name of She

---

[170]Original footnote: This young man, of an extraordinary, marvelous pedantry, and such as I do not believe ever to have encountered before, possessed the art of making himself pardoned for his impertinence, while manifesting himself, many times, as a benefactor, and worming out of me in this way a large number of *confidential* letters. When the lot appeared sufficient, he abandoned me...

My poverty has often been taken advantage of, but this is the most beautiful example I have had of *sentimental usury*.

who weeps on the Mountain, in the name of She who is the hope of captives. Keep in mind that he has been placed under the patronage of Peter, ut Jesum sequatur,[171] *and under that of Lazarus,* ut portetur ab Angelis in sinum Abrahæ,[172] *but a little later, if that is possible. His father would perhaps not have the strength to endure another mourning.*

Your perfectly devoted,

— LÉON BLOY.[173]

Jeanne's dream:

A sort of Mephistopheles showed her an instrument of torture that resembled a glaive, and said to her:

"By this, you will be broken."

---

[171]*Ut Jesum sequatur.* Latin for "that he may follow Jesus."

[172]*Ut portetur...*: Latin for "that he might be carried by the angels into Abraham's bosom." See Luke 16:22.

[173]Original footnote: I present this letter because it appears to have had something prophetic about it.

Recorded on the following 10th of December:

— Our Lady of Loretto. Pierre's death. Pierre-Ange-Lazarus, my second son, was born on September 24, 1895, feast day of Our Lady of Mercy. Jesus, having told him to follow him, just as he had said long ago to the Leader of the Apostles: *Tu me sequere* [Follow thou me], he was carried away by the Angels, as well as by the evangelical Beggar and the Holy House, on the following 10th of December, day of Our Lady of Loretto.

Then, God, pointing to the Cross, said in turn:

"By this, you must die and live."

All this, in the Danish language, according to a very beautiful rhythm.

October

1st. – To a good fellow, perfectly humble, the following:

> *The best "education" that I might give you is to study the Holy Books, to immerse yourself in the Vulgate, to read the New Testament particularly, from morning till night. It is impossible to say – an Archangel would renounce it – at what point it is shameful for these contemporaries of ours, who consider themselves* intellectuals, *to know so many books but to ignore precisely this Book.*
>
> *... Do not trust Huysmans. His Catholicism is a kind of bric-a-brac, and the most suspect I know.*

2. – Spoke with the midwife about vaccinations, which, it appears, are required by law, because every liberty decamps. I express strongly, although quite pointlessly, my horror of this filth, which humanity did so fine without until the last century and which England favored us with. Besides, the modern practice is for every sort of inoculation. We will finish by putrefying our little children with forty types of vaccine.

3. – Psalm XXVIII. Found a concordance between the *Seven Voices*[174] of the Lord and the Septenary. The joy of this find makes me less accessible to anxiety. God knows how much!...

9. – Letters upon letters from my young sot in Marseille. Today, he proposes *Greek* texts to me, to show me that I am on the wrong path. He tells me about his "frankness," about his "sincerity," and our different ways of viewing things. I will quite willingly respond to him that there is only one way to view things: mine. Even more willingly, I would tell him... something else. All this becomes too stupid anymore.

10. – Since morning, the torture of anguish is intolerable. I decide to run to old Gérôme, who may wish to oblige me again. However, I speak with Jeanne, who feels pity for my distress – for this behavior of a beggar makes me despair so, – and she easily persuades me to wait.

At church, I say this in the presence of the Holy Sacrament: Give me a sign, for pity's sake, any sign, an idea. Make me understand your will. I will obey it without hesitation.

Then I remember the text of Saint Matthew, the prince of priests, crying to Jesus, with a surprising vehemence: *Adjuro te per Deum vivum*,[175] and Jesus, who until then was keeping silent, speaking finally.

---

[174]Seven Voices. "The voice of the Lord is upon the waters... the voice of the Lord is in power..." Psalm 28.

Why would I not act like this, given that I have to vanquish the silence of Him who saves, and given so many other cries go unanswered? My prayer then becomes this adjuration, as strong as my feebleness allows it. How not to believe that this idea has been suggested to me, at my request, and that it is really a *sign*? I return home, recomforted, hoping for some happy news.

No news, alas! and the day passes thus. Soon I lose the small moral energy that prayer had armed me with. Any work is impossible, and I feel the most horrible disgust for all things and myself. Towards evening, it becomes so lugubrious for me that I go to seek some succor in a small chapel where I have sometimes found it.

There, I actually obtain a bit of mellowing, but in the midst of what sadness! I think of my poor little ones, of my dear Jeanne, and my thoughts tear me to pieces. How to know what God wants!

– *Domine, salva nos, perimus*,[176] says to the sleeping Jesus his disciples frightened by the storm, and Jesus accuses them of little faith. Now, Faith itself is a gift of God. I firmly believe that we will be saved in the end, but the *unknown* sufferings, which are perhaps still reserved for us, wrench my heart in advance, and I cannot have, in such torments, any other joy than what God will want to give me gratis. I

---

[175]*Adjuro te...*: Latin for "I adjure thee by the living God." Matthew 26:63 (Douay-Rheims).

[176]*Domine, salva...*: Latin for "Lord, save us, we perish." Matthew 8:25 (Douay-Rheims).

think too often of the so recent death of my André.

On return, the dark devil falls on me again and harasses me so much that I appear at home like a desperate man...

How many hundreds of other dark days is this day not the classic example of?

11. – My soul's misery is at its culmination, as is the other misery. I cannot remember having been more miserable, even in the cul-de-sac. What characterizes my present suffering is the feeling of weakness, the consciousness of my perfect exhaustion. I cannot take it anymore.

The poor Savior is still on the cross. He does what he can for the billions of creatures, all that he can, in truth, but *he is on the cross*, and even at the bottom of the pit, one must have pity for him.

14. – Excessive tribulation, but God never stops being adorable.

15. – At Gérôme's house: "Master, I come to ask alms of you." – "Here you are."

> *Beloved sons, said Saint Francis of Assisi to his Blessed flock, have no shame to go and ask for alms. Go with greater confidence and joy than if you were offering one hundred for one, be-*

> *cause it is the Love of God that you of-*
> *fer, by asking for it, when you say:*
> *"Give for the Love of God!"*

It is like that, and not otherwise, that I am tak-
en, this time, out of my landlord's grip.

This latter person, an old domestic and very
old scamp, who thought he read I don't know what
pages of mine, accompanies his ignominious handshake with this decisive judgment, emphasized, moreover, by an admirable wink of his crafty eyes:

"Ah! Ah! monsieur Léon Bloy, you write
naughty things!"

17. – I wonder where, today, is the Christian capable
of taking seriously, in their absolute sense, the words
of Our Lord Jesus Christ touching on the mystery of
Poverty.

Jeanne's churching. Everything has become so
mediocre that the prescription of the Ritual demanding that the priest go and find, "outside the church,
the woman kneeling at the threshold and holding a lit
candle," and whom he introduces; – this old and penetrating ceremony is no longer observed, at least not
in Paris.

20. – Reading Barbey d'Aurevilly's letters to me, of
which I fortunately have a copy,[177] made ten years

---

[177]Original footnote: The originals, 70 in all, pawned, for a
derisory sum, to a merchant of hand-written manuscripts, and

ago. Sad memory.

These letters are, for the most part, very medi-ocre. The reason, doubtless, being to interest the pub-lic, if they should ever be published.

If d'Aurevilly had not had the gift of a verita-ble kindness that only his most intimate friends were able to know, few men would have been more diffi-cult to support. If ever this collection were one day published by me, I will tell all in the preface. How to do otherwise? One owes the truth, *primarily to the dead*, and the poor great artist whom I so greatly loved, at the bottom of the abyss, expects it from me perhaps.

It is enormous to think of the suffering that I endured beside him, *for him*, for nearly a quarter of a century, without his even suspecting it!

I often appeared ridiculous to him, and he had nothing to offer me but jokes instead of any spiritual comfort. Nothing less than death was needed to fix his soul.

Excessive bitterness to plunge myself into this past again. Ah! how many times have I sobbed inter-nally, when that old child whom I naïvely tried to win over to God, offered me, guilelessly, the idiotic balderdash that brought him joy!

---

which I was unable to buy back, were finally lost to me, in 1896, and dispersed, I do not know where, with many other more or less precious souvenirs...

What does it matter? seeing as everything passes.

23. – In a journal, read about the astonishing catastrophe at the Montparnasse train station. A train, traveling at full speed, crashing through the facade, falling onto the pavement and crushing, miraculously, just one person. Someone told me about it yesterday evening, and I had difficulty believing it. As is usually the case on such an occasion, nobody has any idea how it happened.

26. – Heavy, dark, desolate day.

Why, at certain hours, are we assailed by dark and malicious sadness, just as what the remorse for some crime would fill us with?

Would it not be the case that a human or *angelic* being, perfectly unknown to us and, nevertheless, mysteriously bound to us by the closest of spiritual bonds, comes to accept the guilt for this crime, which becomes *ours* by solidarity of remorse?

28. – Introduction to the *Letters of Barbey d'Aurevilly to Léon Bloy (1872-78)*, to be published in a very uncertain epoch in the future:

> *"The Gods are thirsty!" said Montezuma. – "The dead are thirsty!" said the doleful Spirit charged with grazing, in dark valleys, on past generations. But who thinks of the* thirst of the dead?

*In the famous Parable of the Beg-
gar,[178] the wicked rich man implores in
vain, amidst the flames, for a drop of
water to refresh his tongue; he would
like, at least, that his brothers who are
still alive, be informed of his frightful
thirst...*

*"Have pity on me, Lazarus!" the great
Dead Man cries to me, from the bottom of his pit, "have pity on me! for I
burn in the furnace of the Desire for
Truth. A drop, nothing but a drop, I
beseech you, by God's entrails!*

*"I have always been compassionate
towards you, you must remember.
Even though I was not a rich man,
adorned in purple and fine linen, as
spoken about in the Gospel, and even
though my meals each day lacked
magnificence, I have given you, often,
much more than the crumbs that might
have fallen from my table. I did not always leave you lying at my door, and
you cannot say that only the dogs had
compassion on your wounds.*

*"Quench me. We others, the dead, we
have need of the Truth to rain down on
us, and this need, which the living are
unaware of, is absolutely terrible, ab-*

---

[178]Parable of the Beggar: or the Parable of Dives and Lazarus.
Luke 16:19-31. (An illustration of which is on the cover of this
book.)

solutely inexpressible.

"If you have loved me, Lazarus, you who have known me so well, deliver me of the crucifying admiration and the barbarous praise. The Holy Truth, the only Truth, give it to me, I beg you!

"Because the homicidal vanity of some men or women who did not pray for me, wants, at all costs, that my poor name should shine with their *glory, do not hesitate to divulge my profound misery, my certain misery, my too unknown misery.*

"It is the only thing I thirst for, – but a thirst eternally to die for.

"You can never say enough about my frivolity, my inconstancy, my childishness, and the infernal insanity of some of my literary attitudes.

"One would need the dilated intelligence of the Angels to know how rigorously the dead are judged, and how celestial and refreshing a just blame appears to them, as they thrash about in the insomnia of the tombs!..."

Here then, integrally, are the letters that I received from Barbey d'Aurevilly in the span of a few years. Let it be understand that this publication,

which each person will judge for him-
self, is a sort of preliminary design
that I formed to tell ALL, – a little lat-
er.

– *LÉON BLOY.*

29. – "Making Art for money!" de Groux wrote to
me. "Working in order to live! What horror!... when it
can only be a question of having money to make Art
and living in order to work."

It is very hard, in fact, poor de Groux's life! Suffering
is necessary for him, clearly. But what a soul! Humility and magnificence, that is what I find in him.

31. – There is, in the Tarn-et-Garonne department, a
commune that is called Our Lady of Miseries...

November

2. – Read, in the *Journal*, an interview, by correspondence, among several important individuals to whom it was asked *what they think about death* (!!!)

I do not recall ever having read anything more mediocre, or more abject. The only good response, I believe, is that of Gérôme saying that death has at least this going for it: that it is agreeable, that it delivers us of all the scoundrels with whom one is forced to be in contact with.

Jeanne tells me: "Human nature is such that one cannot not fear death. But when that redoubtable moment has passed, a person will say to himself: 'How simple it was! and how is it we could not see how simple it was?'"

6. – To an individual whom I believed to be my friend:

> ... *I am compelled to begin with a complaint. "I strongly desire from you a work of pure glorification, detached from all earthly accidents!" you write to me. You have already expressed this desire, in previous letters, as if it were completely accepted and completely incontestable that I have never done anything of the sort.*
>
> *But that is profoundly unjust, and it*

appears all the harsher to me given that, as a friend, you ought to feel that I have, more than any other, a need for justice. Have you not read, then, Salvation Through the Jews, *not to mention my two works on Christopher Columbus? It is, without comparison, the most considerable book of mine, the one I am most proud of and the only one, to this day, that I would dare to present to God, without any fear. It is the ripe fruit of fifteen years of biblical exegesis or sacred hermeneutics, and of an even greater number of years of suffering,* chosen by me for the love of God, *which you can have absolutely no idea of, for there was even more involved then just misery.*

That work of "pure glorification" had no success and could not have had any. God alone was a witness to my struggles and the unique judge of the appalling difficulties that I had to overcome in order to concentrate, in so few pages and in so penetrating a format, the vastest theme that might exist. At that distant time in the past when men did not scorn these things, such a work would have been noticed, doubtless. Today it appears that it is quite impossible, as my friends themselves are ignorant of it. Let it be then uniquely for the glory of God, like a

*poor little star lost and indiscernible
in the depths of the night.*

*It was necessary to let out that com-
plaint, without any bitterness besides,
before passing on to an explanation of
the "benefit" that your so amicable letter had for me. It is very simple. I am
practically alone in the world. I would
have been able to have, like so many
others, numerous and even innumerable friends. In the beginning of my
career, which was, miraculously,
rather boisterous, I obtained applause
from the get-go. Those who love
strength, even among atheists, were
with me. But I was not yet the author
of* The Desperate Man. *When people
understood my calling, when it was
notorious that I was a man of the Absolute, nobody wanted to follow me...*

9. – After an interruption of three days:

(In haste.)

*... Impossible to continue this letter
which I was so happy to write to you.
Since Wednesday, my days and nights
have been spent entirely caring for my
dear wife, fallen ill suddenly and
whose condition, today,* frightens *me;
taking care of the two little children,
feeding bottle, toilette, etc. needs*

which I have no knowledge of; strug-
gling finally at every household task...
Without any assistance, moreover, de-
prived of all rest, ill myself, troubled
to the bottom of my soul with anxiety
and disappointment, deprived espe-
cially of my daily communion without
which I am used to regarding life as
impossible; abandoned finally by ev-
eryone, I fear that I will go completely
mad. Have pity on me!

– LÉON BLOY.

"You are the man I love most," a poor child wrote to me, "because I have noticed that each time I think of you my thought turns into prayer."

Haunted by mournful thoughts, here is what came to me yesterday and today:

Our infirmity is so great that we cannot *understand* anything, least of all the death of a loved one. The enormous sorrow of André's death, for example, – it is impossible for me to grasp it fully. But everything, in the end, must be understood. Later, doubtless, when our bodies are dust, we will have the *substance* of that pain which we could not know or feel anything but the *accident* of.

12. – To Henry de Groux:

Henry,

My wife has received, this morning,

the Viaticum and the sacrament of Extreme Unction.

We do not know whether she will live, nor even whether she will live another day. She has made her last wishes.

I will never forget the terrible night that just passed, and the unfortunate woman continuously crying the Name of Jesus while invisible torturers, whose arrival we had had a foreboding of, piteously and pitilessly tormented her.

The day before yesterday, in a fit of deliriousness, she spoke to me about you, my Henry, having heard *your voice. It was about 3 in the morning.*

"God is so good," she said, "to have sent us our one friend!"

Henry, I am dead-drunk with grief, lassitude, and fright! It is more than sixty hours already and I am almost alone taking care of two little children and their mother, not eating, not sleeping, riddled with sorrow, and no money!

I am an anvil at the bottom of the abyss, the anvil of God, who makes me suffer in this way because he loves me, well do I know it.

The anvil of God, at the bottom of the abyss!...

So be it. It is a good place from which to call out to him.

Everything that happens is adorable, perfectly adorable, and I am burnt by tears...

Your LÉON BLOY.

* * *

That's enough. I cannot continue. Let's go! Eat, dogs. Here are a man's entrails.

To be sure! She must have been particularly and terribly chosen to meet me, the noble Scandinavian daughter, the eldest and beloved daughter of the poet Christian Molbech!

Anywhere else, it is quite certain, the sufferings and bitterness of death would have rushed at her, like *exiles* to a place of refuge, like the lovers of God to a holy place filled with lights. Was she not infinitely designated for voluntary penance and *propitiation*?

But it was necessary, undoubtedly – how necessary, and since what eternity! – that I should be the occasion and *privileged configuration* of her holocaust.

Could she have descended any lower, that soul ambitious to be immolated?

To choose to be the companion of a universally detested poor man! To share the ignominy and the rare bread of a writer of books, whom the lowest rogue of letters believes he has the right to cover in filth! To bring on herself perfect neglect, basest outrage, ridicule, contempt, calumny!

All that, – and more than all that even, if God requires it, – so as not to incur the blame, which makes the Columns [of Heaven] tremble, of having spent time beside the Abandoned One and not having discerned Greatness in him.

The magnanimous woman wanted to do what *no* man had the courage or thought to take on, and here she is now, dying... and what a death!

Epilog

The wheel of several weeks, as heavy as the Prophets' chariots, has crushed my heart.

My beloved wife will not die, it is true. The cup of torments is still too full, and who would help me to drink it?

But there is, somewhere, one more small tomb, and we are made to hear, sometimes, amidst the human cries of the populace that surround us, the plaintive and heart-rending threnody of our innocent Véronique, the last child remaining to us:

My little brother André is dead.

My little brother Pierre is dead.

My little mama is dead.

There is no garden anymore.

There is no house anymore.

The little girl is all alone in the street.

I see her, I still hear her, the dear child, sitting on one of the steps of our humble doorway, lost in her dream, and singing – for whom, O Lord? – these dolorous words that she herself had arranged, – in the inexpressibly sweet and serious voice of a turtledove that is dying!...

Here is what someone told me:

An individual, more or less known in Brussels, but whom the laws forbid me, unfortunately, to name, was apparently tasked with remitting to me, in Paris, in 1893, a sum of *Three thousand francs*, entrusted to him by various subscribers.

Having been unable, or not having wanted, to find me immediately, this ambassador would have offered himself the said sum, considering that a poor person's property is good for the taking.

I find, in fact, in my "memoranda," on the date of August 31, 1893, the following note:

> *Letter notifying me that a Belgian journalist asks to see me and that* I am urged to be at his disposition. *Admirable! This individual is recommended on a card by Henry Carton de Wiart!!!*

Much to my regret, I cannot find that letter again. But I remember very well that the presumptuousness of a like message revolted me, all the more so because it was backed up by the recommendation of a man whom I despise more than anyone.

Did I respond or did I not respond? It is impossible for me to remember. In any case, there was no follow up, I am quite sure of it, and I decided to wait until that person might deign to trouble himself, or that he might more civilly inform me of his intentions.

But if the information that I am given today is correct, there is reason to believe that this gentleman had *calculated* his insolence, with a view to taking advantage of my indignation, expressed or not, so as to take off at once with the cash.

My God! I know my duties. I know that the poor are made to be eaten. Nevertheless, in this adventure, there are subscribers unknown to me, who were perforce *robbed*, and who could be surprised, on reading the preceding pages, to hear me crying misery, after such a secours.

I add that the death of my two little children, and the atrocious grief that this secours might have prevented, are not precisely, in my eyes, what would be needed to attenuate the surprising infamy of that abuse of trust.

The individual, who will perhaps recognize himself in the above, and whom I still wish to suppose slandered in the most indignant manner, is invited to justify himself.

LÉON BLOY.

August 1897.

He has to fall, the wretch! Nothing would save him, for God himself wants him to fall.

Vainly, he attempted to cling to heaven. But the shivering stars recoiled.

Vainly, he summoned the Angels and the Saints, and the Leaders of the Angels and the Leaders of the Saints.

Vainly, he supplicated the sorrowful Virgin.

The Four Rivers of Paradise flowed back to their sources, so as not to hear his clamor...

Ah! you there! you wanted to say something. You have taken the Words and the Promises seriously, and you have scorned men, forgetting that they themselves have become Gods! You sought Mightiness, Justice, Splendor! You sought Love!

Well now! here is the abyss, here is *your* abyss. It's name is SILENCE...

It is not an ordinary pit, this one. No need to ask it for that mercy of a bed of hard rock where the wretch, hurled down into it, might be broken. Its walls are ever expanding, on the contrary, its gob grows vaster and vaster, and the fall becomes infinite. There is no adieu comparable to that swallowing.

He has fallen, the blasphemer of the Riffraff, forever, undoubtedly. One dares to believe it.

Who knows, however? In the places of the deep there are, sometimes, strange surprises.

Who knows, really, among the Riffraff, the satisfied and reveling Riffraff, whether that Poor man will not reappear, one day, on the surface of the darkness, holding a mysterious flower in his hand, – the flower of Silence, the flower of the Abyss?

Other Books by the Publisher

Fanchette's Pretty Little Foot by Restif de la Bretonne

Je M'Accuse... by Léon Bloy

My Hospitals & My Prisons by Paul Verlaine

Salvation Through the Jews by Léon Bloy

Words of a Demolitions Contractor by Léon Bloy

Cellulely by Paul Verlaine

Ecclesiastical Laurels by Jacques Rochette de la Morlière

Flowers of Bitumen by Émile Goudeau

Songs for Her & Odes in Her Honor by Paul Verlaine

On Huysmans' Tomb by Léon Bloy

Ten Years a Bohemian by Émile Goudeau

The Soul of Napoleon by Léon Bloy

Blood of the Poor by Léon Bloy

Joan of Arc and Germany by Léon Bloy

A Platonic Love by Paul Alexis

The Revealer of the Globe: Christopher Columbus & His Future Beatification (Part One) by Léon Bloy

An Immodest Proposal by Dr. Helmut Schleppend

The Pornographer by Restif de la Bretonne

Style (Theory and History) by Ernest Hello

On the Threshold of the Apocalypse: 1913-1915 by Léon Bloy

She Who Weeps (Our Lady of La Salette) by Léon Bloy

The Sylph by Claude Prosper Jolyot de Crébillon (*fils*)

Voyage in France by a Frenchman by Paul Verlaine

Ourigan, Oregon by William Clark, Richard Robinson, and anonymous

Drowning by Yu Dafu

Cull of April by Francis Vielé-Griffin

The Misfortune of Monsieur Fraque by Paul Alexis

Fêtes Galantes & Songs Without Words by Paul Verlaine

Joys by Francis Vielé-Griffin

The Son of Louis XVI by Léon Bloy

Septentrion by Jean Raspail

The Resurrection of Villiers de l'Isle-Adam by Léon Bloy

Poems Saturnian by Paul Verlaine

The Biography of Léon Bloy: Memories of a Friend by René Martineau

Fredegund, France: A Book of Poetry by Richard Robinson

The Good Song by Paul Verlaine

Swans by Francis Vielé-Griffin

Constantinople and Byzantium by Léon Bloy

Enamels and Cameos by Théophile Gautier

Four Years of Captivity in Cochons-sur-Marne: 1900-1904 by Léon Bloy

Dark Minerva: Prolegomena: The Moral Construction of Dante's Divine Comedy by Giovanni Pascoli

What is Fascism: Discourses and Polemics by Giovanni Gentile

The Desperate Man by Léon Bloy

Meditations of a Solitary in 1916 by Léon Bloy

The Ride of Yeldis & Other Poems by Francis Vielé-Griffin

Silvie & The Chimeras by Gérard de Nerval

Italian Nationalism by Enrico Corradini

A Silver-Grey Death and *Drowning* by Yu Dafu

Doctrines of Hatred, Part I: Anti-Semitism by Anatole Leroy-Beaulieu

Rhymes of Joy by Théodore Hannon

Windows and Doors by Richard Robinson

The Perverted Peasant by Restif de la Bretonne

Early Poetry by Auguste de Villiers de l'Isle-Adam

Antisthenes: The Founder of Cynicism by Charles Chappuis